IMAGES
of America

SHAWNEE AND POTTAWATOMIE COUNTY

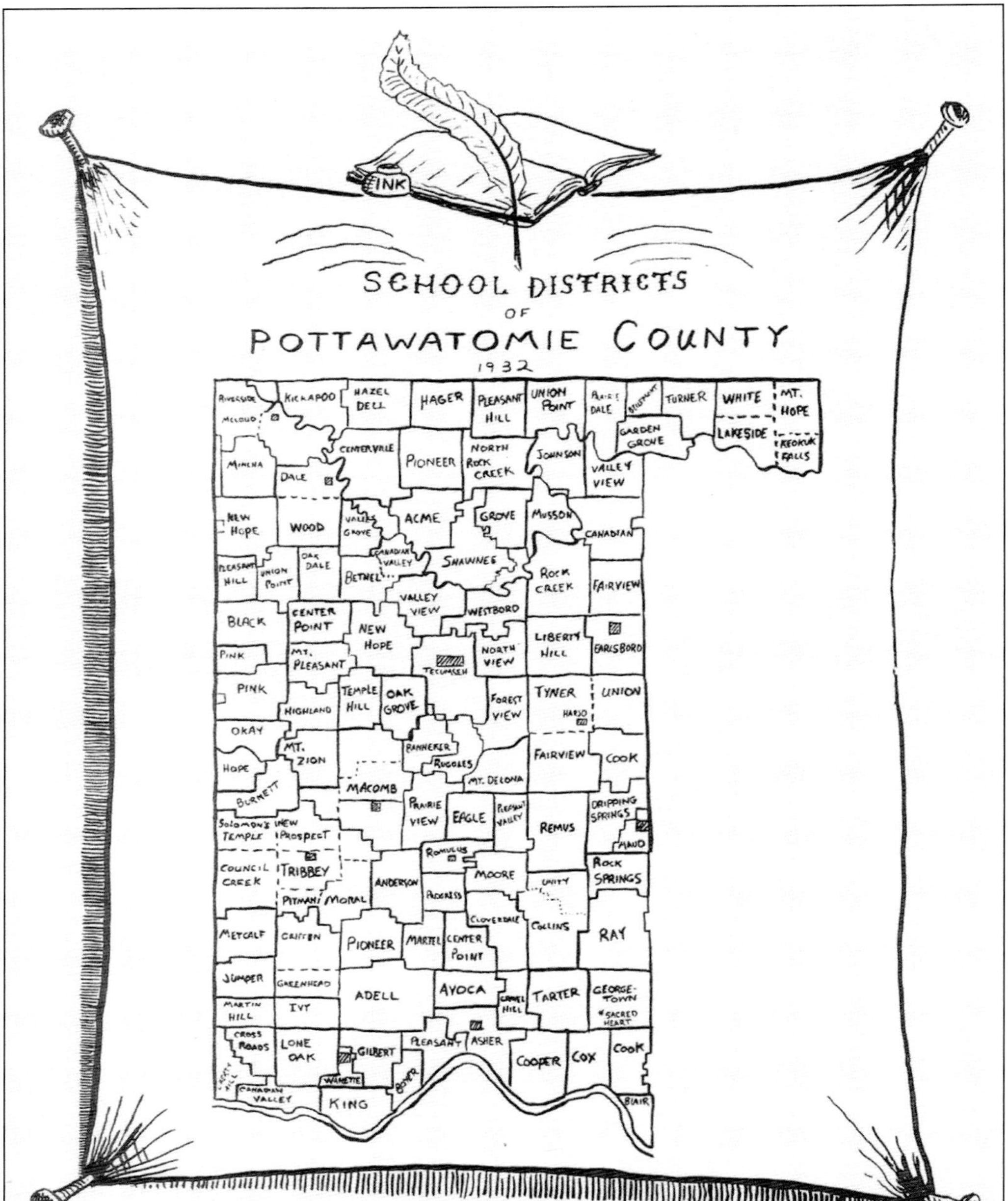

1932 School Districts. This hand-drawn 1932 map of Pottawatomie County illustrates the numerous school districts of the time, many of which have long been forgotten. Over 100 school districts are marked on this map. In comparison, Pottawatomie County today has fewer than 20. (Courtesy of Pottawatomie County Historical Society.)

On the Cover: A Close Shave. Barbers and their sharply dressed clients pose for a photograph in the Aldridge Hotel Barber Shop in Shawnee. This barbershop is typical of ones to be found in almost every town in the county. (Courtesy of Pottawatomie County Historical Society.)

IMAGES
of America

SHAWNEE AND POTTAWATOMIE COUNTY

Brad A. Holt

ARCADIA
PUBLISHING

ISBN 978-1-4671-2546-8

Published by Arcadia Publishing
Charleston, South Carolina

Printed in the United States of America

Library of Congress Control Number: 2016954290

For all general information, please contact Arcadia Publishing:
Telephone 843-853-2070
Fax 843-853-0044
E-mail sales@arcadiapublishing.com
For customer service and orders:
Toll-Free 1-888-313-2665

Visit us on the Internet at www.arcadiapublishing.com

This book is dedicated to the person who encouraged me to compile it and who has encouraged me through every step of my life—my mom, Jennifer Holt. And to my dad, Bruce Holt, for without his presence in my life, I wouldn't be the person I am today. Miss you, Dad. Love to both.

Contents

Acknowledgments

First, my sincere thanks to the Pottawatomie County Historical Society, Santa Fe Depot Museum, Ken Landry, and the rest of the staff that works so hard to document and preserve the history of Pottawatomie County. Without access to their immense collection of photographs and knowledge, this book would not be possible. Ken Landry is an absolute wealth of information and an outstanding resource to the community.

Special thanks to Jones Theatres and Ronny Jones for a large majority of the photographs and information that comprises the "Theaters" chapter. It is so rare that a family is as continuously and passionately involved with a community and an industry as the Jones family is. I greatly appreciate his time in locating photographs and answering my questions.

Thank you to those other businesses and individuals who contributed photographs and information. I hope you find satisfaction in seeing your family photographs and businesses in the book. I am grateful to Karen Dorrell and my wonderful former high school teacher Sylvia Elaine Sachs for proofreading the book for grammar. I appreciate both of you immensely.

I must acknowledge my late, great Aunt Betty, who first piqued my interest in genealogy and local history many years ago, as well as the late Doris Browder, who passed down much of the history and pictures of the Asher area. I believe both would have loved seeing this book come to reality.

Thanks to Brian Ferrell for his support and encouragement to complete the book.

Finally, I would like to express my gratitude to my editor at Arcadia, Caitrin Cunningham, for her guidance and patience through this new experience.

INTRODUCTION

Early in the morning of Tuesday, September 22, 1891, in a scene that today might remind us of Black Friday shoppers lining the sidewalks of a big box store, restless pioneers, all with the goal of staking prime land, surrounded the border of what would become Pottawatomie County, Oklahoma. They made their preparations and were sure to be ready when the border opened at noon. The crowd was diverse, some looking to make quick money, some looking to start a new life. The mass was not always well behaved. While trying to stake his claim, a man was trampled by a horse and killed. Others got into confrontations about who staked a particular lot first. Chaos eventually turned to order. Tents quickly went up, and wood-frame houses and structures soon followed. The first businesses opened within days. The citizens went to the polls in November 1892 to name their county, known up this point only as "County B." They chose Pottawatomie, after the Pottawatomi tribe, which was previously resettled to the land along with the Iowa, Sac and Fox, Absentee Shawnee, and Kickapoo tribes. The citizens also elected their first officials.

Of great interest to the pioneers was the town site of Tecumseh, which was already designated the county seat. Obtaining this honor was simply a matter of location—traditionally, county seats were in the geographic center of the county. Tecumseh thrived as the county seat, but it was soon disputed. When the railroad chose to run a line to nearby Shawnee instead of Tecumseh, a fierce court battle followed. Early Shawnee settlers knew that the success of their still-young community depended on the railroad. In the end, Shawnee got the line, and there was a great celebration there on July 4, 1895. This began a long rivalry between Tecumseh and Shawnee. Tecumseh held its own as it was, for a time at least, the more developed of the two cities. The matter would not be settled for another 30 years.

As Shawnee and Tecumseh were feuding, other, smaller towns were quickly popping up. By the end of the decade, Pottawatomie County was home to just over 43,000 people. In the 1920s, the county experienced an oil boom. Nearly 20 cities and towns had established post offices. Shawnee continued to grow steadily and even had aspirations of becoming the state capital; however, it finished a distant third in a 1919 vote. The city did finally prevail by taking the county seat from Tecumseh, however, in 1930.

Pottawatomie County today is home to just over 70,000 citizens. Many of the towns built seemingly overnight are just a memory, but Asher, Earlsboro, Macomb, Maud, McLoud, St. Louis, Tecumseh, Shawnee, Wanette, and a few others persevered in their own ways and still bring a unique version of small-town charm to Pottawatomie County.

Shawnee, still the county seat, is home to a prestigious college and university and is known as the birthplace of SONIC Drive-In. Tecumseh, no longer the county seat but still a significant city, was once home to Gov. Mary Fallin. Asher has long been a center of baseball interest. Earlsboro is known for its 1920s oil boom that, at least temporarily, brought thousands to the city. Macomb was once dubbed the "Queen City of South Pottawatomie County," but hardships kept it from living up to its nickname. Maud proudly claims Wanda Jackson as one of its own. McLoud has long been recognized as the "Blackberry Capital of the World." St. Louis once enjoyed proximity to one of Oklahoma's "giant" oilfields and profited greatly from it.

The county is home to 16 sites listed in the National Register of Historic Places, including the Aldridge Hotel, Bell Street Historic District, Pottawatomie County Courthouse, Sacred Heart Mission Site, the Santa Fe Depot, and St. Gregory's University. Some well-known former residents of the county include Governors Brad Henry and Mary Fallin, athlete Jim Thorpe, astronaut Leroy Gordon Cooper Jr., country and western recording artist Wanda Jackson, actor Brad Pitt, and novelist Tony Hillerman.

This book concentrates on Shawnee and Pottawatomie history from the 1891 Land Run up to the 1950s. Chapter one, "The Railroad," looks at the importance of the railroad to the development of the towns and cities of Pottawatomie County. Chapter two, "Banks," details the history of some of the important banking establishments of the county and touches on a few bank robberies of the time. The third chapter, "Business and Industry," illustrates the many ways county citizens built their lives and how the rural towns differ from cities like Shawnee. Chapter four, "Theaters," gives a look back in time to the many beautiful theaters the county had. The fifth chapter, "Churches and Community," takes a look at the abundance of houses of worship in the county, as well as important community buildings like city halls and courthouses. The final chapter, "Schools and Activities," concentrates on the numerous schools of Pottawatomie County and the sports and other activities connected to them. Whenever possible, if a building is pictured, the caption will reveal the current state of that structure.

Compiling this book brought some sadness and frustration in seeing that many of the county's great buildings have either been razed or covered over by uninteresting, if not downright ugly, facades. It is satisfying though to see an interest in removing many of those false fronts and renovating those buildings to their previous glory, especially in downtown Shawnee.

One

The Railroad

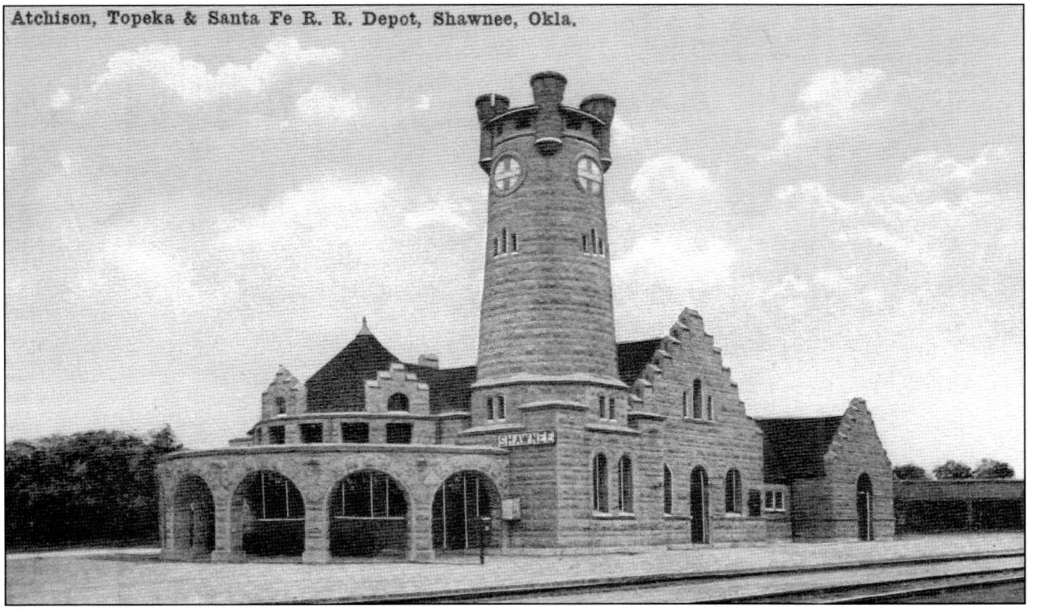

A Unique Depot. The railroad was a vital link for early towns. Not only was it a convenient form of transportation for residents, it was also, perhaps more importantly, vital in the transportation of crops and other goods. Shawnee attained its first railroad line in 1895. The railroad was later extended to almost every town in the county. The Santa Fe Depot, pictured, was opened in Shawnee in 1904. (Courtesy of Pottawatomie County Historical Society.)

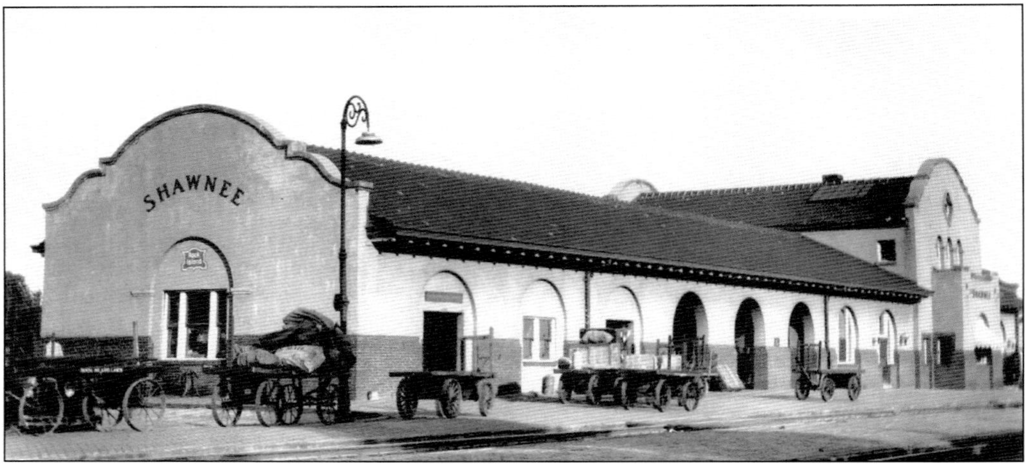

Rock Island. The Rock Island Train Depot in Shawnee above was one of the city's three train depots. This depot was built shortly after Rock Island absorbed the Choctaw Railroad in 1902. In 1948, Gov. and presidential candidate Thomas Dewey stopped in Shawnee on his "whistle stop" campaign. Below, many Rock Island employees pose for a photograph in 1917 at the roundhouse. According to a company magazine, Rock Island had almost 1,000 employees in Shawnee at the beginning of 1920. Shawnee lost the repair shops in 1937, and eventually the trains quit coming. The depot was razed around 1970. (Both, courtesy of Pottawatomie County Historical Society.)

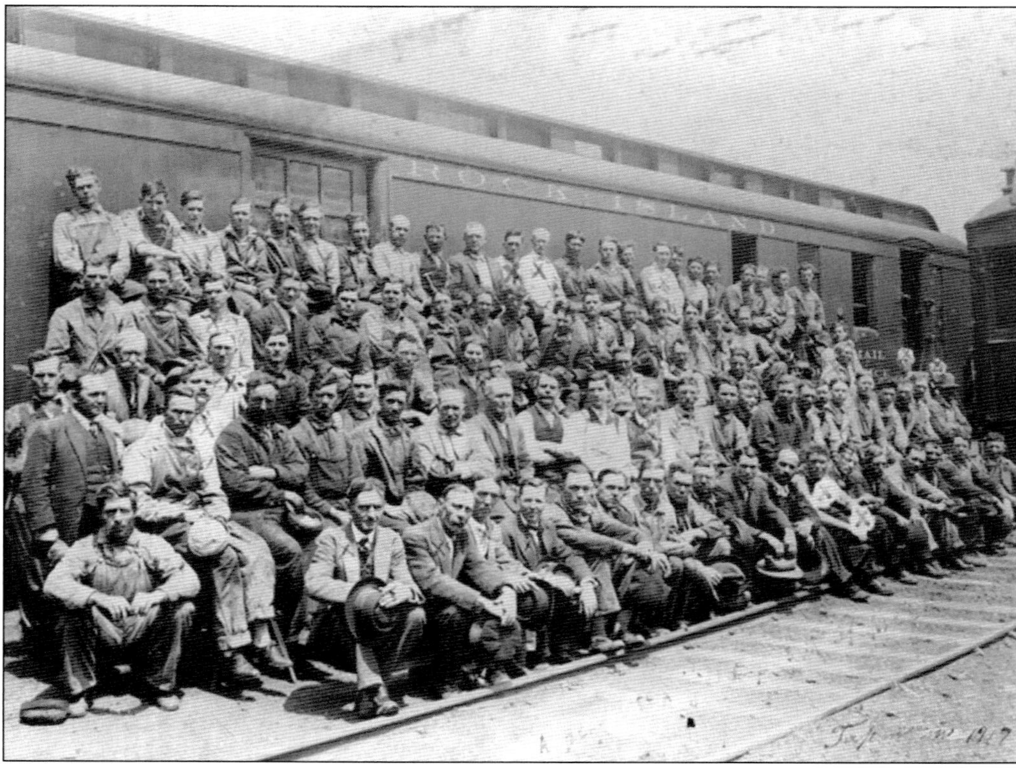

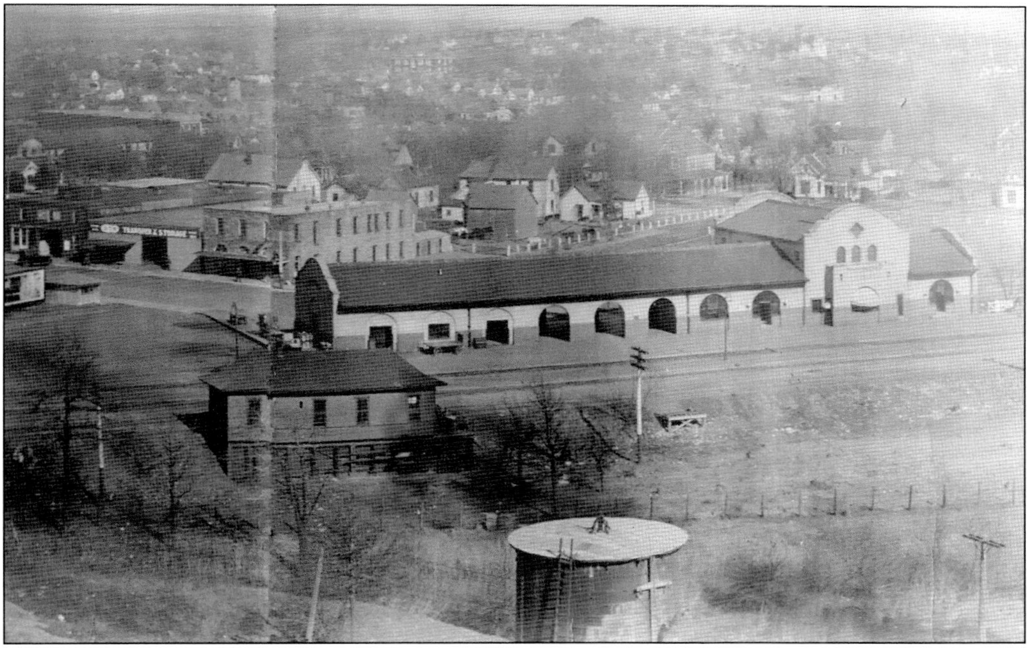

ANOTHER VIEW. The photograph of Rock Island and the surrounding area (above) was possibly taken from Shawnee Milling Company. The passenger depot was located at the end of Union Street, south of Main Street. The shops and roundhouse occupied significant property south of the intersection of Main Street and Louisa Avenue. A few of these shops still exist. Rock Island employees (below) show off an engine during a parade on Shawnee's Main Street. This photograph is undated but was probably taken around 1910. (Both, courtesy of Pottawatomie County Historical Society.)

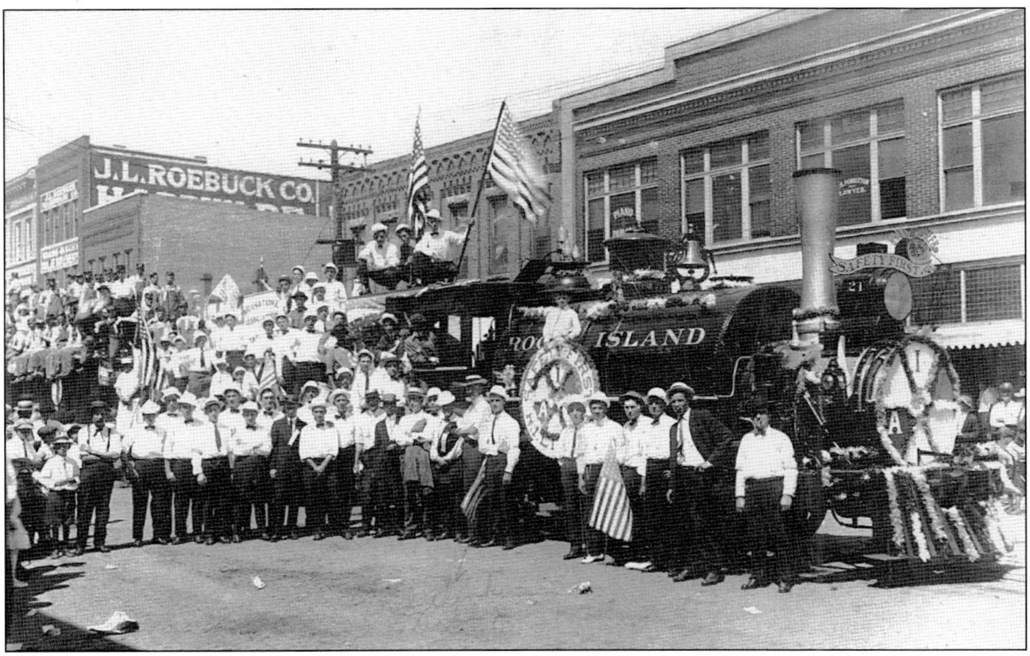

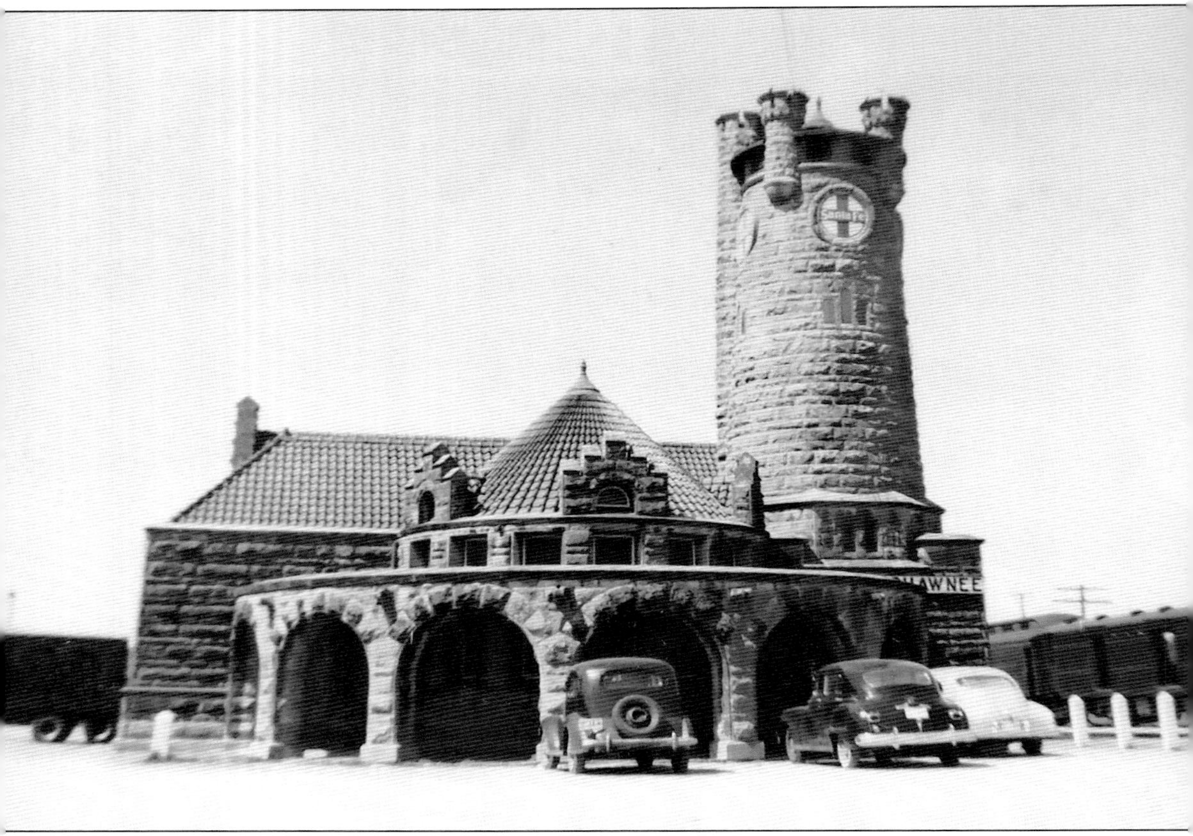

Santa Fe Depot. The unique and visually striking Santa Fe Depot in Shawnee opened in 1904. Its architecture is classified as Romanesque Revival, and the structure is comprised of limestone blocks two to three feet thick. This picture of the depot dates to about 1950. The depot was active until 1956, after which it sat empty for over two decades. In 1979, a fund drive began to remodel the building into a museum. On May 30, 1982, the restored depot welcomed its first visitors as a museum. The Pottawatomie County Historical Society and Museum now operate from this location. The building is in the National Register of Historic Places. (Courtesy of Pottawatomie County Historical Society.)

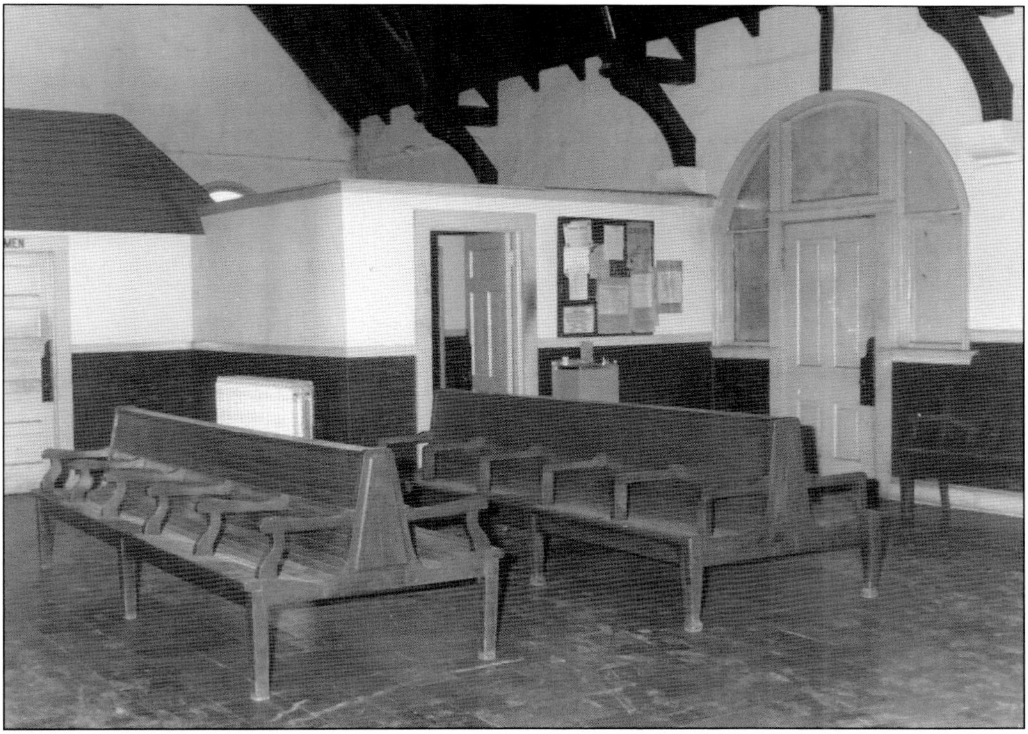

Santa Fe Interior. This is a view of the interior of the depot. Although this picture was taken in the 1970s, it provides a good idea of how the depot looked when it was active. Pictured is the general waiting room. Ladies had a separate waiting room. (Courtesy of Pottawatomie County Historical Society.)

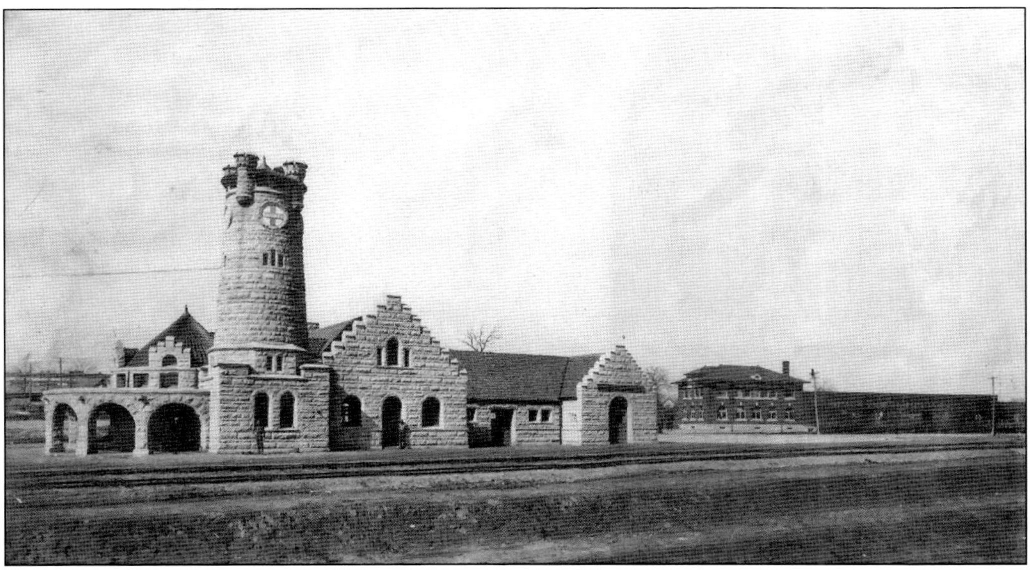

Santa Fe Freight Depot. A rare photograph shows both the Santa Fe passenger depot and the lesser-photographed Santa Fe freight depot in the background. (Courtesy of Pottawatomie County Historical Society.)

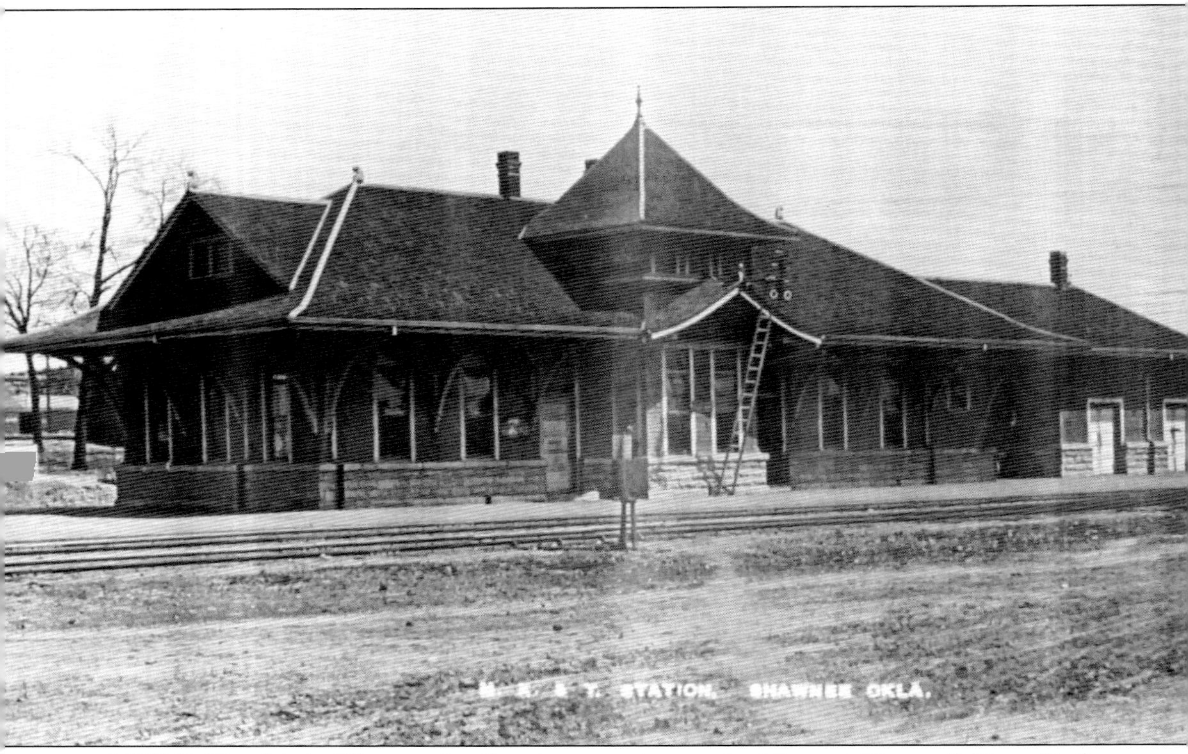

MK&T. The third of Shawnee's railroad companies was the Missouri, Kansas & Texas Railway (also known as MK&T or Katy). The Shawnee depot of the line is featured in this 1920s postcard. The passenger depot was located between Broadway Avenue and Bell Street south of Seventh Street. The freight depot was located west of the passenger depot near Beard Street. (Courtesy of Pottawatomie County Historical Society.)

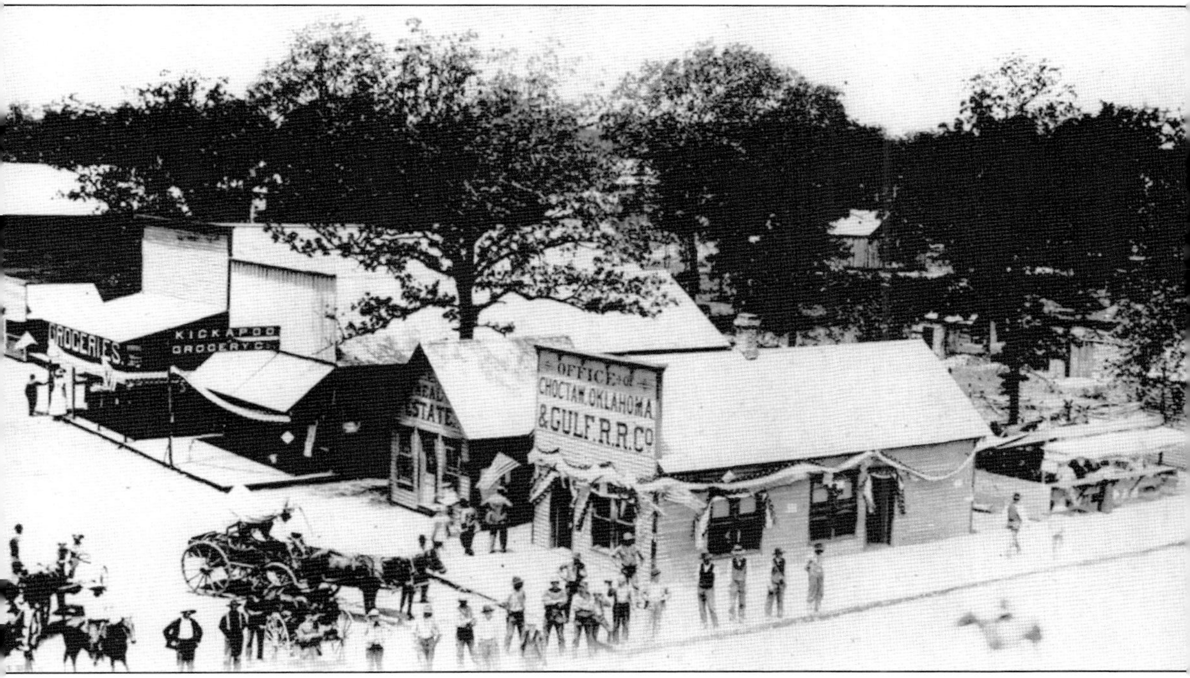

CO&G. This photograph, showing the northwest corner of Main Street and Broadway Avenue in Shawnee, was taken on July 4, 1895. Local establishments, including a pair of grocery stores and an estate office, are ready for the holiday. Also pictured is the office of the Choctaw, Oklahoma & Gulf (CO&G) Railroad Company. The CO&G was the first to commit to Shawnee and completed tracks to Oklahoma City the day this photograph was taken. John Beard, who participated in the 1891 Land Run, was instrumental in convincing the railroad to come to Shawnee. This was a considerable task, as Tecumseh had already been declared the county seat. The Choctaw Railroad would later relocate its repair shops to Shawnee, spurring significant growth. (Courtesy of Pottawatomie County Historical Society.)

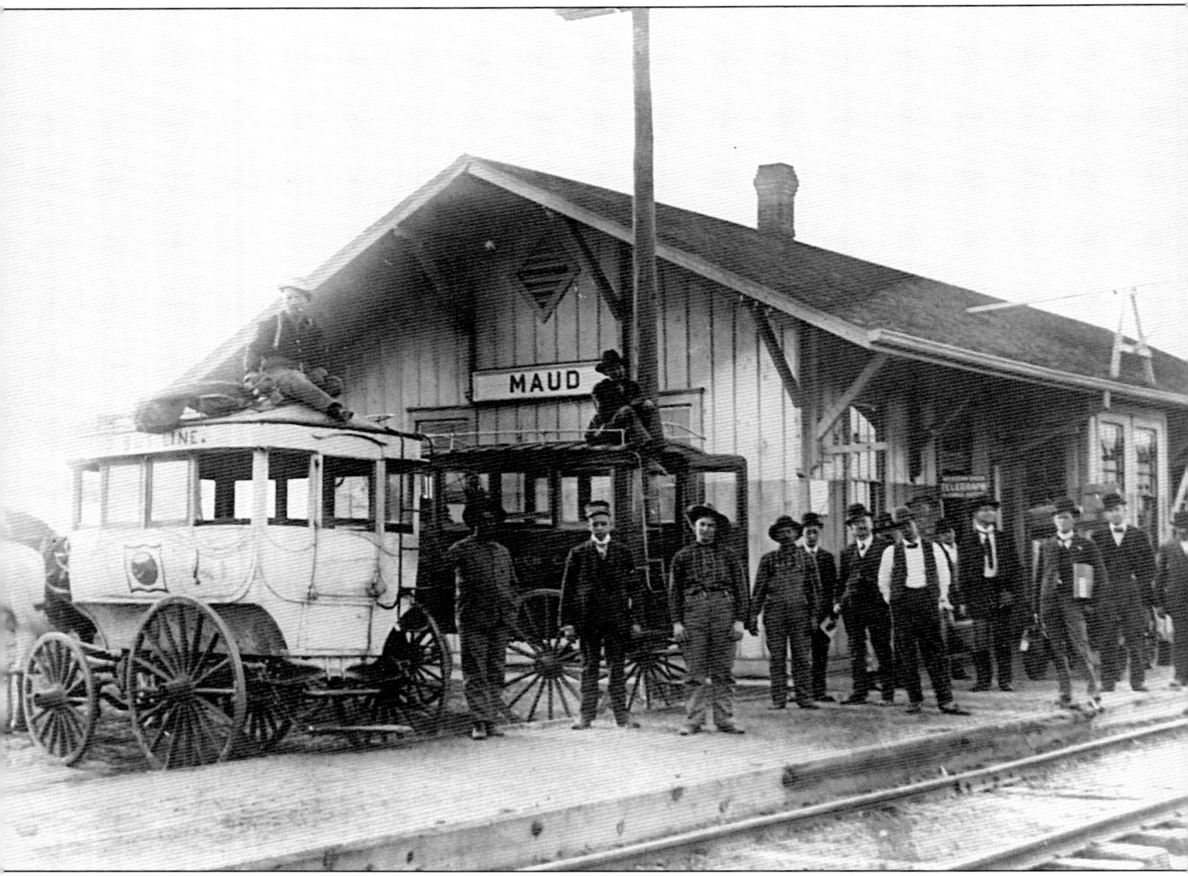

Rural Depots. The picture above is of the Maud Railway and Telegraph Office in 1902. The depot served passenger and freight trains on the Missouri, Kansas & Texas Railway. Maud's depot design was typical of rural Pottawatomie County towns, being more functional than monumental. The depots located in Asher, Maud, McLoud, Romulus, Tecumseh, and Wanette all had similar practical designs. (Courtesy of Pottawatomie County Historical Society.)

Two

BANKS

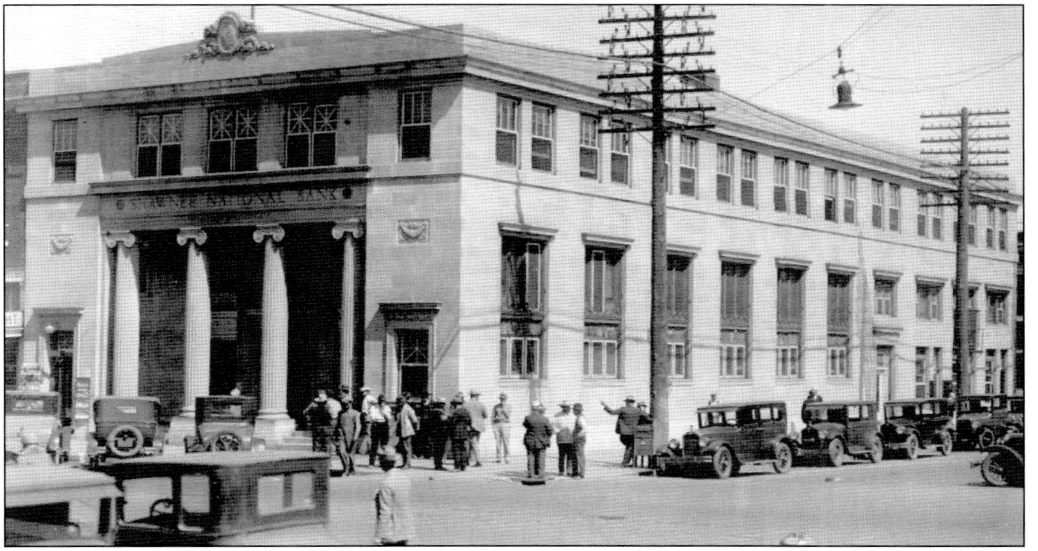

A BANK ON EVERY CORNER. As Pottawatomie County was developing, banks were constructed in almost every community, and sometimes it seemed on every corner. Early banks were usually small private establishments, and most bankers resided in the community where their banks were located. Sadly, most of the pre-statehood bank buildings have been lost, but some early buildings still stand, like the Shawnee National Bank building above. (Author's collection.)

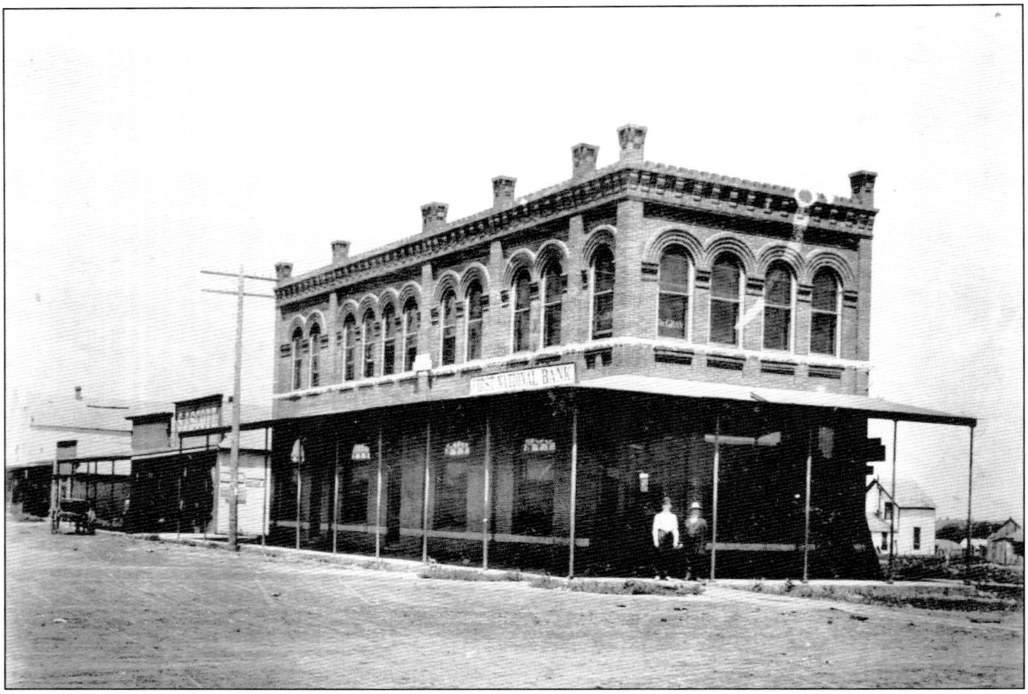

Tecumseh First National Bank. James H. Maxey, a former captain in the Confederate army, came to Tecumseh in 1892 and organized the Tecumseh First National Bank. Two men stand outside the bank building above. Judging from the surrounding buildings, this was most likely a very early Tecumseh structure. This bank stood at the corner of Main Street and Park Avenue. An advertisement for Dr. Gray is in an upper-floor window. This building no longer exists. A $10 currency note issued by the Tecumseh National Bank in 1912 is pictured below. (Above, courtesy of Pottawatomie County Historical Society; below, courtesy of Carl Cochrane.)

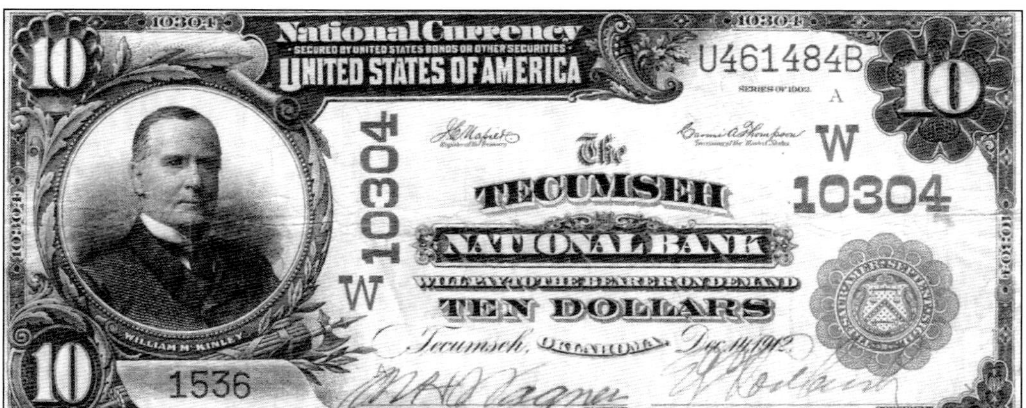

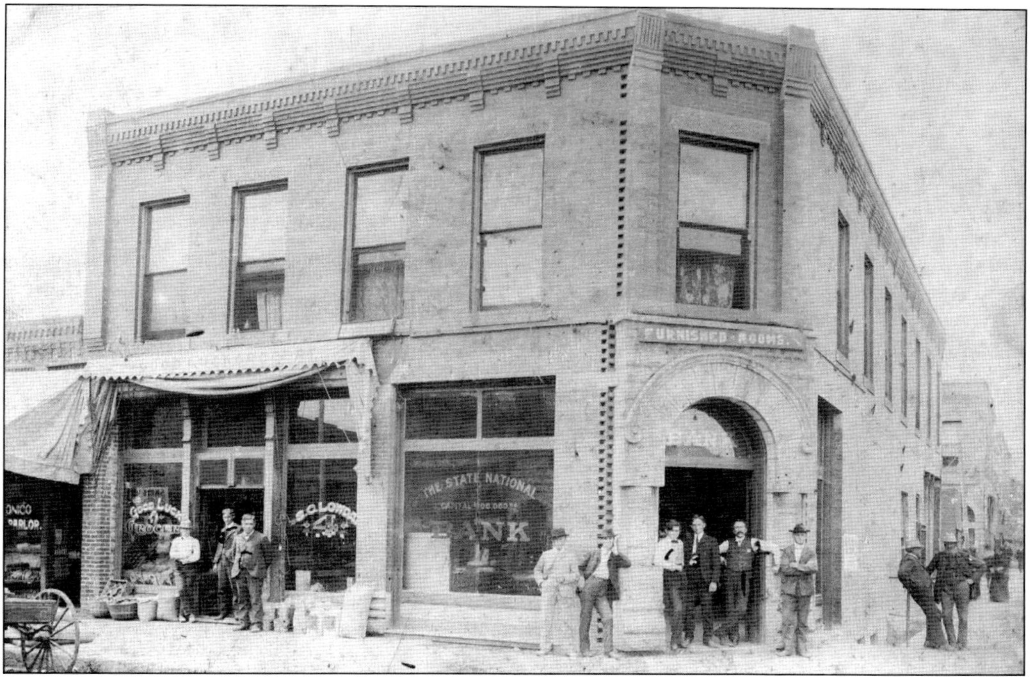

State National Bank. The State National Bank was organized in 1902 and was originally located at the corner of Main Street and Broadway Avenue in Shawnee. The photograph above was taken in 1903. Several members of the Lowdan and Johnson families are outside the building. S.C. Lowdan Grocery shares part of the structure. The bank moved to a new building across the road in 1929. The photograph below shows how the original bank building appeared about 60 years later, when it was the home of Central Drug. The building remained a Shawnee landmark until it was damaged and subsequently removed after a 1999 tornado. (Both, courtesy of Pottawatomie County Historical Society.)

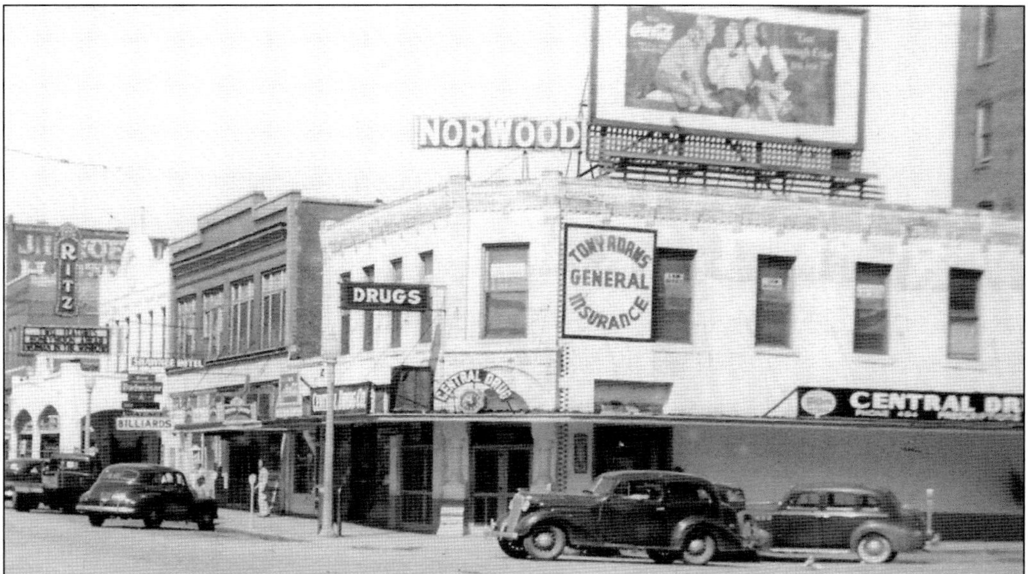

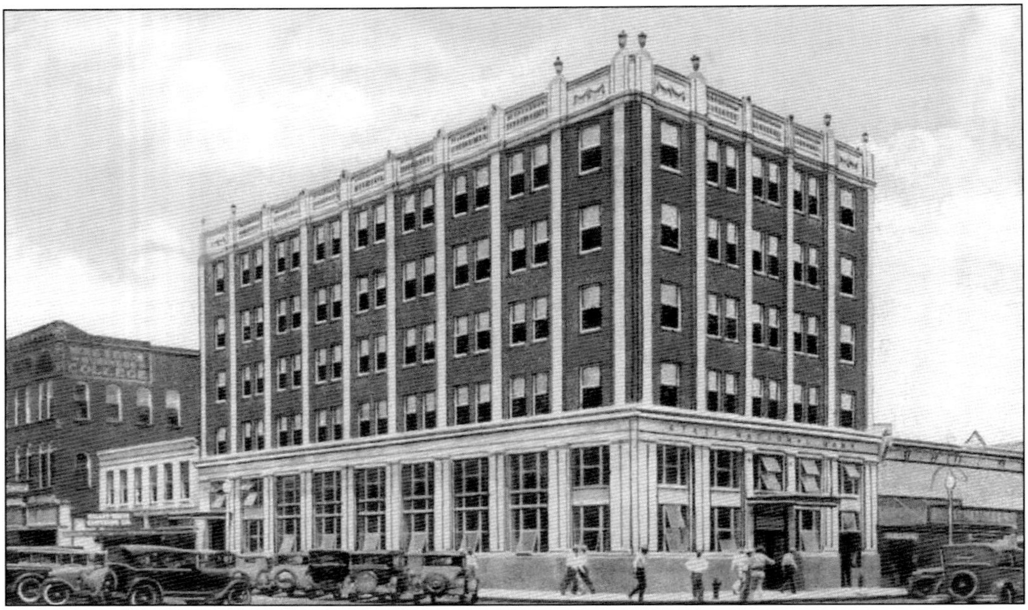

State Makes a Short Move. State National Bank moved into a much larger building across the street from its original location in 1929 and can be seen in the postcard above. The Western Business College is visible on the left side of the photograph. The bank suffered during the Great Depression and was closed by a bank moratorium in 1933. It reopened under a new charter in 1934 as American National Bank of Shawnee. The bank moved to the corner of Ninth Street and Broadway Avenue in 1965 and is now known as Arvest. The Main Street building still stands downtown and is currently known as the KIRC Building. Most of the upper floors are vacant. Below is a $20 currency note issued by the State National Bank of Shawnee. (Above, author's collection; below, courtesy of Carl Cochran.)

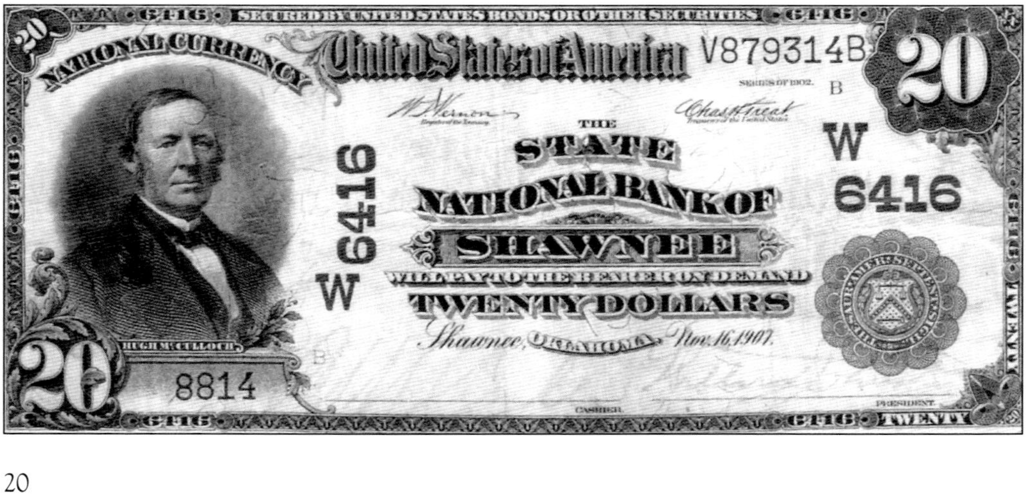

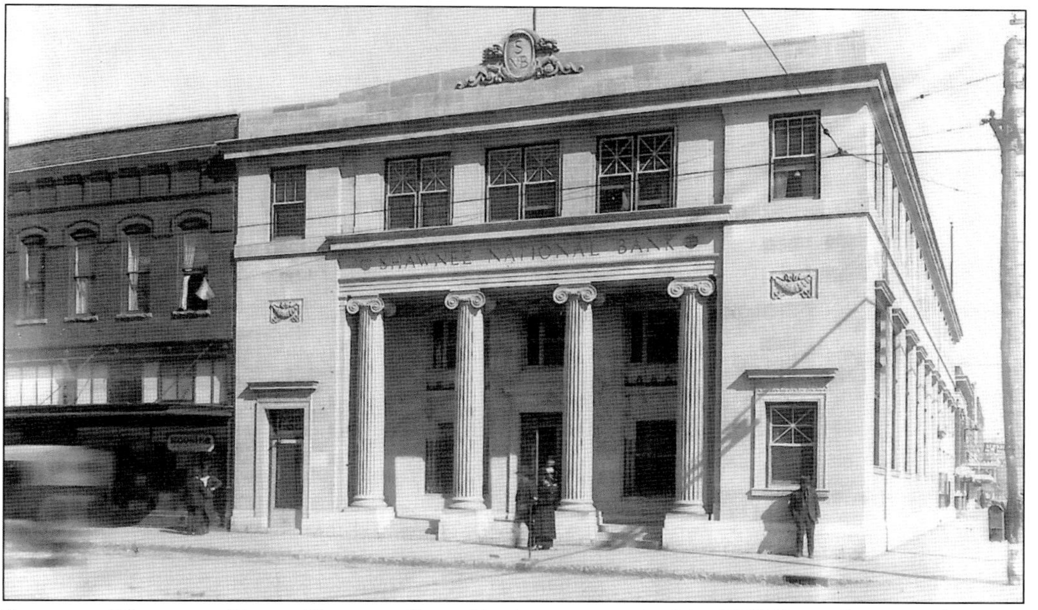

SHAWNEE NATIONAL BANK. Shawnee State Bank was organized in 1895. Just a few years later, in 1898, it was reorganized as Shawnee National Bank. The Shawnee National Bank building above was constructed in 1909 at the corner of Main and Bell Streets. The bank conducted business out of this building until it was closed by the national bank examiner in November 1932. A short time later, Oklahoma Gas and Electric (OG&E) took over the building, as shown in the photograph below. Note that "Shawnee National Bank" and "SNB" from the emblem have been removed. OG&E stayed in the building until about 1950. About the time OG&E vacated the building, the front of the bank was reworked and additional floors were added. Shortly thereafter, First National Bank moved to this location (Both, courtesy of Pottawatomie County Historical Society.)

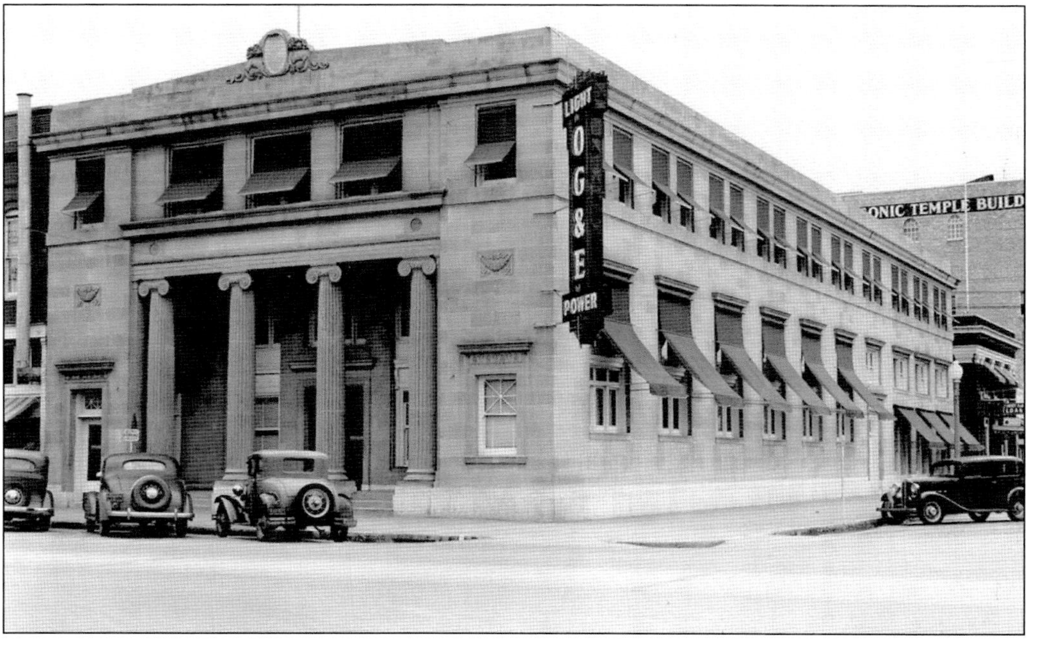

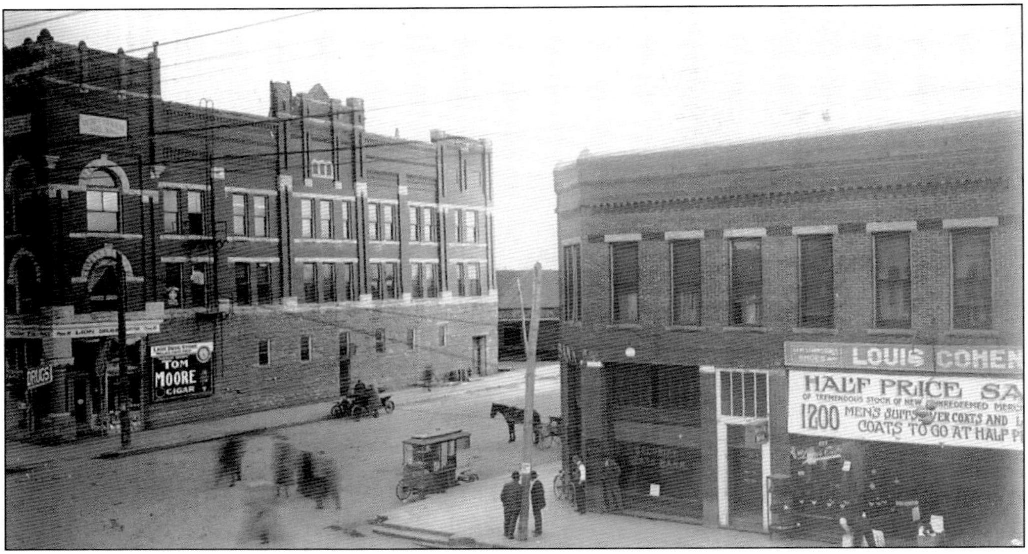

Security National Bank. The Security National Bank above was located at Main and Union Streets. In the 1920s, the name was changed to Guaranty State Bank. In 1923, it was converted to Federal National Bank. At a different point, the building housed the Arcade Bar and the English Kitchen, as seen in the photograph below. These photographs were taken by A.F. Martin, who had a studio at 112½ East Main Street. It is possible to see how this intersection changed over time, as Martin took numerous photographs of it. Also at this intersection were the Whittaker Building (which can be seen in these photographs), the Burt (later Walcott) Hotel, and another corner bank. None of these buildings survives today. (Both, courtesy of Pottawatomie County Historical Society.)

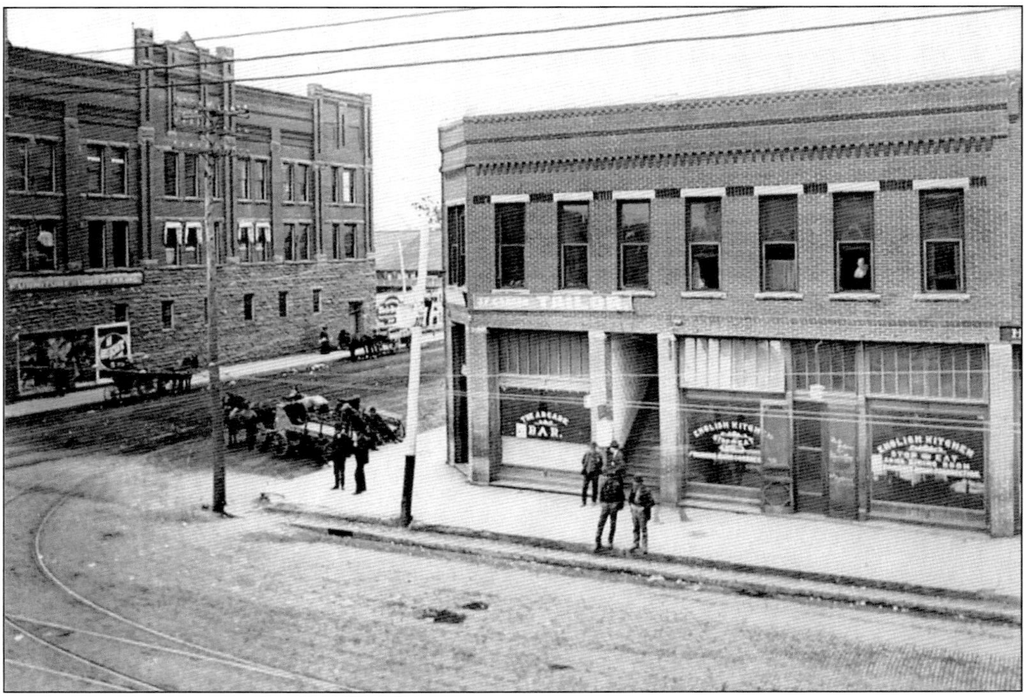

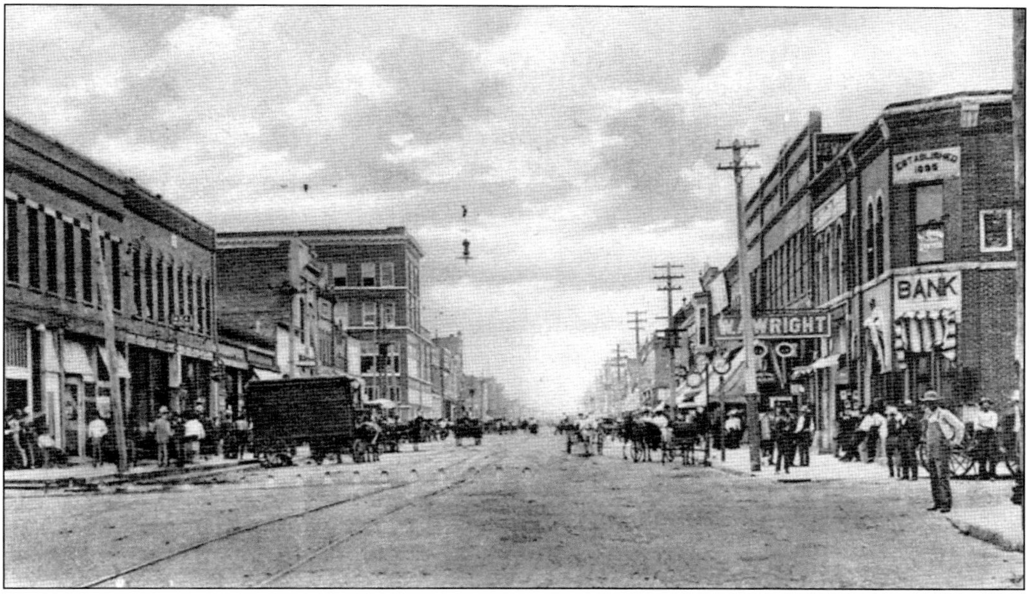

Bank of Commerce. In its advertisements, the Bank of Commerce claimed to be the "oldest bank in the city." It opened for business in 1902. Prior to 1911, it was housed in the East Room of the Whittaker Building at Main and Union Streets. In 1911, it absorbed the Oklahoma State Bank and moved into that building on the northwest corner of the same intersection. It was known thereafter as the National Bank of Commerce. This bank can be seen in the c. 1910 photograph above (the "Established 1895" refers to the Oklahoma State Bank). Later the old building was removed, and the bank moved into a new building on the same site. Eventually, it was bought out and the name changed to Federal National Bank, as seen in the picture below. (Above, author's collection; below, courtesy of Pottawatomie County Historical Society.)

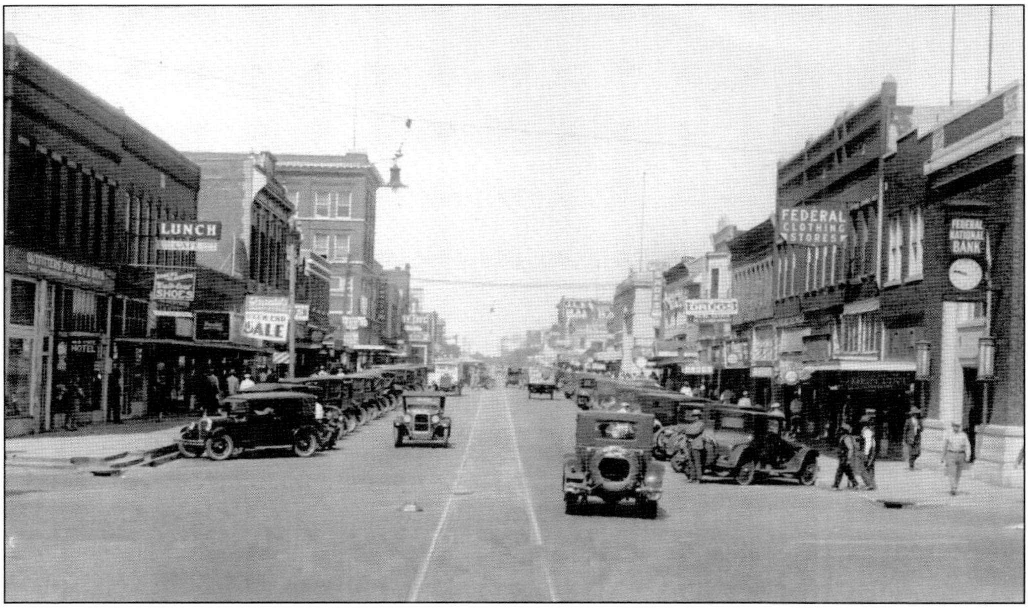

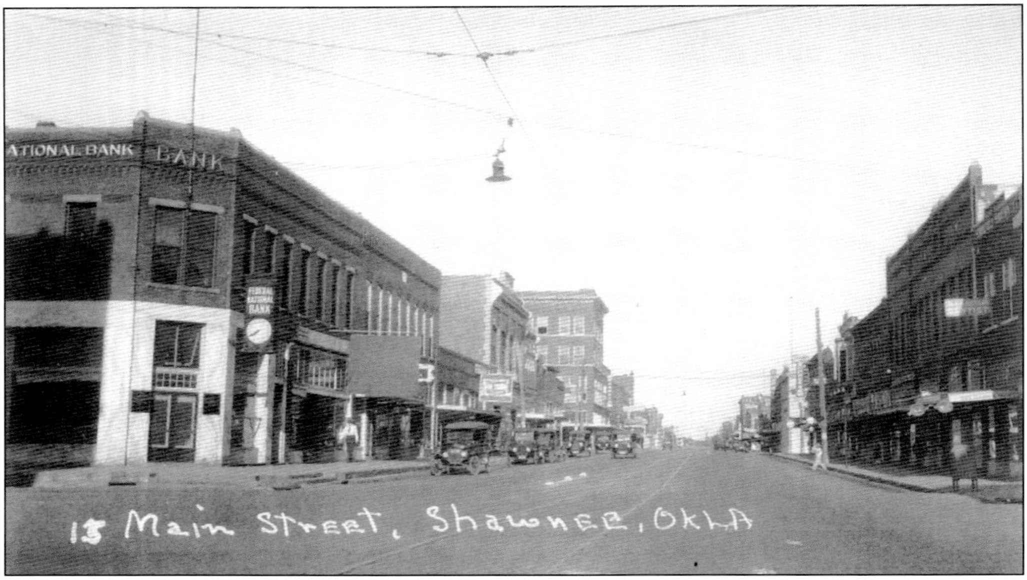

Federal National Bank. Directly across the street from the old Bank of Commerce was the Federal National Bank. It was established as a national bank in 1920. It took over the Security State Bank building, located on the southwest corner of Main and Union Streets. The photograph above shows it at this location with portions of the lower half of the building now covered in marble slabs. The bank later moved across the street when it purchased the National Bank of Commerce and took over its building (which can be seen on the previous page). In June 1949, Federal National Bank moved again to the old Shawnee National Bank building at Main and Bell Streets. Below is a $10 currency note issued by the Federal National Bank of Shawnee. (Above, courtesy of Pottawatomie County Historical Society; below, courtesy of Carl Cochran.)

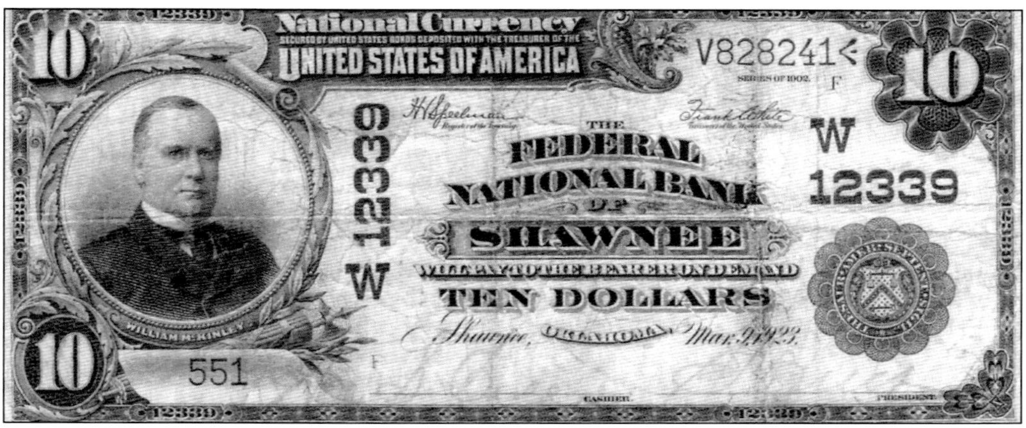

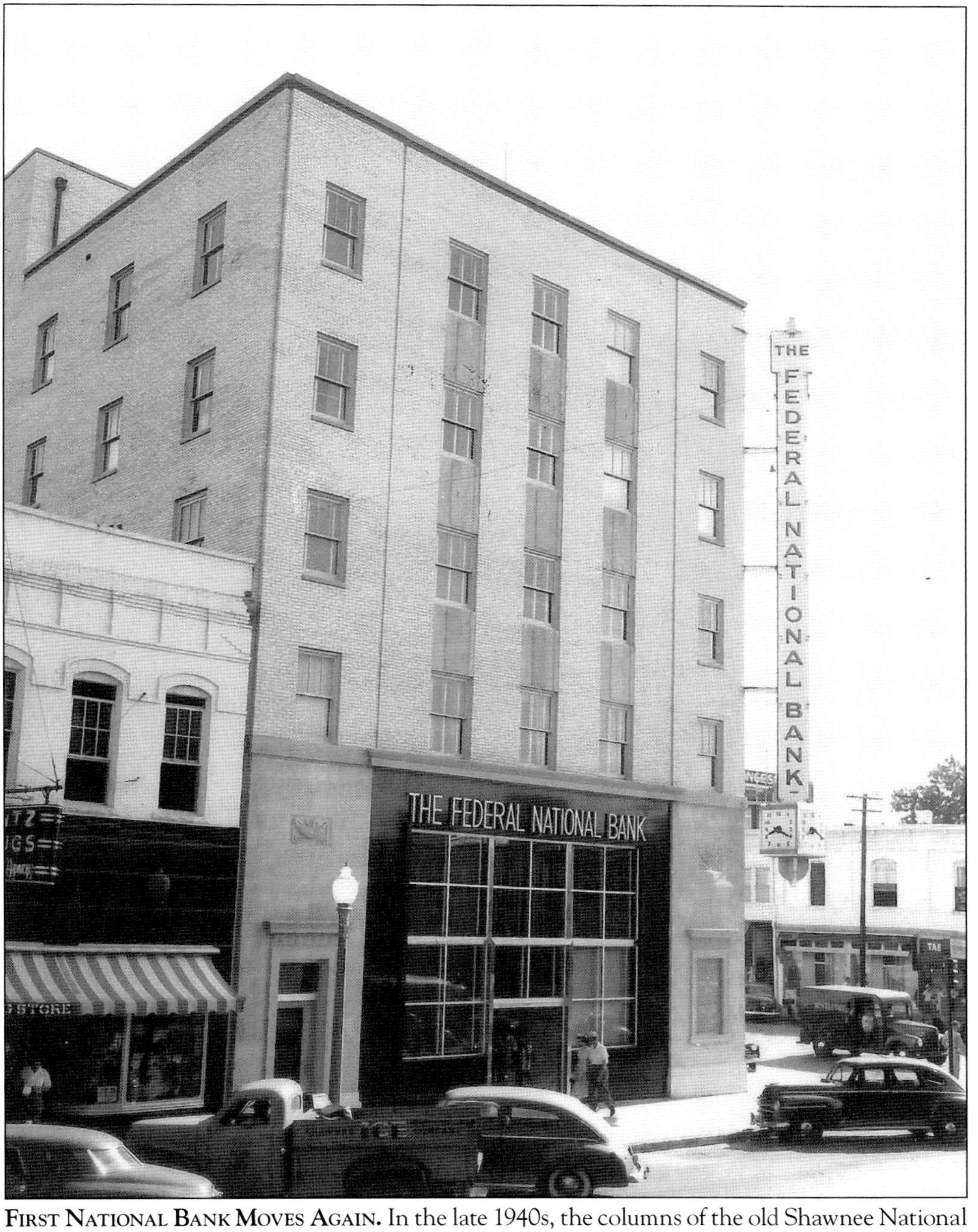

First National Bank Moves Again. In the late 1940s, the columns of the old Shawnee National Bank at Main and Bell Streets were removed, and the front of the building was reworked. In addition, four more floors were added. The final result can be seen above. Shortly after the expansion, Federal National Bank moved into the building. Federal National was acquired by BancFirst in 1989, and the bank became a branch of BancFirst. The branch closed in 2000. The structure is listed in the National Register of Historic Places as part of the Bell Street Historic District. (Courtesy of Pottawatomie County Historical Society.)

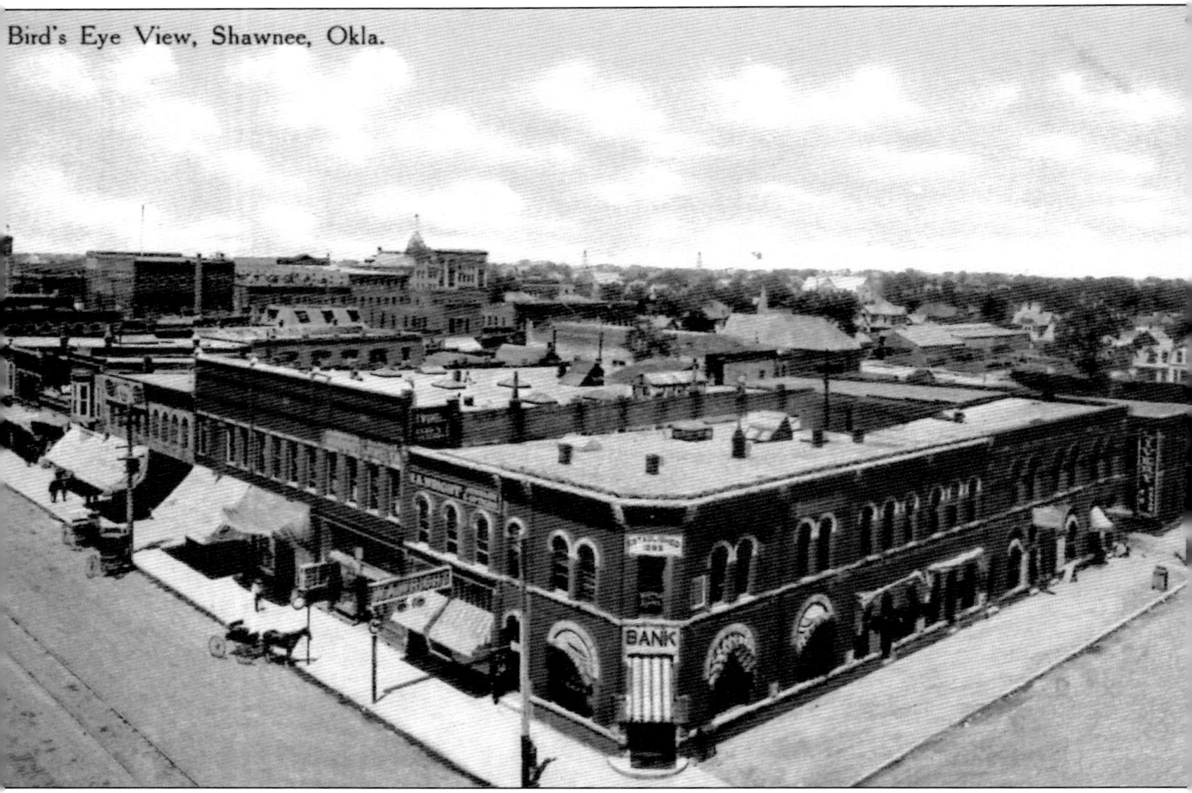

MAIN AND UNION STREETS. There were banks on two corners of Main and Union Streets in the early 1900s. One was the Security National Bank, and the other was the Bank of Commerce. This bird's-eye image of the intersection provides a nice view of the Bank of Commerce. City hall can be seen in the far back of the photograph. Wording on the bank building dates it to 1895, although the photograph used in this postcard was most likely taken some years later. (Author's collection.)

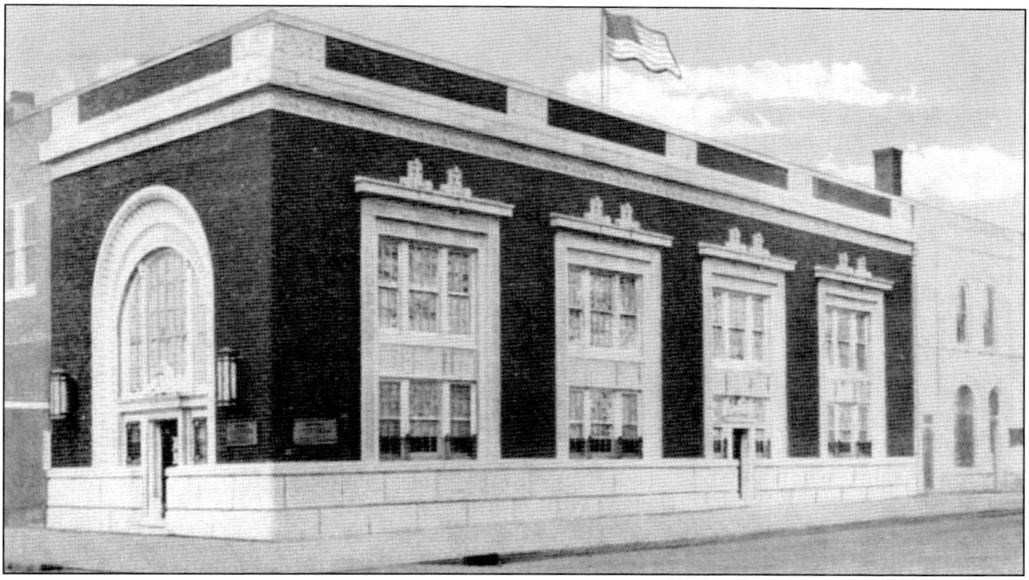

A New Building. The Bank of Commerce was located at the corner of Main and Union Streets in Shawnee. The building in the postcard above replaced its original structure at the same site. Federal National Bank took over the building, moving from across the street in December 1925. First National Bank moved again to Main and Bell Streets about 1951. The building at Main and Union Streets was later razed to make room for a new J.C. Penney store. Below, a parade celebrating the Pottawatomie County Courthouse dedication passes by the bank in July 1935. (Both, courtesy of Pottawatomie County Historical Society.)

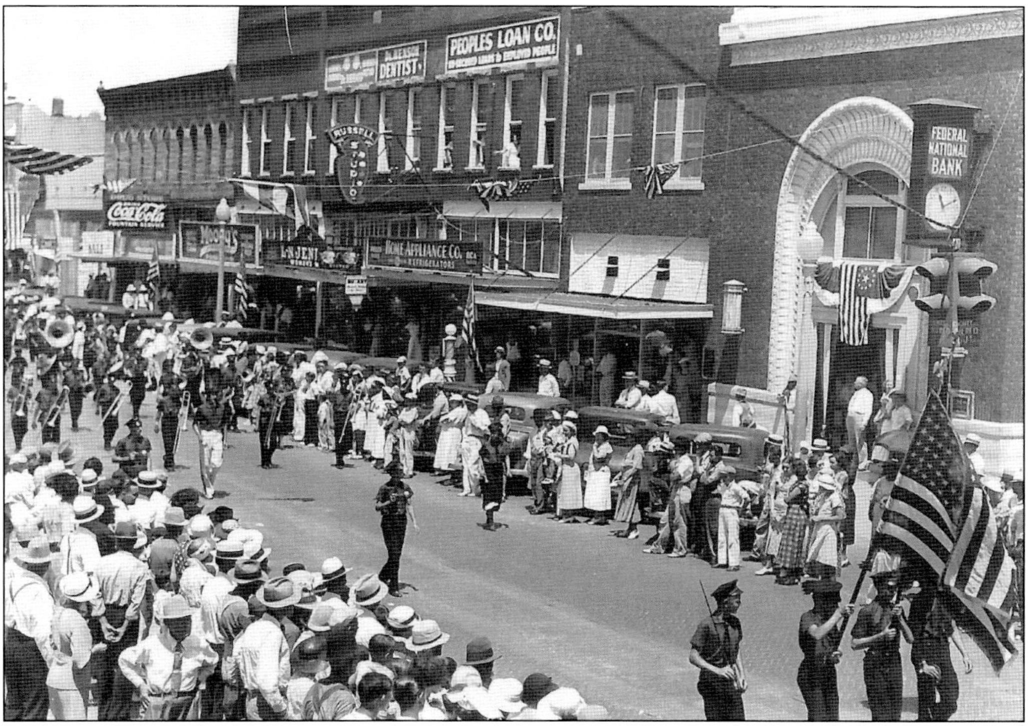

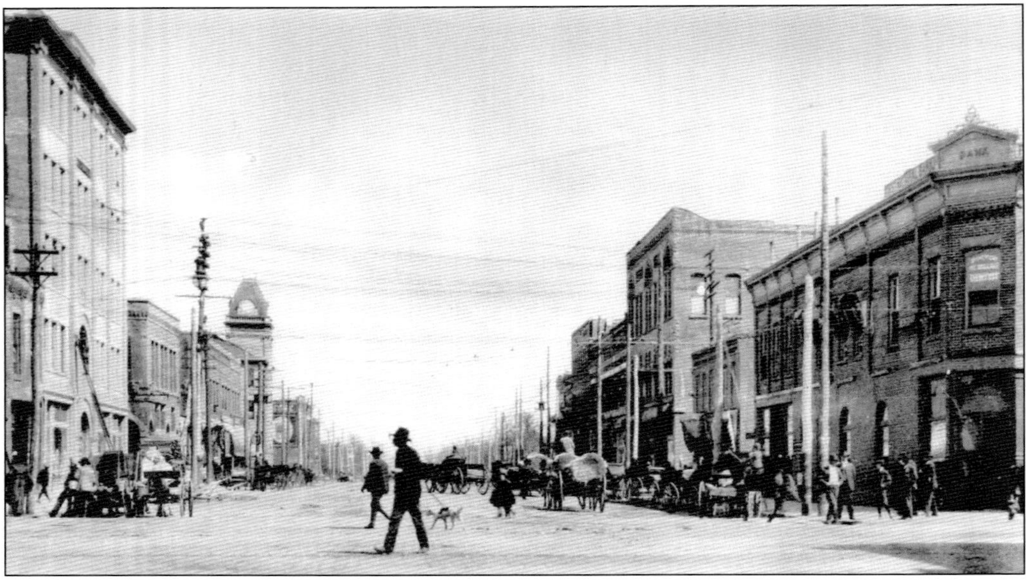

First National Bank. First National Bank started out in 1895 as the Bank of Shawnee, but it was changed to First National Bank in 1898. The bank was located at the corner of Main Street and Broadway Avenue in Shawnee. The photograph above, looking east down Broadway Avenue, shows the bank on the corner. Farther down is the post office building. Across the street, the top of city hall is visible. The photograph below shows Main Street looking east, and First National Bank is visible on the left. This building was razed, and State National Bank was built here in 1929. (Both, author's collection.)

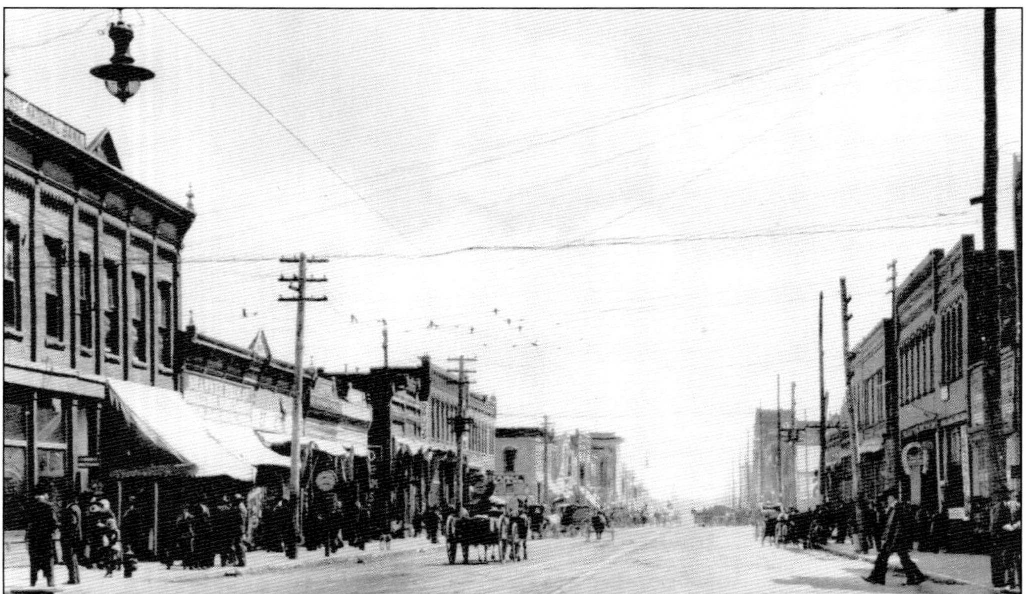

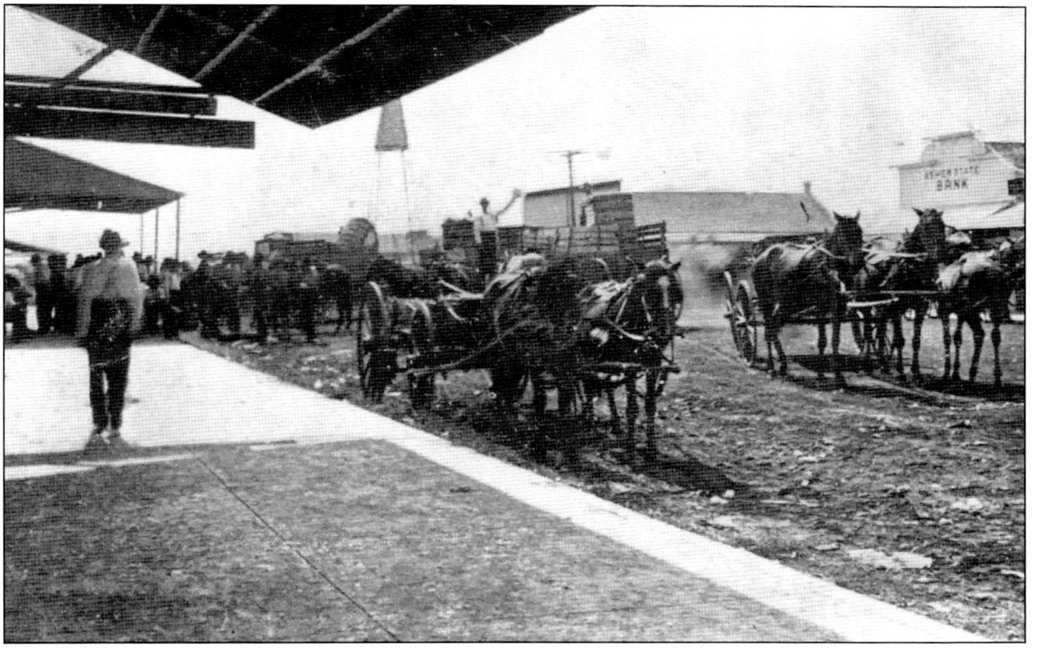

Asher State Bank. An early 1900s photograph of Asher's Main Street is shown above. Asher State Bank can be seen at far right. According to the *Ada News*, in December 1906, the Ben Cravens gang entered the First State Bank and left with $4,000 cash. Drops of blood thought to have belonged to an injured robber were followed from the bank to the Rock Island depot. The men headed north on the Rock Island Railroad and were believed to have made their escape on a handcar. One hostage, Roy Leham, was found in a boxcar several hours later. Two men, Dave McCullough of Wichita and A.W. Franks of Higginsville, Missouri, were arrested the following Saturday at the Frisco Hotel in Oklahoma City. Below is a blank Asher State Bank check that would more than likely bounce today. (Both, author's collection.)

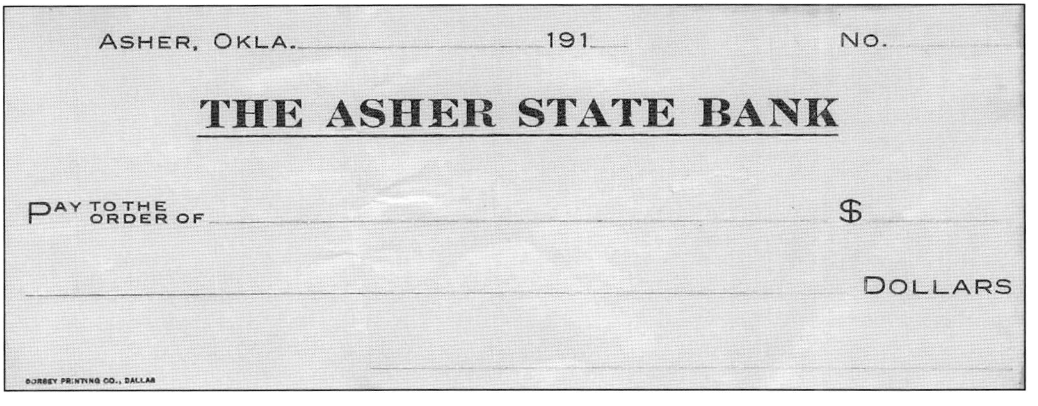
ASHER, OKLA. __________ 191__ NO. ______

THE ASHER STATE BANK

PAY TO THE ORDER OF __________ $ ______

__________ DOLLARS

DORSEY PRINTING CO., DALLAS

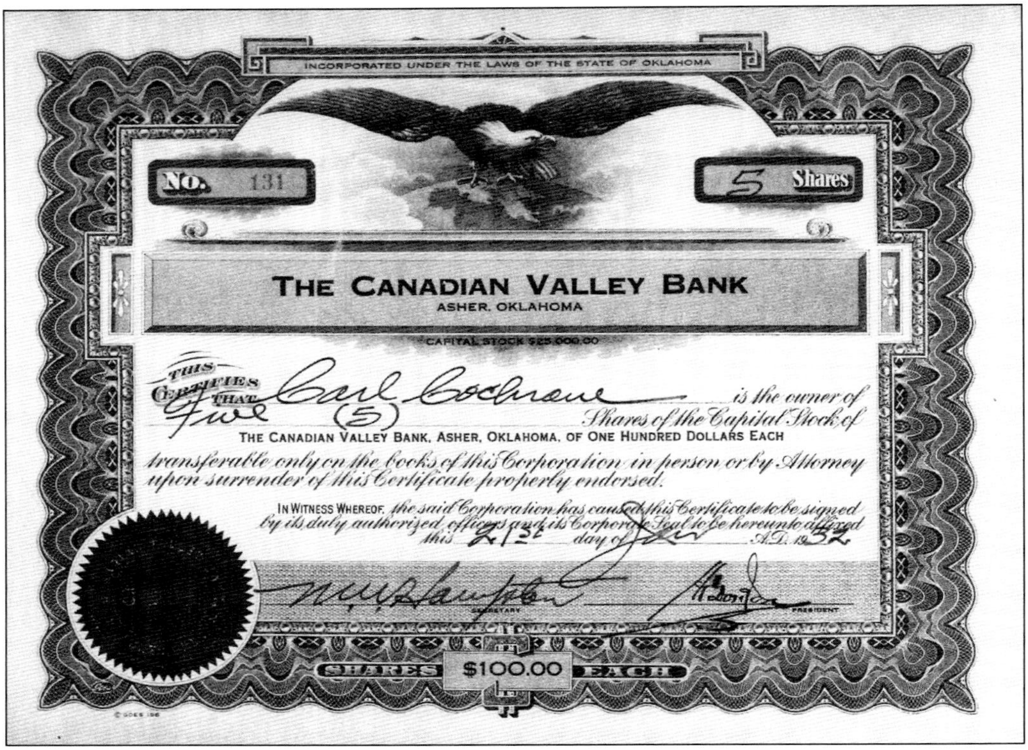

Canadian Valley Bank. The Canadian Valley Bank was located on Main Street in Asher. According to various newspaper articles, the bank was robbed in 1927, 1928, and 1929. In the 1927 robbery, an Asher druggist, Bailey Browder, was shot and later died of his injuries. After the 1929 robbery, the bank moved to a more secure location and did not experience any more robberies but was closed in November 1932. The building stood for many years after closing but has since been removed. Above is a bank stock certificate issued the year the bank closed. Below is a canceled 1923 check written on the bank by W.H. Wilsie. (Both, courtesy of Carl Cochrane.)

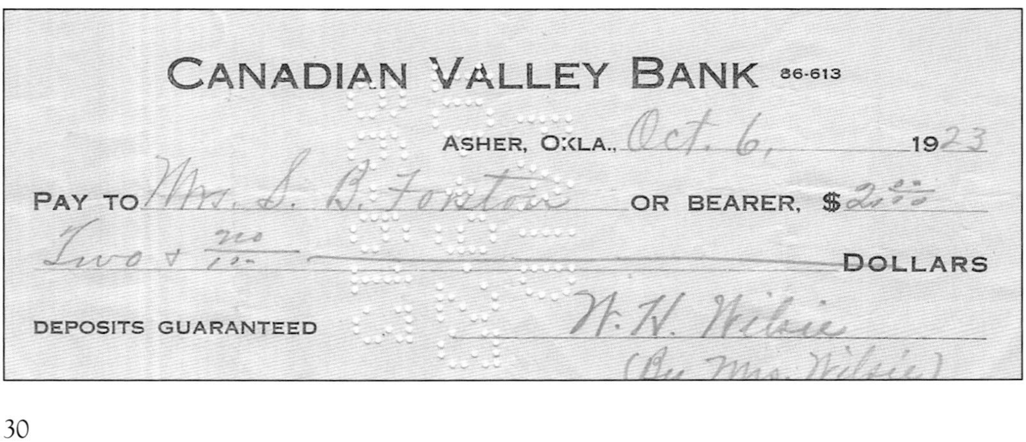

Three

Business and Industry

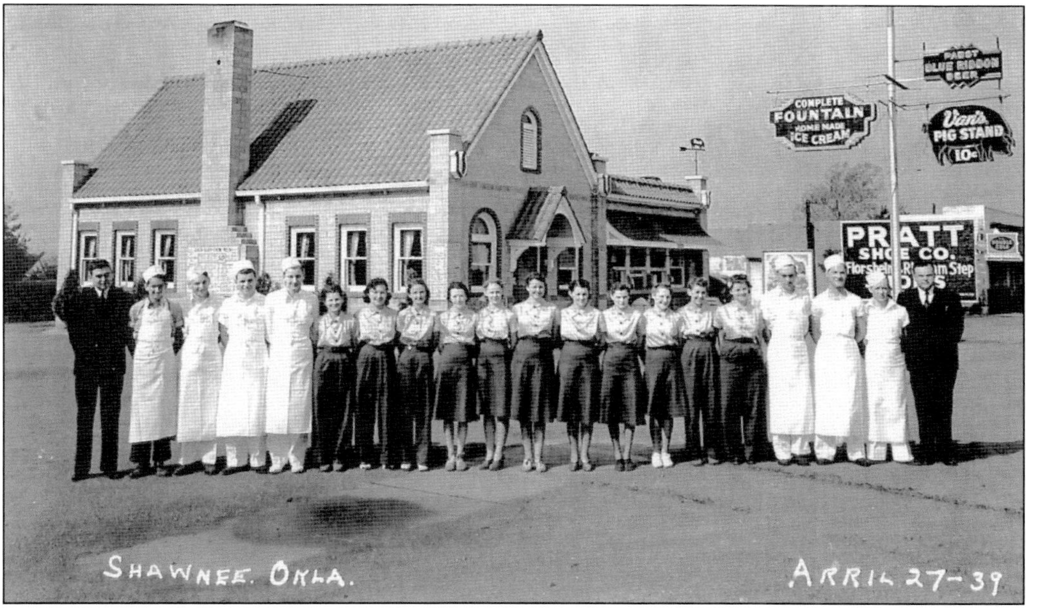

Van's Pig Stand. Pottawatomie County has always experienced a divide when it comes to business and industry. While south Pottawatomie County has relied more on agriculture and oil, Shawnee and Tecumseh have enjoyed more hospitality, shopping, and restaurant options like Van's Pig Stand (pictured in 1939). This Shawnee mainstay was opened in 1930, and it continues to welcome barbecue lovers today. (Courtesy of Pottawatomie County Historical Society.)

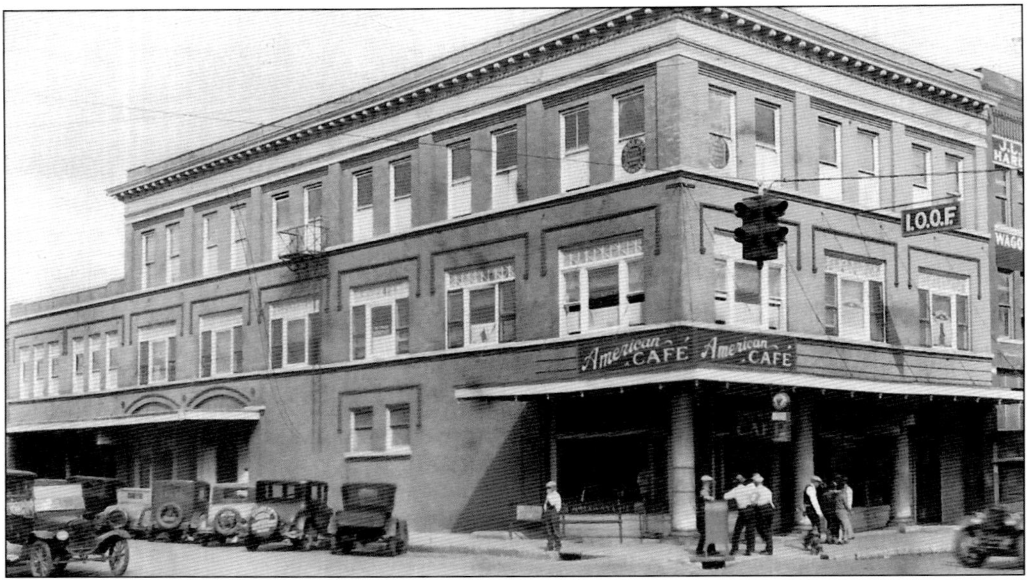

CHRISNEY BUILDING. The American Café and the Independent Order of Odd Fellows are two tenants of the Chrisney Building at Main and Beard Streets in Shawnee. Buildings like this went up rapidly in Shawnee in the early 1900s. This building is one of the lucky ones that remains standing and is currently undergoing the long process of restoration. (Courtesy of Pottawatomie County Historical Society.)

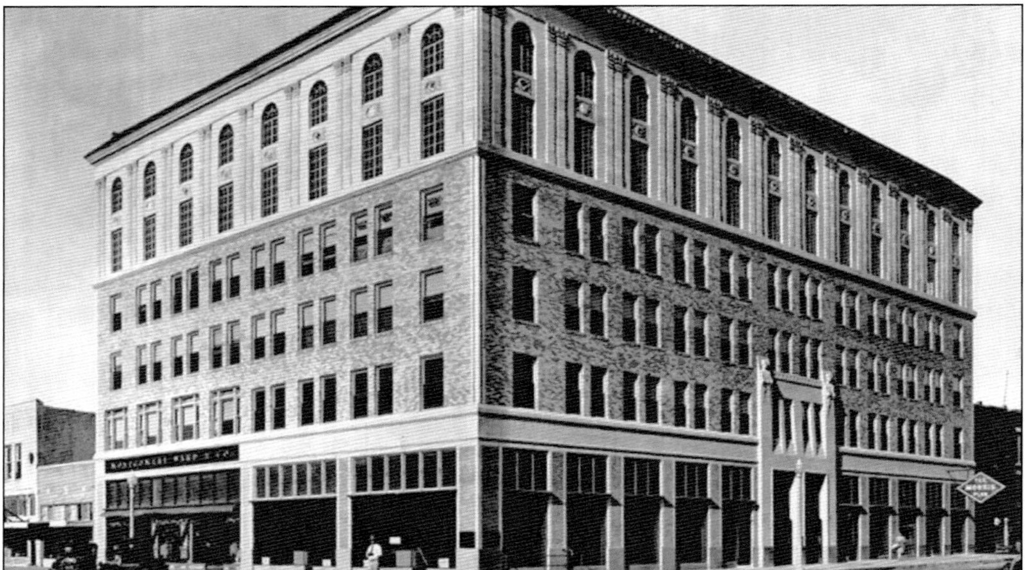

THE BILLINGTON BUILDING. The Billington Building is a seven-story building on the southwest corner of East Ninth and Bell Streets. It was constructed in 1929 by C.B. Billington at a cost of $300,000 and is recognized as one of the first skyscrapers in Shawnee. Billington was a Mason, and the top two floors were used as a meeting hall for the Shawnee Masonic Lodge. Those floors are adorned with decorative arches over the windows with Masonic symbols. (Courtesy of Pottawatomie County Historical Society.)

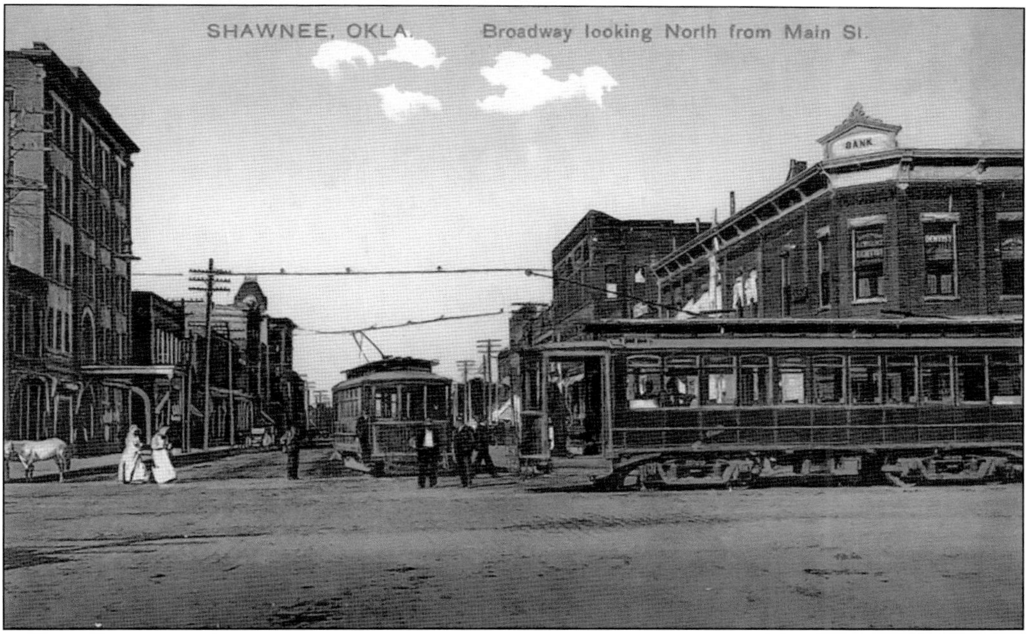

BROADWAY AVENUE AND MAIN STREET, SHAWNEE. A nice view of Broadway Avenue looking north from Main Street can be seen in this postcard from 1910. Streetcars can be seen traveling the roads. A bank is on the corner, and the post office building can be seen about halfway down on the right. City hall is farther down on the left. (Courtesy of Don Taylor.)

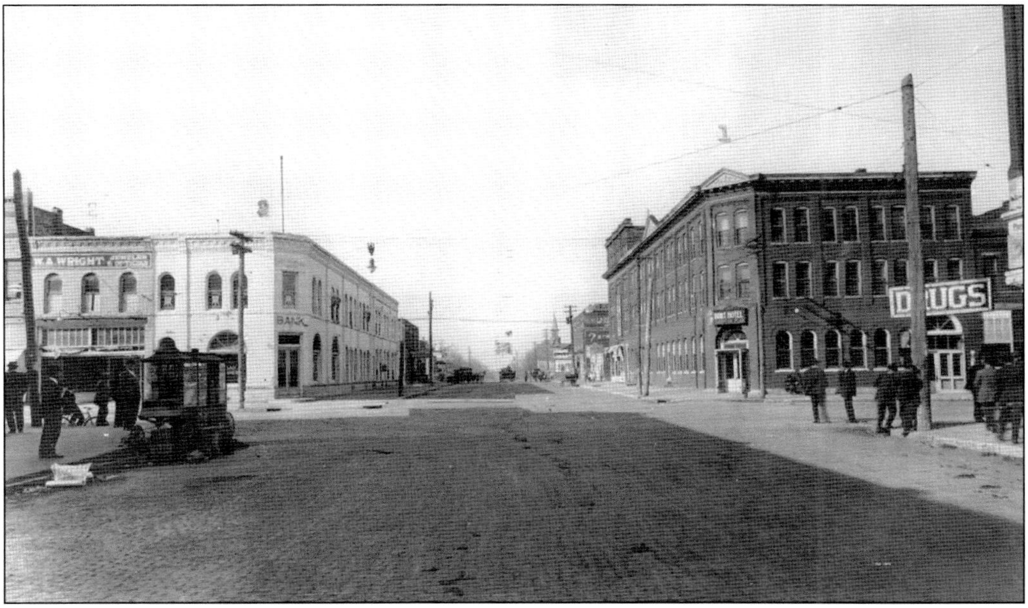

MAIN AND UNION STREETS. The building pictured proclaims itself to be the Burt Hotel, but it is better known by most people as the Walcott. The hotel was located at Main and Union Streets. The Security State Bank is across the street, and next door is W.A. Wright's Jewelry and Optician Shop. (Courtesy of Pottawatomie County Historical Society.)

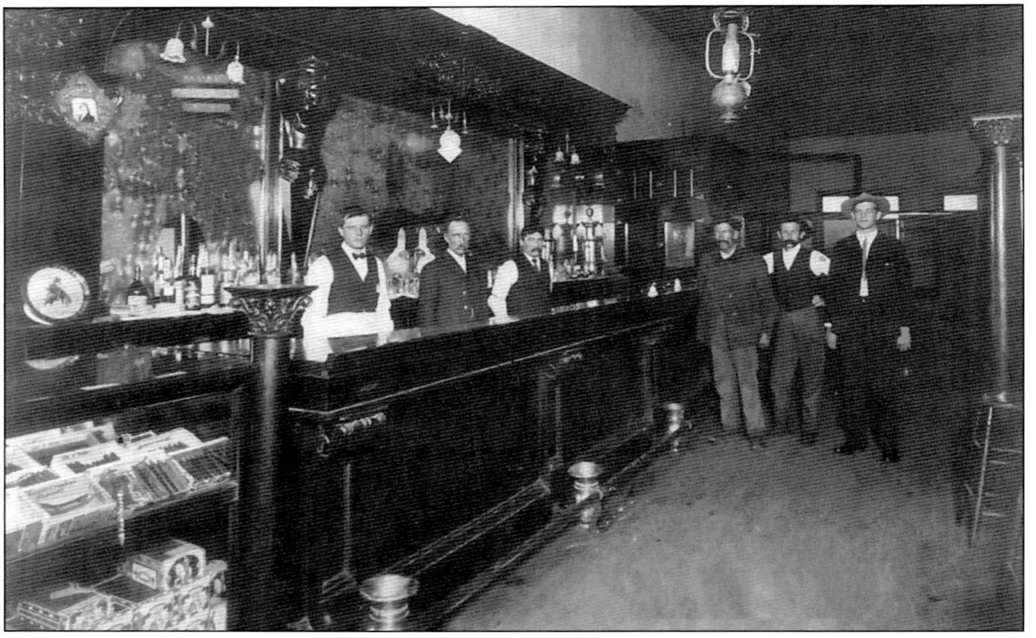

The Owl Saloon. Impressive woodwork and a few interesting characters fill the Owl Saloon in this c. 1901 photograph. The saloon was located at 305 East Main Street in Shawnee. Photographed behind the bar are John Julius Berger and Gustava Berger, co-owners of the establishment. (Courtesy of Pottawatomie County Historical Society.)

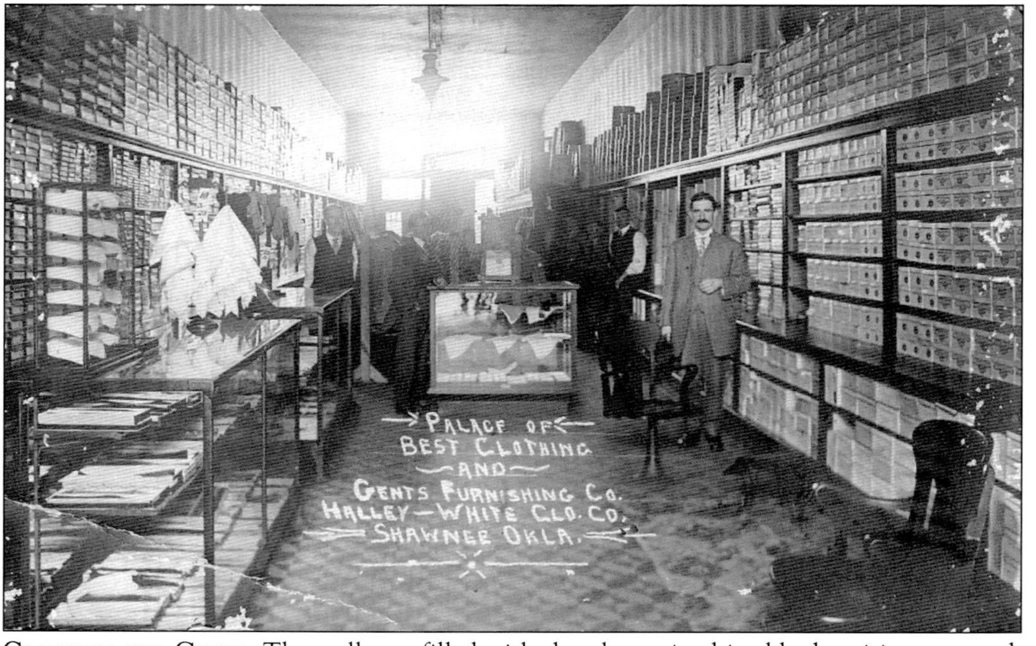

Clothing for Gents. The walls are filled with shoe boxes in this old advertising postcard. Featured is the interior of the Palace of Best Clothing and Gents Furnishing Company and Halley-White Clothing Company in Shawnee. This postcard was mailed on December 22, 1910. (Courtesy of Don Taylor.)

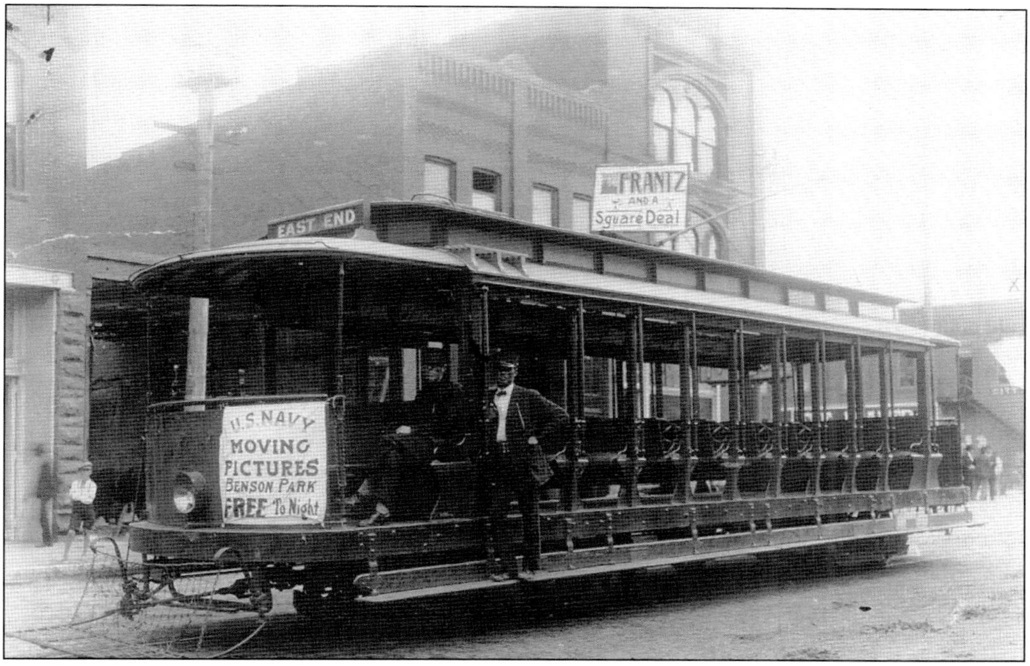

STREETCARS. The Shawnee City Council and the mayor approved an ordinance for streetcars in 1905. The first cars came some time after, just two at first, and they made such a rumbling sound when they went by that people would run to the windows to see. Tracks stretched from St. Benedict's on Kickapoo Street up to Broadway Avenue and Main Street as well as down Broadway Avenue. A line to Tecumseh was added later. In the photograph above, two men show off one of the streetcars that served early Shawnee. This one advertises a movie that night at Benson Park, located between Shawnee and Tecumseh. In the photograph below, tracks are being laid in Shawnee at the intersection of Main and Bell Streets. (Both, courtesy of Pottawatomie County Historical Society.)

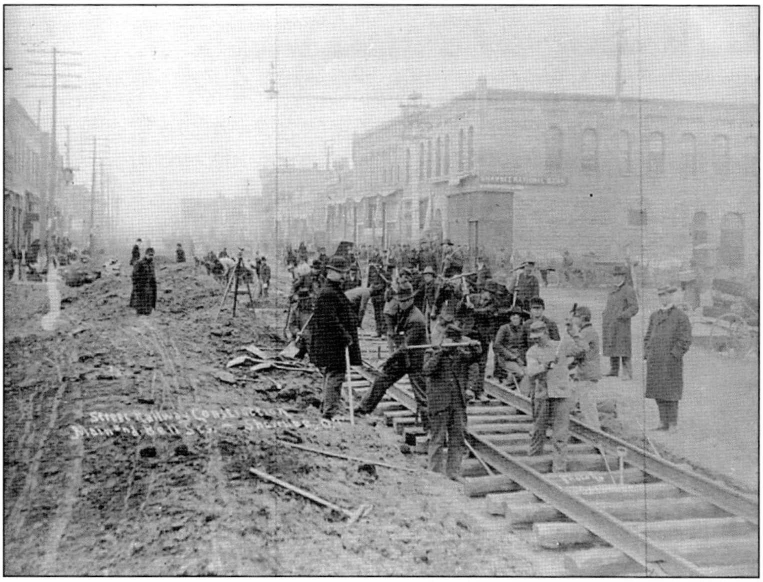

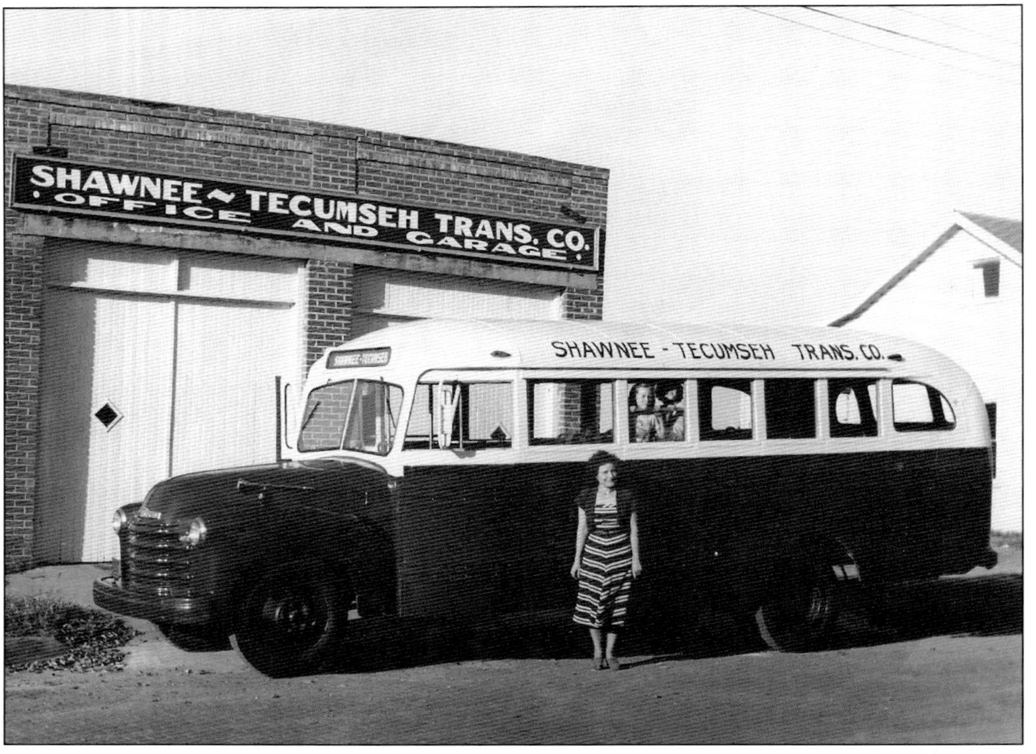

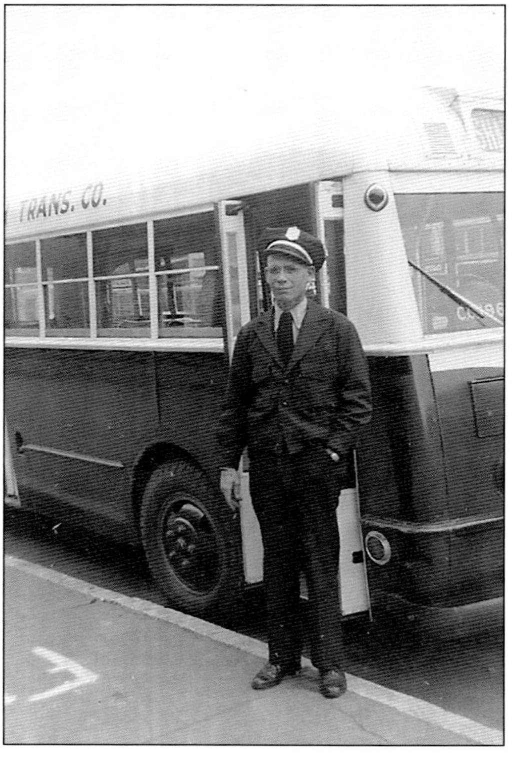

More Modern Transportation. After the trolley era, the Shawnee-Tecumseh Transportation Company offered a more modern transportation option between Shawnee and Tecumseh. Initial pricing to or from Shawnee was 25¢. Commuter round-trip tickets were $1 for one week. Twenty-ride tickets sold for $3. The business was sold in 1959 to Shawnee City Lines and was discontinued shortly thereafter. In the 1952 photograph above, Thelma Mason shows off a new bus with daughters Sue Ann and Jane Kay sitting by the windows. The office and garage were located on Park Street in Tecumseh. The photograph at left shows Buford McGee, a bus driver, in 1957. (Both, courtesy of Sue McDaniel.)

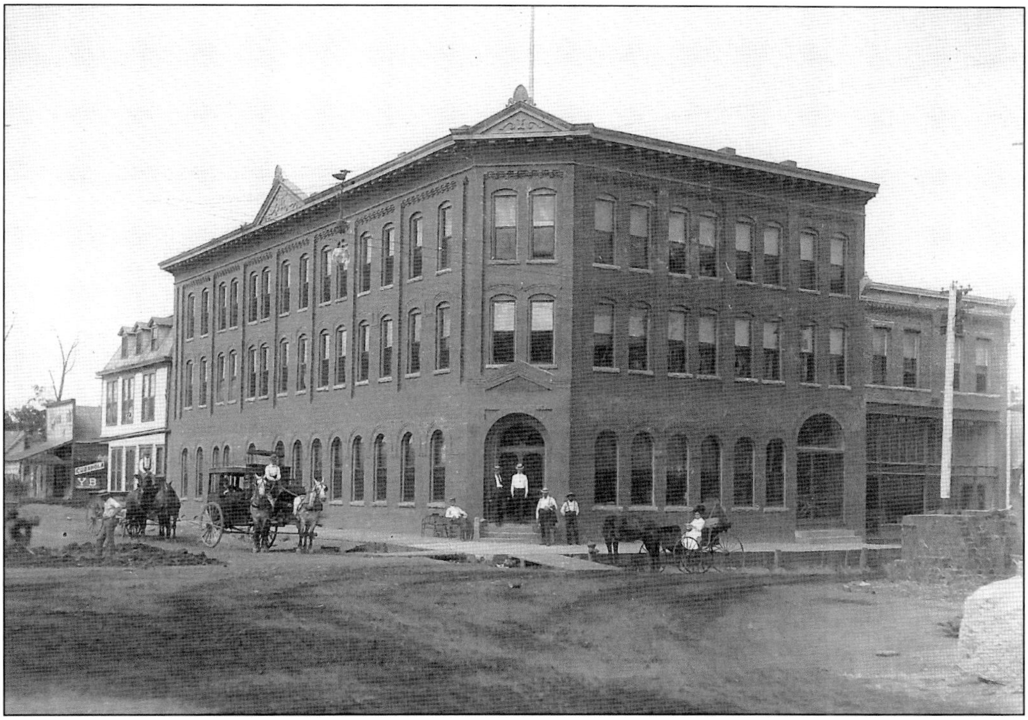

WALCOTT HOTEL. The Burt Hotel, later renamed (and better known as) the Walcott Hotel, was at the corner of Main and Union Streets in Shawnee. Built by Cowan Construction Company, the hotel had 82 rooms—35 with a shower, 15 with a bath, and 32 without a bathroom. The photograph above was taken in the early 1900s. Since Shawnee never had a "town square," hotels like this as well as other businesses jockeyed for the best position they could find on Main Street and its arterials. The photograph below, taken later, shows Bear Drugs and Walcott Barber Shop, along with the neighboring Keller's Feed Store. The Walcott burned in the 1970s or 1980s. (Both, courtesy of Pottawatomie County Historical Society.)

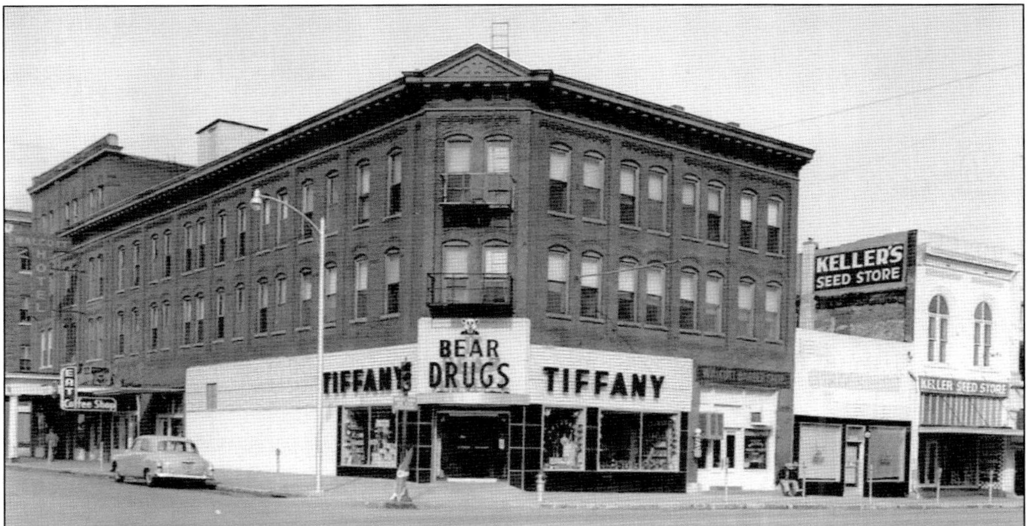

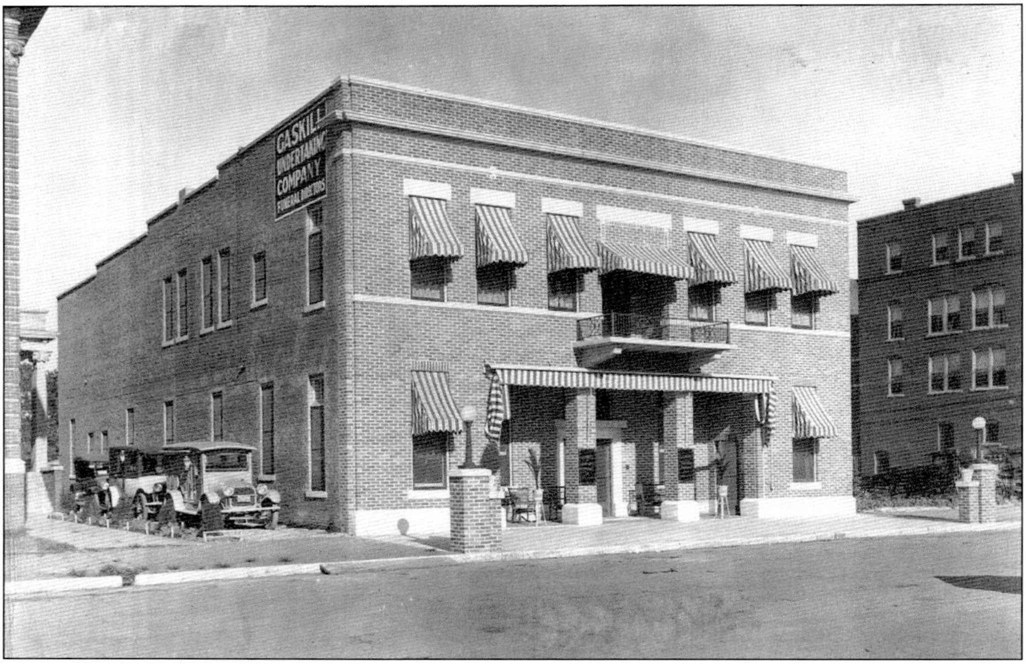

Gaskill Funeral Home. Gaskill Funeral Home, above, was located on Union Street between the Convention Center and the Walcott Hotel. Prior to becoming a funeral home, the building was occupied by the Carey Bus and Boarding Stable. Built in 1905, it is one of Shawnee's oldest standing buildings. In a 1927 photograph of Union Street looking south, below, the Gaskill building can be seen flanked by the convention center and the Walcott Hotel. In the background, the Rock Island depot is visible. (Above, courtesy of Pottawatomie County Historical Society; below, courtesy of Don Taylor.)

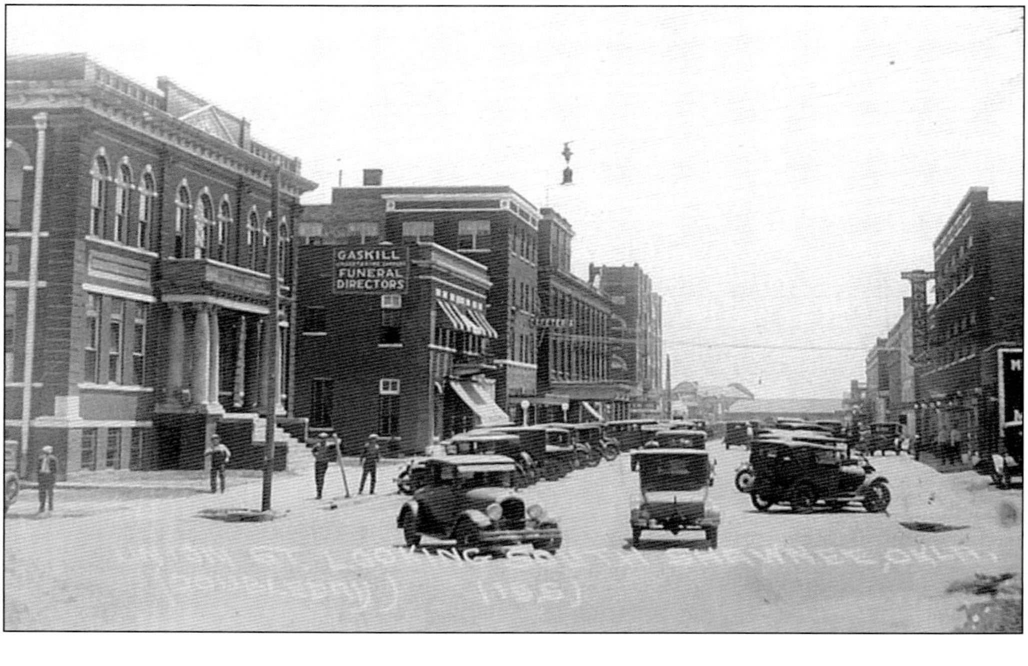

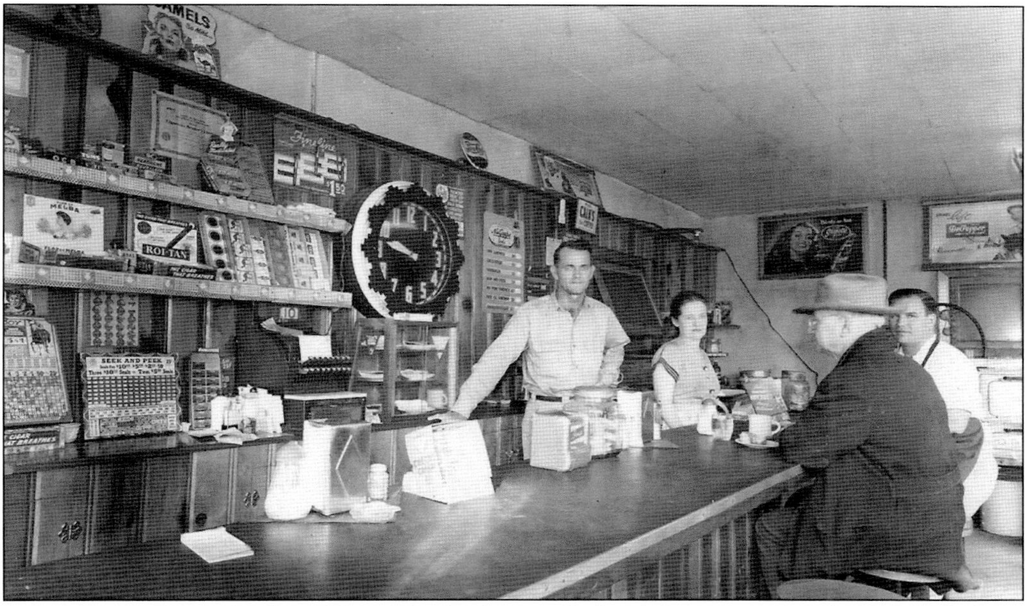

Asher Café. Ernest Holt and his wife, Archie, are behind the counter at the Asher Café on Division Street. Two unidentified customers are enjoying their morning coffee. This 1950s photograph shows a wealth of interesting items in the background, including a few punch board games tempting patrons to find prizes up to $10. The building that housed the café also included a station and market. (Author's collection.)

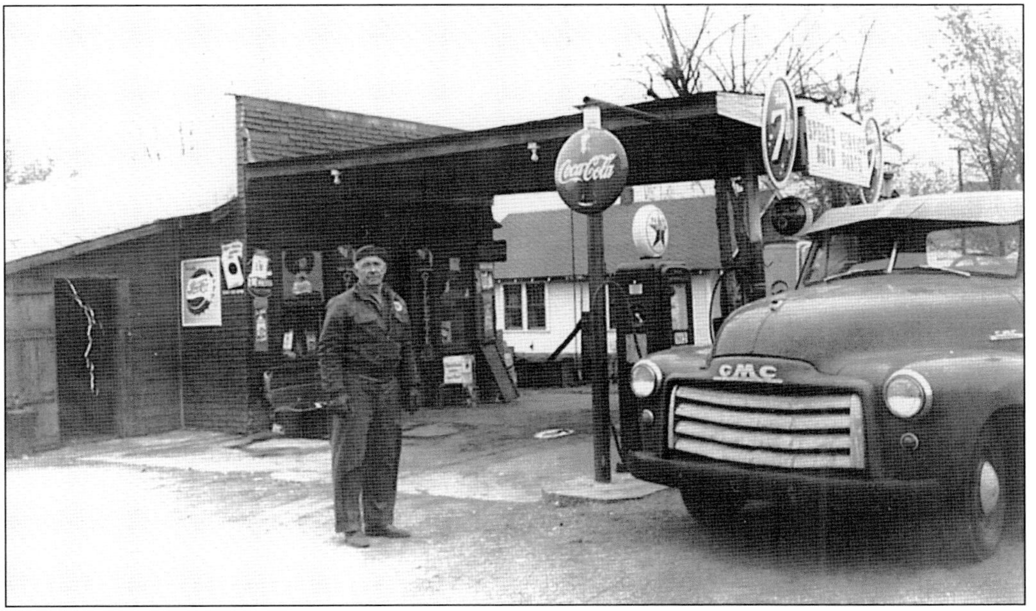

Asher Station. Joseph Lessie "Dick" Speers stands outside his service and auto parts station in Asher in 1956. Signs for many iconic brands, such as GMC, Coca-Cola, 7-Up, Texaco, and Pepsi-Cola, contribute to this interesting photograph. Early gas stations like this often had a small market and a service station where several needs could be taken care of by one or a few proprietors. (Author's collection.)

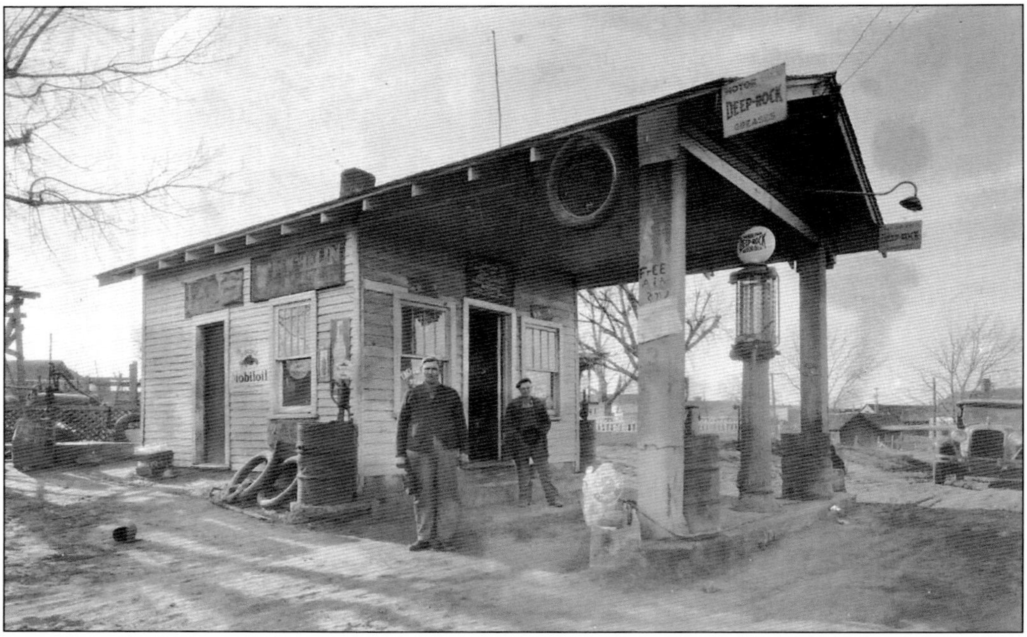

McLoud Stations. Mobiloil, Deep-Rock motor oil and greases, and Michelin tires are advertised at Charles Haley's Station, above, which was located at the east end of McLoud. The two gentlemen are not identified, nor is the photograph dated, but it is probably from the 1910s or 1920s. Gasoline is a mere 16¢ at Martin Held's Station, below, which was photographed in 1928. (Above, courtesy of Pottawatomie County Historical Society; below, author's collection.)

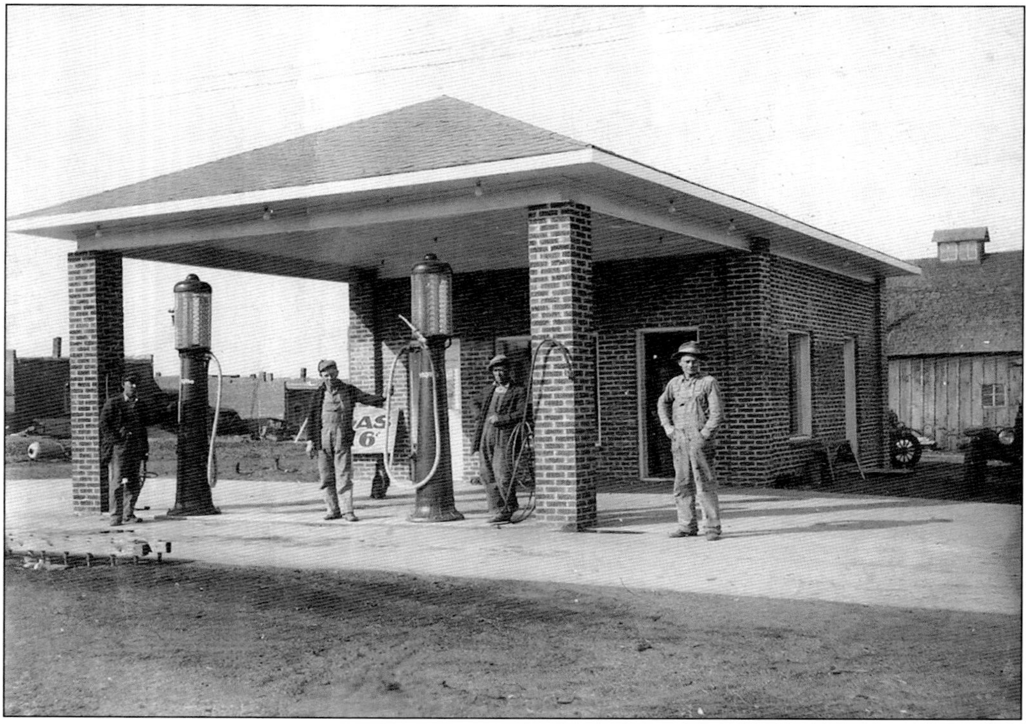

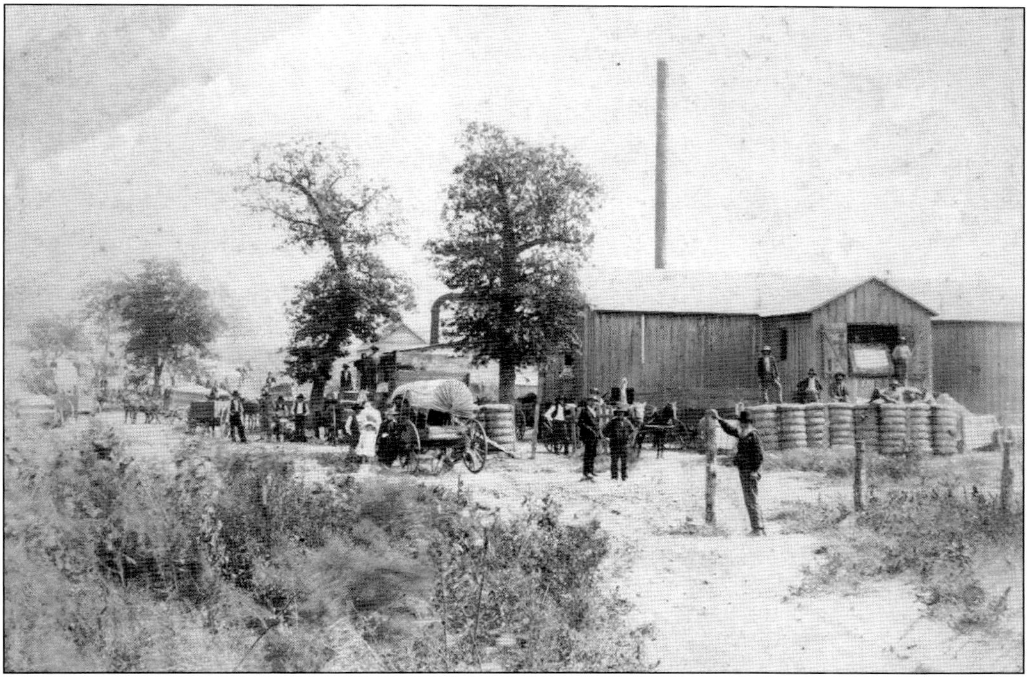

An Important Crop. Two of McLoud's cotton gins are pictured. The above photograph is from 1899, and the photograph below is from 1901, both when McLoud was part of Oklahoma Territory. Cotton was a major agricultural commodity in Oklahoma and Pottawatomie County at this time. It is estimated that almost a quarter of the cultivated land in the state was being used to grow cotton. (Both, courtesy of Pottawatomie County Historical Society.)

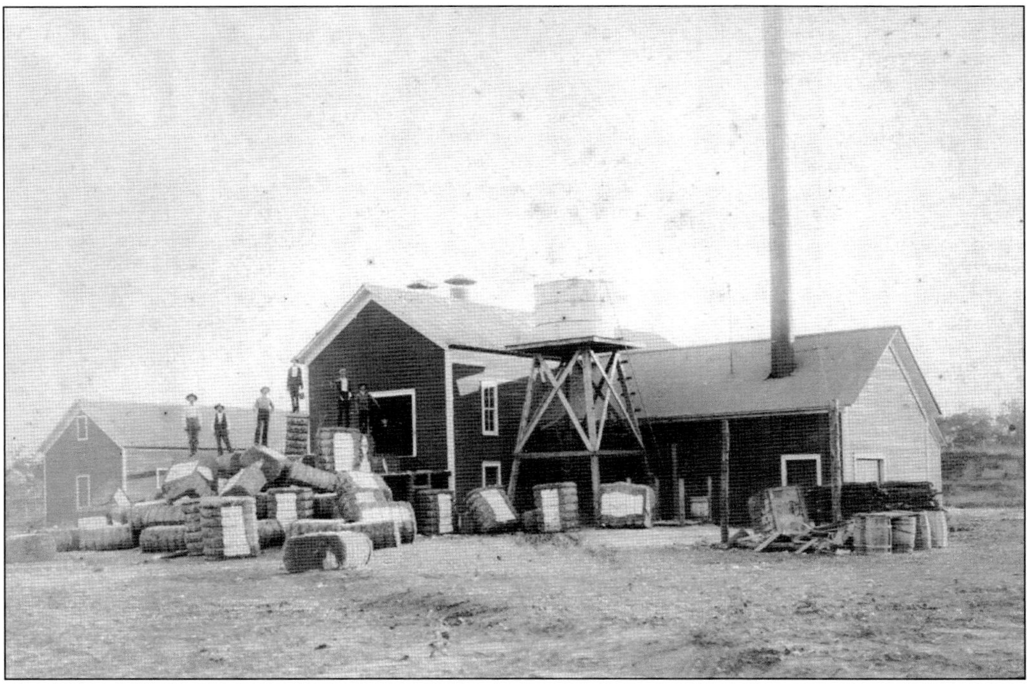

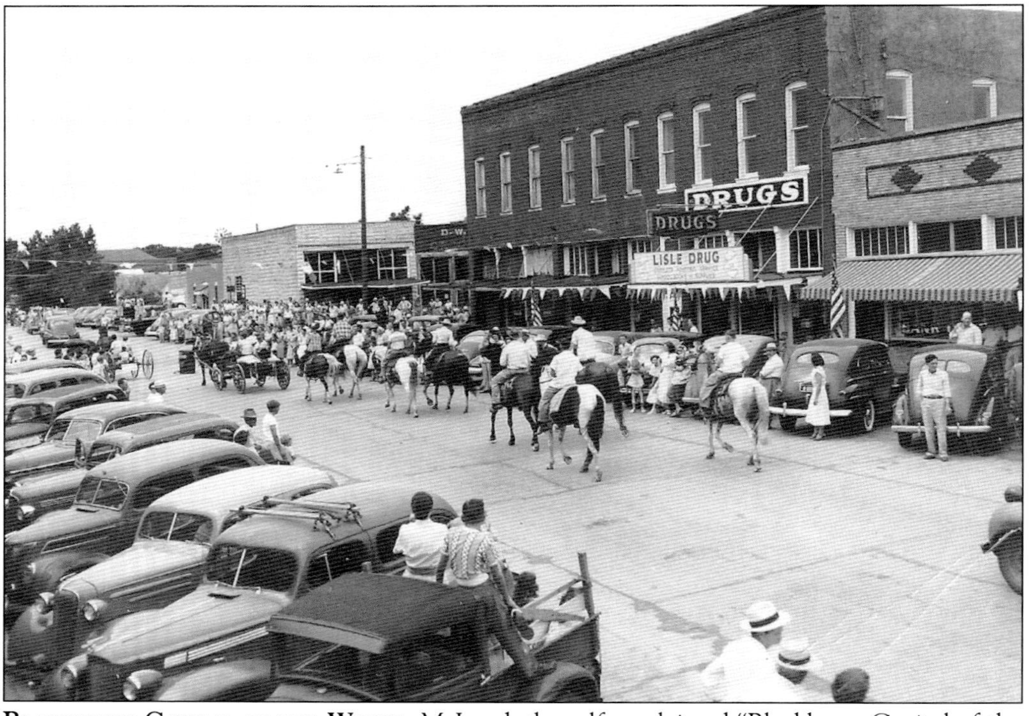

Blackberry Capital of the World. McLoud, the self-proclaimed "Blackberry Capital of the World," chooses to celebrate the end of the harvest season with a Blackberry Festival. The first festival was held in the 1940s, and it was later combined with the town's Independence Day celebrations. It is one of the oldest continual festivals in the state. A parade during one of the first festivals is shown above. Below, a group of men inspects a batch of berries. While blackberry farming is no longer an agriculture strength for the town, the festival has continued. (Both, author's collection.)

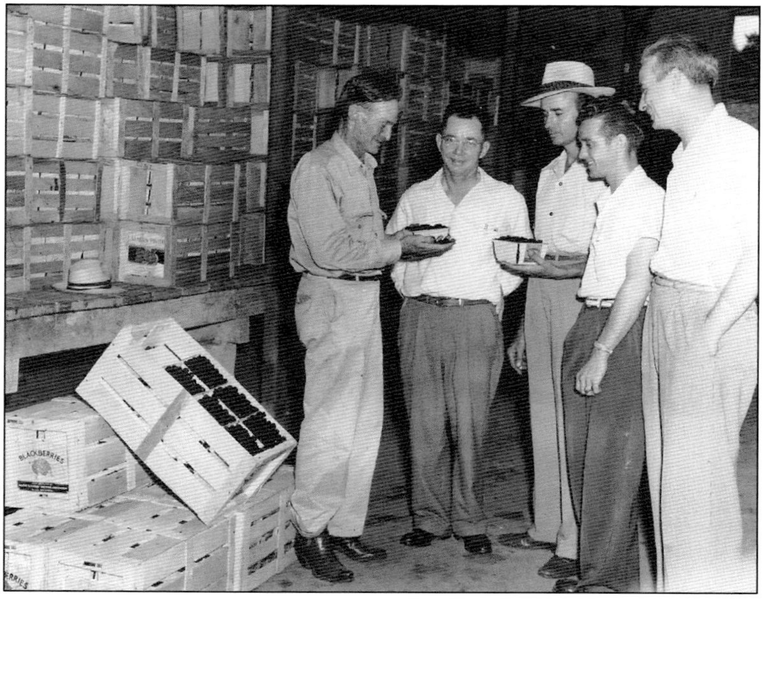

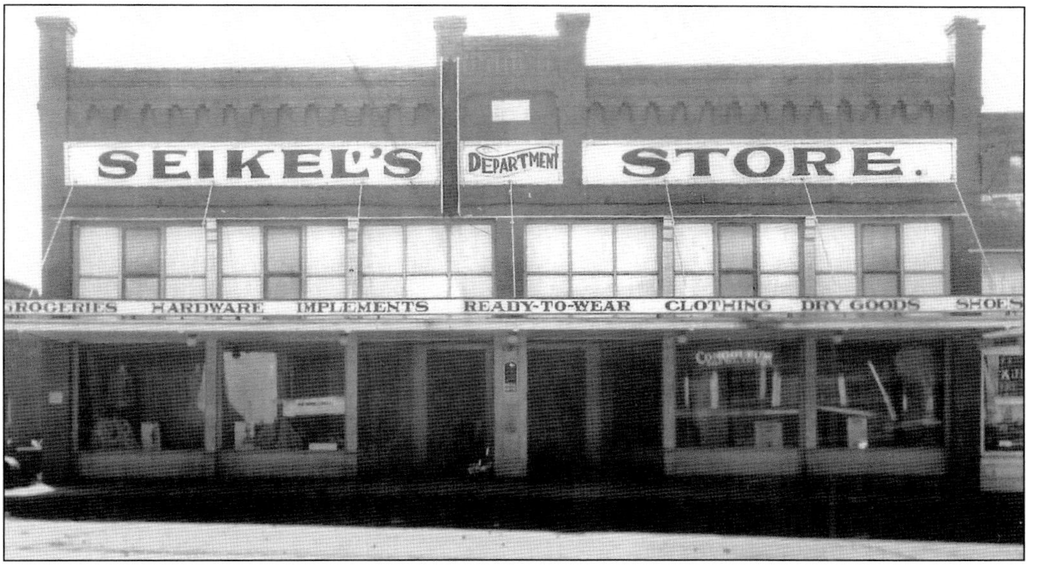

SEIKEL'S IN MCLOUD. Seikel's Department Store, founded by John Sylvester Seikel in 1901, is shown in this photograph, undated but probably taken in the 1950s. Seikel's had almost everything the McLoud community needed: food, hardware, clothing, a shoe department, and even flooring. The store continued to be operated by the Seikel family until 1984. (Courtesy of Pottawatomie County Historical Society.)

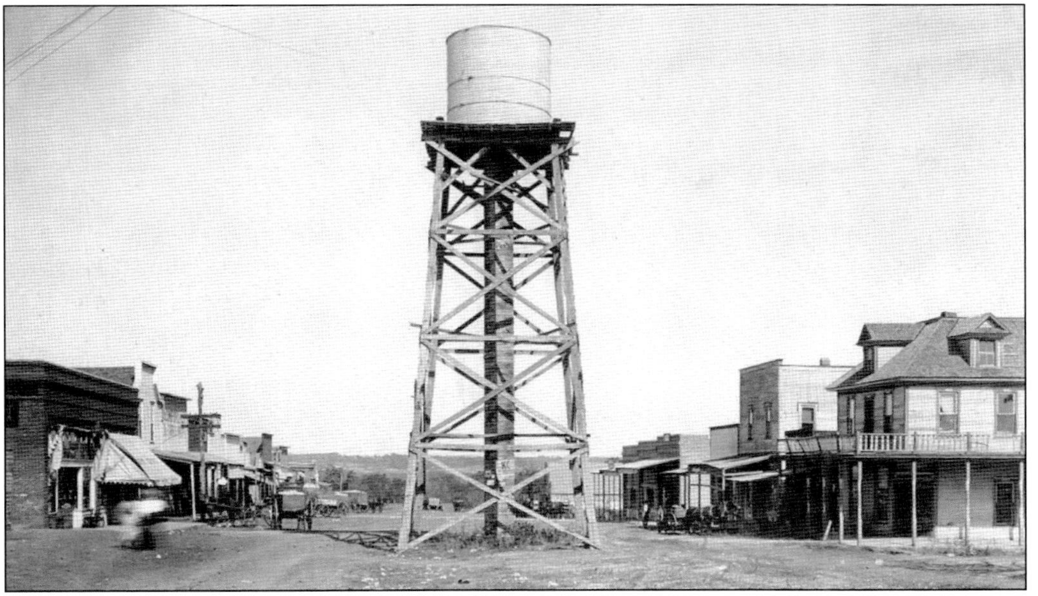

THE QUEEN CITY. Macomb opened a post office on May 29, 1903, named for a Santa Fe engineer named Macomb. This photograph of Macomb shows Main Street and the water tower in 1912. Although once nicknamed the "Queen City of South Pottawatomie County," a prolonged drought causing agricultural failures made it difficult for the town to grow to a sizable city. (Courtesy of Don Taylor.)

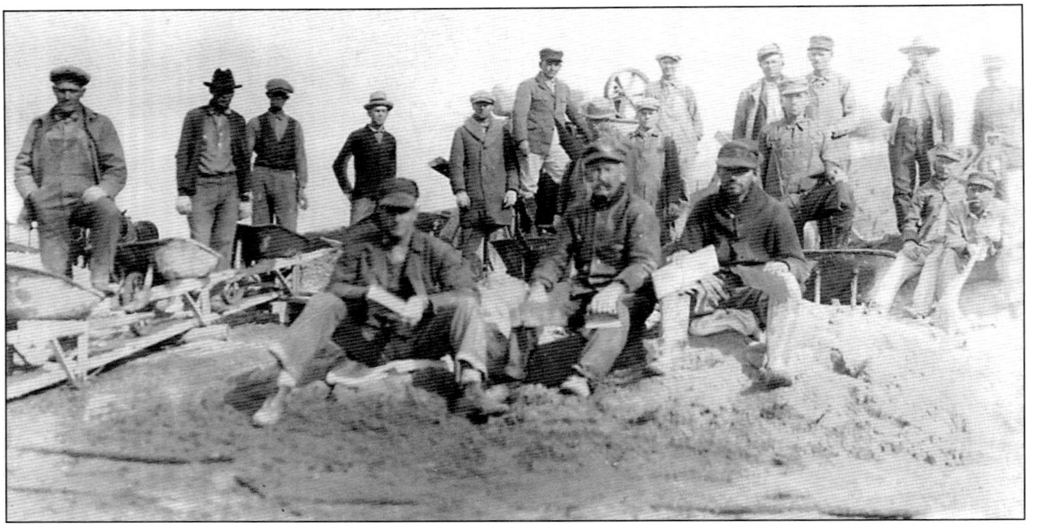

South Canadian River, Asher. Above, a group of workers pauses for a photograph near the South Canadian River in Asher. This photograph was taken in the 1920s, during the construction of the first bridge to cross the river. Each worker has a wheelbarrow to haul concrete for the piers. Before the bridge was built, the river could only be crossed when the water was low enough. After the construction, as seen below, south Pottawatomie citizens had easier access to Pontotoc County and Ada, which opened up new trade possibilities. This bridge and the one that replaced it have both been removed. (Above, courtesy of James Kreuzberg; below, courtesy of Pottawatomie County Historical Society.)

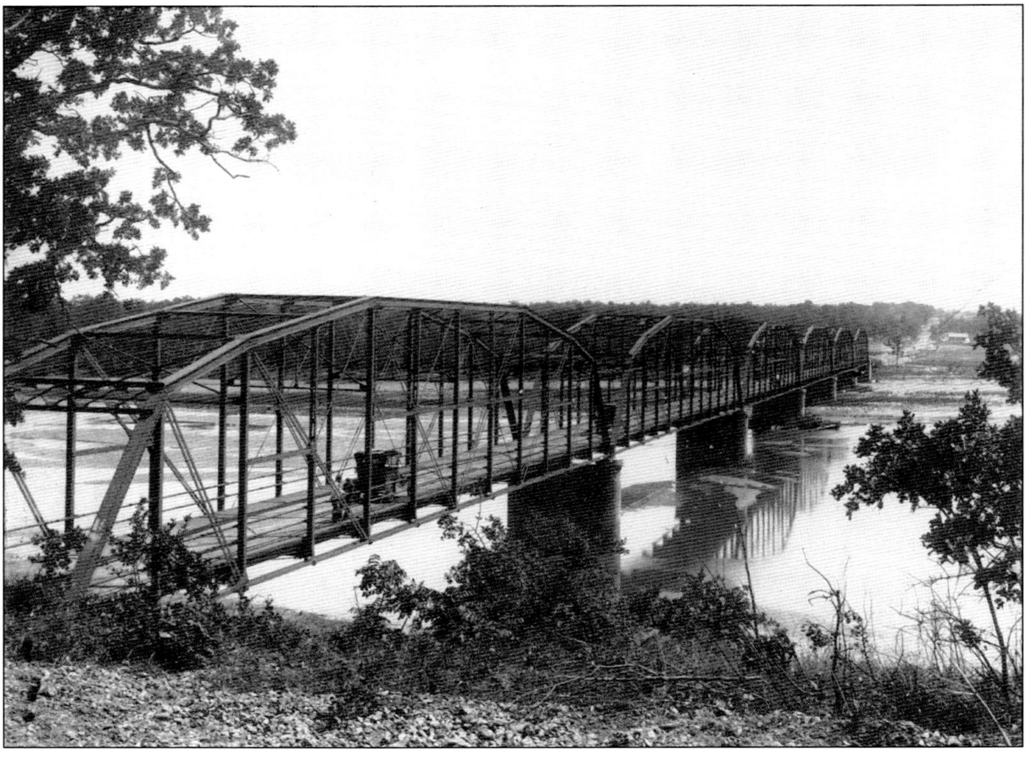

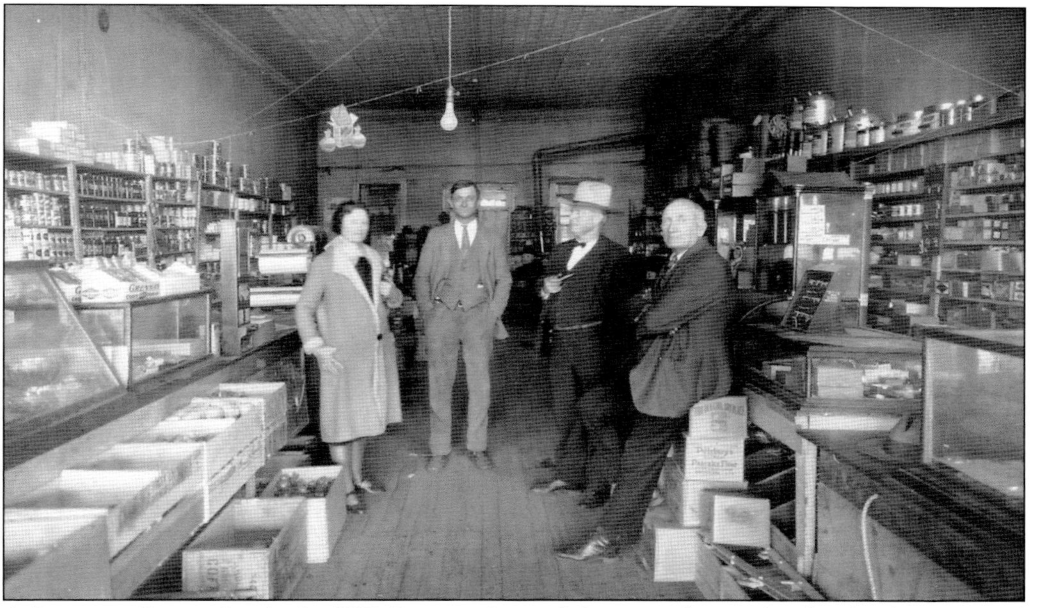

A Strange Store. Inside the W.T. Strange General Store on the north side of Asher, pictured from left to right are a Shawnee news reporter, Pat Ryan, Constable Charlie Bush, and W.T. Strange. General stores like these were often the first places of business to be established in a community and carried household items, groceries, and dry goods, among other supplies. (Author's collection.)

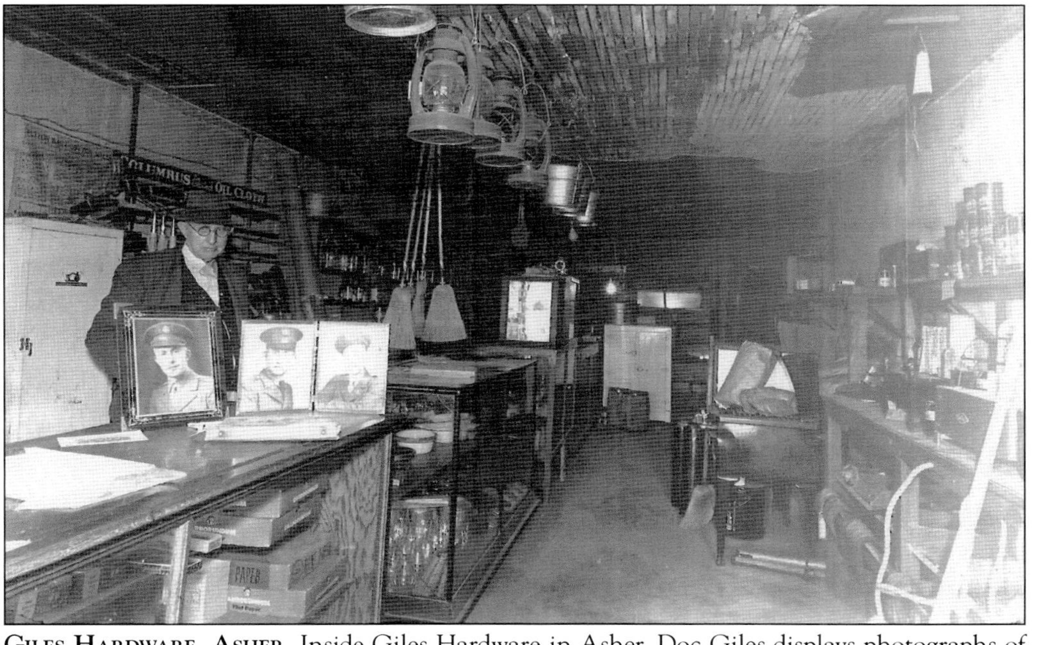

Giles Hardware, Asher. Inside Giles Hardware in Asher, Doc Giles displays photographs of his three sons, Less, Stan, and Frank, who served in World War II. Hardware stores, like general stores, were very often hubs of the community and carried buckets, brooms, gas lanterns, and other essential hardware items. (Author's collection.)

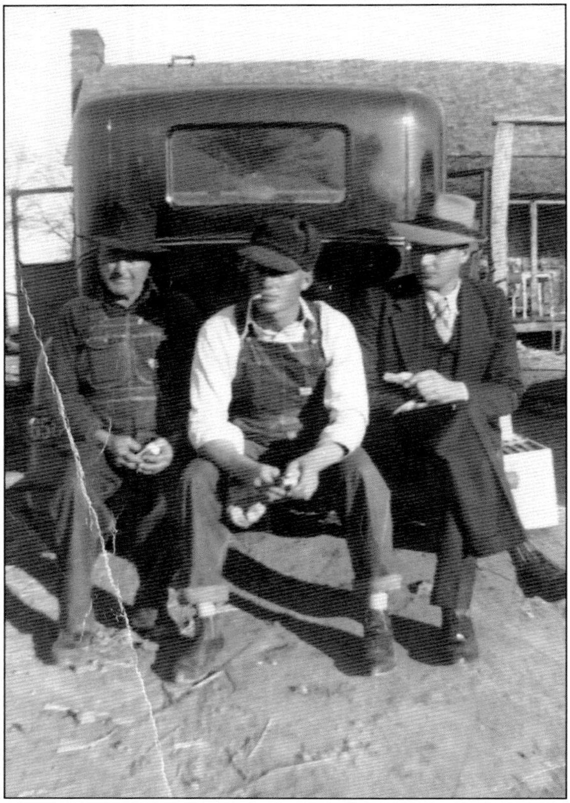

Farming. Pictured from left to right, Tom Owen, Hal Owen, and Grady Owen sit on the back of a pickup truck at their home place between Asher and Pearson. Grady was visiting from Kansas City and had just purchased the truck in the photograph. The Owen farm included cows and pigs. The family also grew corn, baled hay, and had a large vegetable garden. (Courtesy of Reta Bowen.)

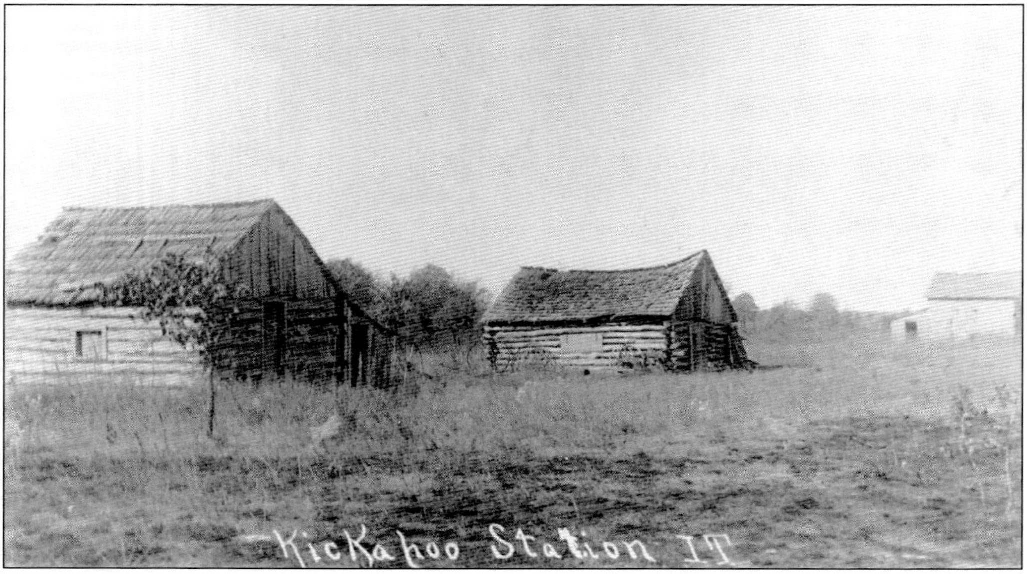

Kickapoo Station, Indian Territory. Kickapoo Station was a small community established in 1876 about three miles northwest of Shawnee. The town was named after the Kickapoo tribe and was mostly comprised of Mexican Kickapoos removed to Indian Territory. The community had a post office until 1900. (Courtesy of Pottawatomie County Historical Society.)

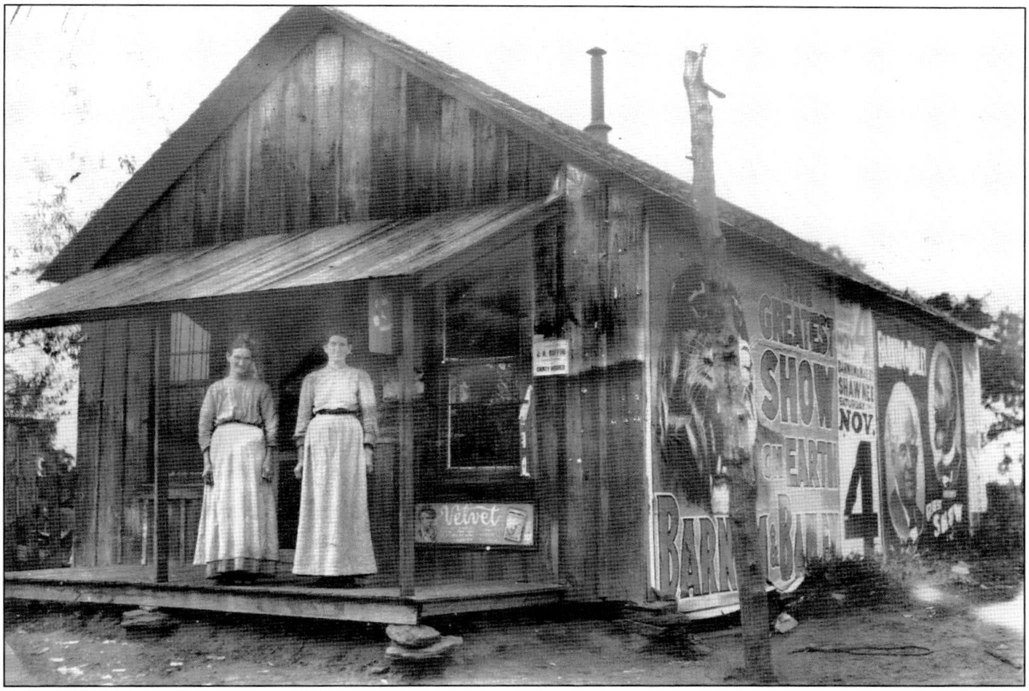

COUNTRY STORE. Two ladies stand on the porch of a little country store near New Hope No. 41 School District, Tecumseh, in 1916. Mrs. M.E. Geralds, perhaps one of the two women in the photograph, is recorded as being in charge of the store. (Courtesy of Library of Congress.)

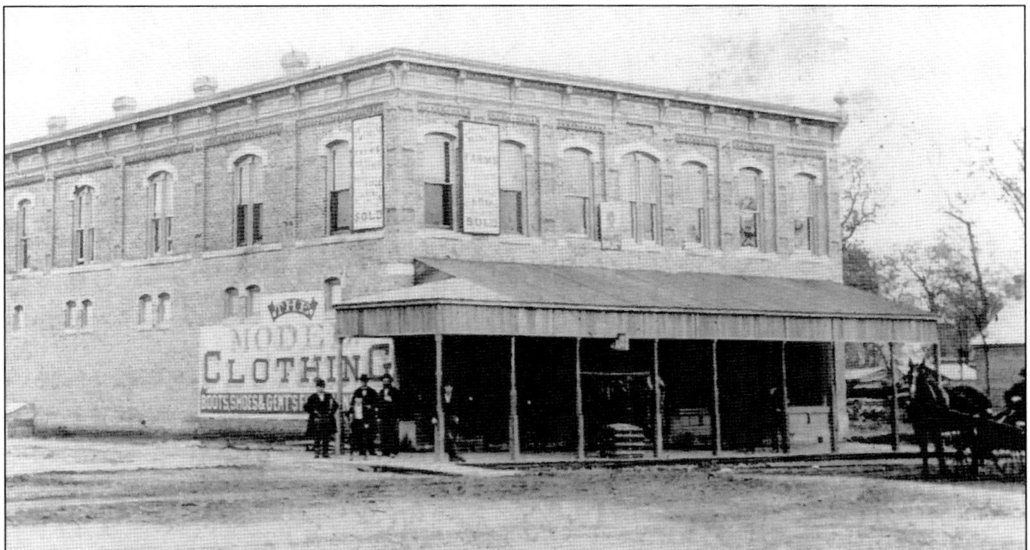

DEXTER BUILDING. The Dexter Building is at the corner of Main and Bell Streets. This two-story building was constructed in 1895 and is the second oldest building in the downtown core. Restoration efforts, including the removal of a false facade covering the second floor, began in 2012. The structure is listed in the National Register of Historic Places as part of the Bell Street Historic District. (Author's collection.)

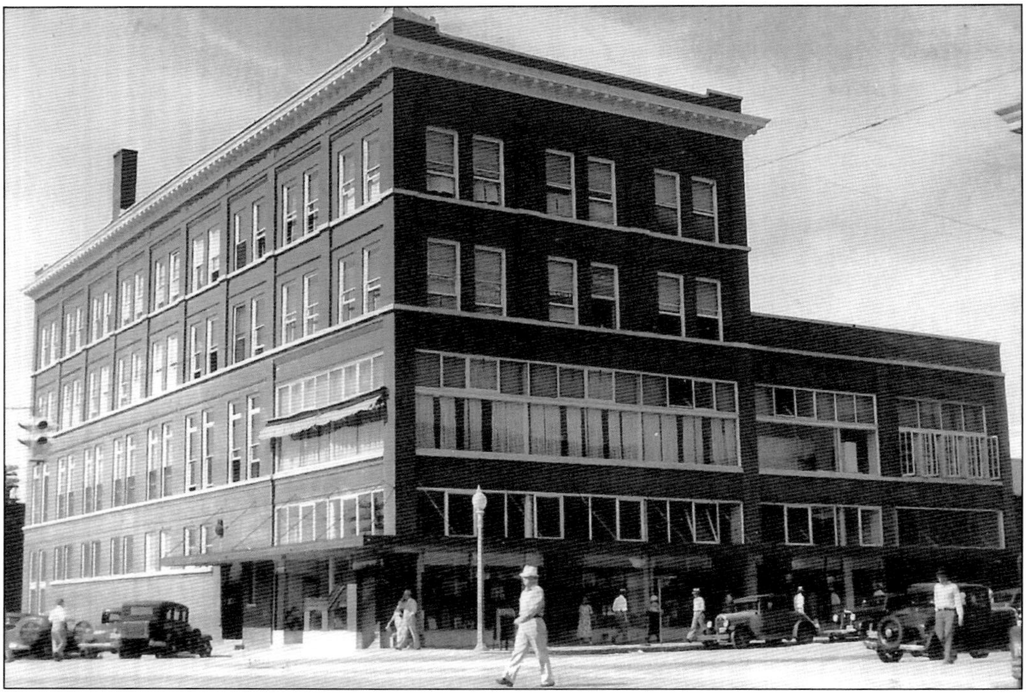

The Mammoth. With four stories, the Mammoth Department Store (shown above) was one of the largest department stores in the area. Located on the southwest corner of Main and Bell Streets, the store carried clothing, shoes, men's and ladies' hats, housewares, bedding, furniture—almost everything. Originally a smaller store, the Mammoth moved to this location around 1900. In the 1940s, it became Montgomery Ward (below). The building is now a home furnishings store. (Both, courtesy of Pottawatomie County Historical Society.)

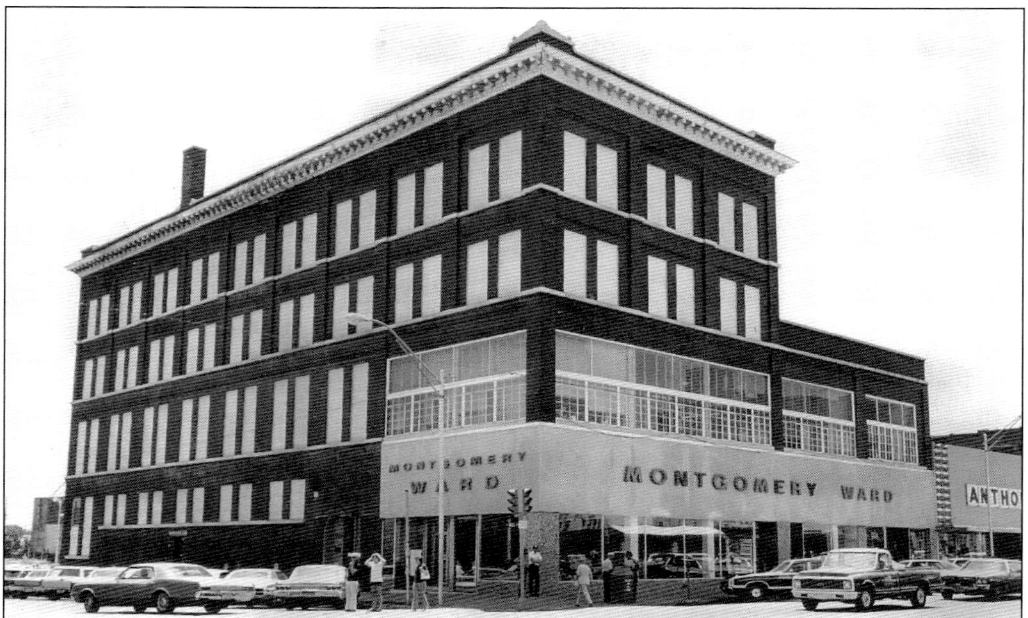

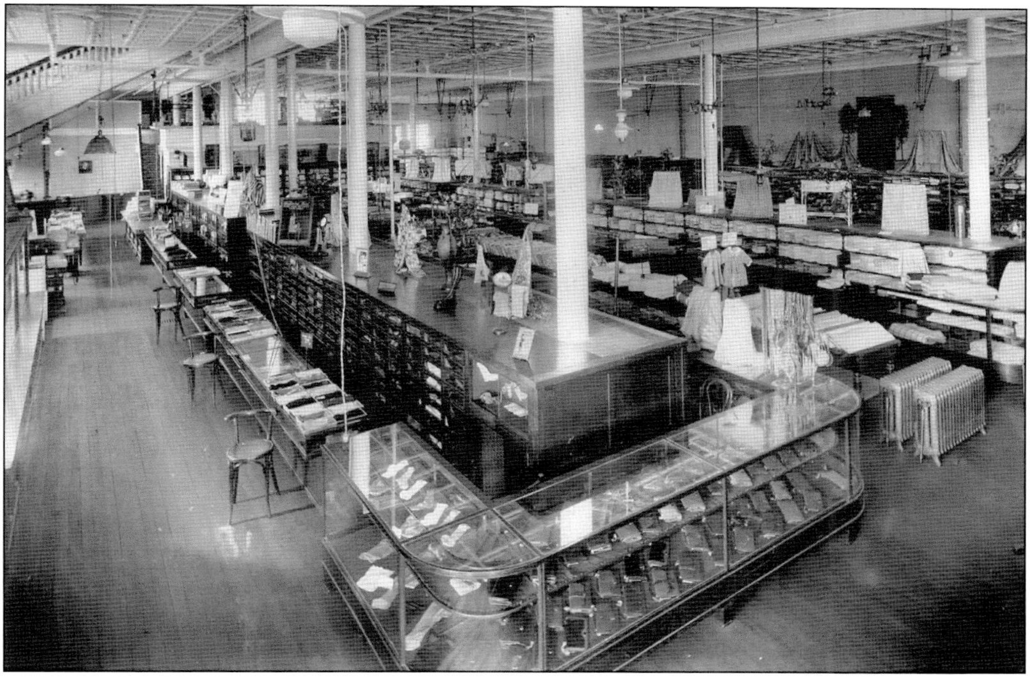

Inside the Mammoth. These two photographs show just a glimpse of what the Mammoth had to offer its patrons. In the above photograph, there is a large collection of ladies' bags behind the glass case, as well as a good assortment of fabric to make clothes and dresses. Below, an impressive gathering of handsome men's hats is displayed. Of course, one could also find shoes, suit coats and pants, and much more. (Both, courtesy of Pottawatomie County Historical Society.)

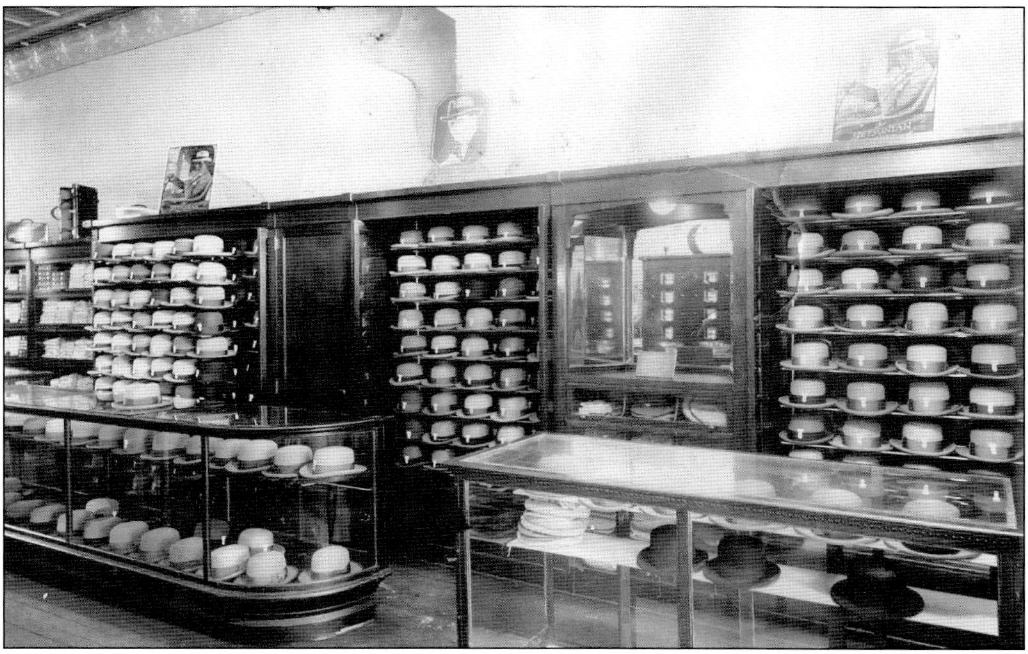

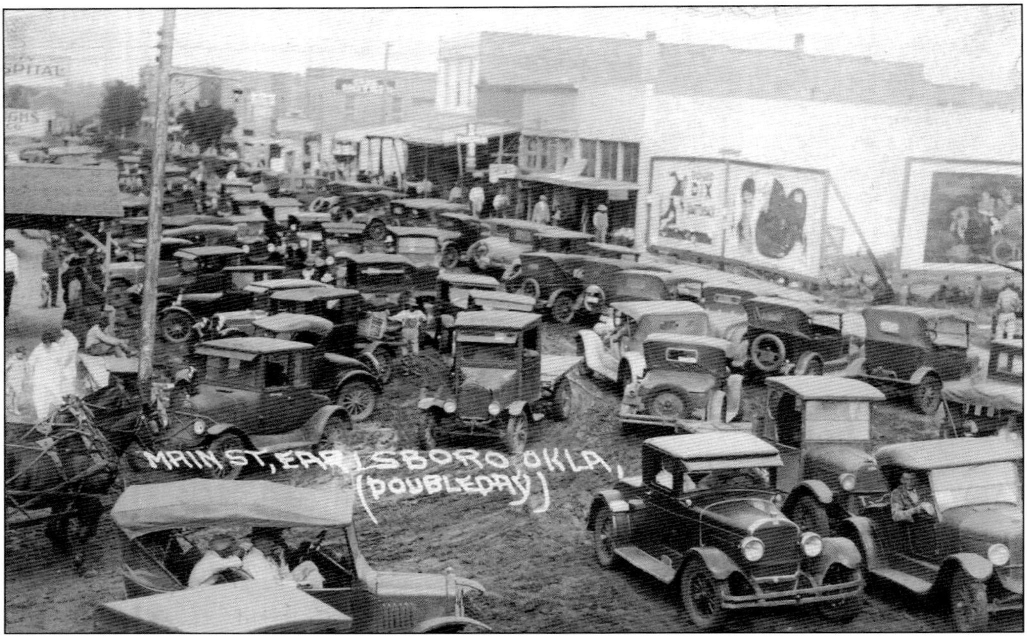

EARLSBORO SCENES. Earlsboro, which the *Daily Oklahoman* referred to as "the town that whiskey built and oil broke," has seen its highs and lows. Located just on the other side of dry Indian Territory, Earlsboro had an economic boom by building saloons. Prohibition stopped that, but an even bigger boom came when oil was struck in the 1920s. Production declined in the 1930s, which caused a bust and bankrupted the town. Above, Main Street in Earlsboro is packed with cars. Although undated, this photograph was probably taken in the mid-1920s, during the town's oil boom. Below, another view of Earlsboro shows the Rose Hotel as well as some other shops. Also undated, it was most likely taken later in the 1920s or 1930s. (Both, courtesy of Pottawatomie County Historical Society.)

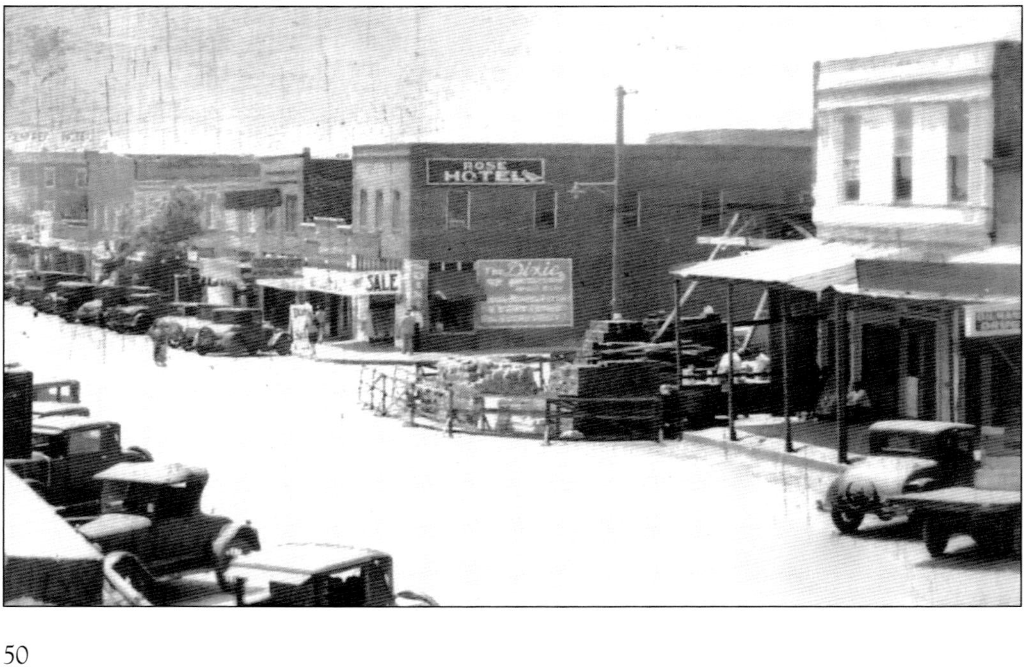

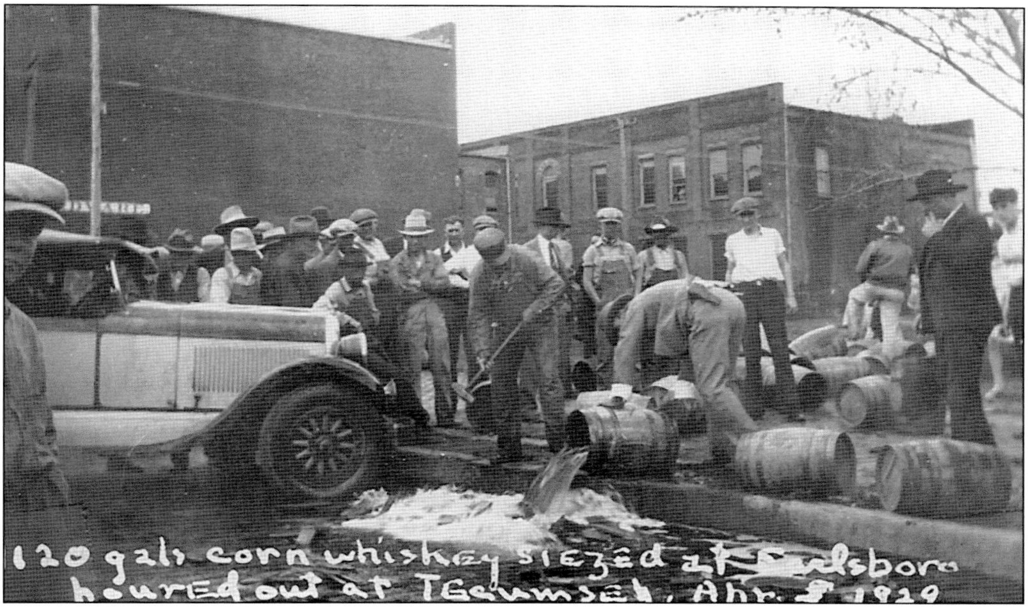

WHISKEY DOWN THE DRAIN. Prohibition forced many Pottawatomie County saloons and distilleries to close. The action even created a number of ghost towns in the county, as the main reason these towns were established was to sell alcohol to the bordering dry Indian Territory. In this April 1929 photograph, 1,120 gallons of corn whiskey seized at Earlsboro are being poured out by officials in Tecumseh. (Courtesy of Pottawatomie County Historical Society.)

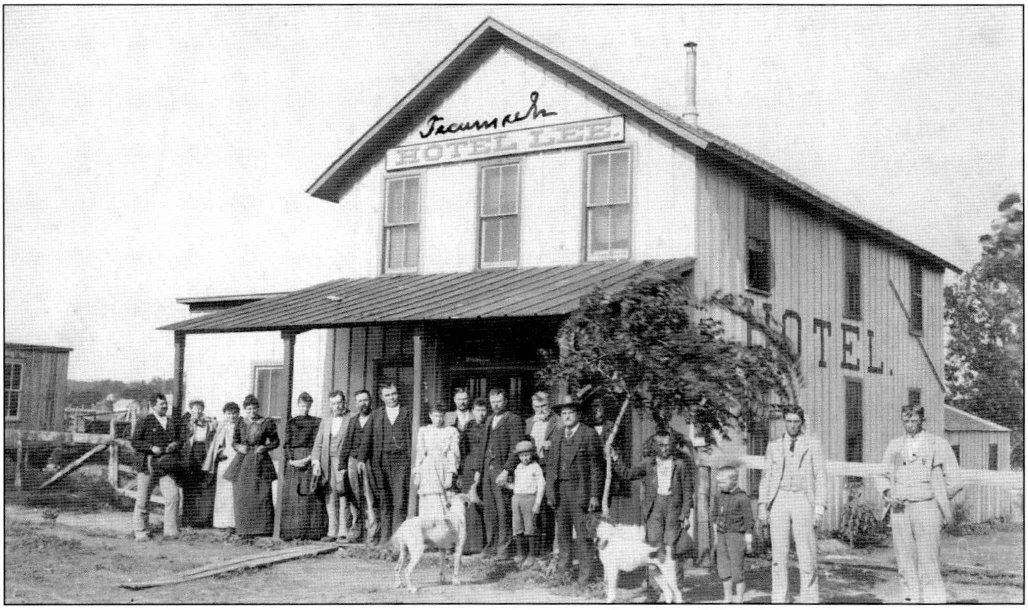

HOTEL LEE. A large group of men, women, children, and a couple of dogs stand outside one of Tecumseh's first hotels, Hotel Lee. The hotel was established in the 1890s with Marion Lee as the proprietor and was located at the corner of Park and Fifth Streets, conveniently just east of the tracks. Advertisements for the hotel boasted it had the "best accommodations in town." (Courtesy of Pottawatomie County Historical Society.)

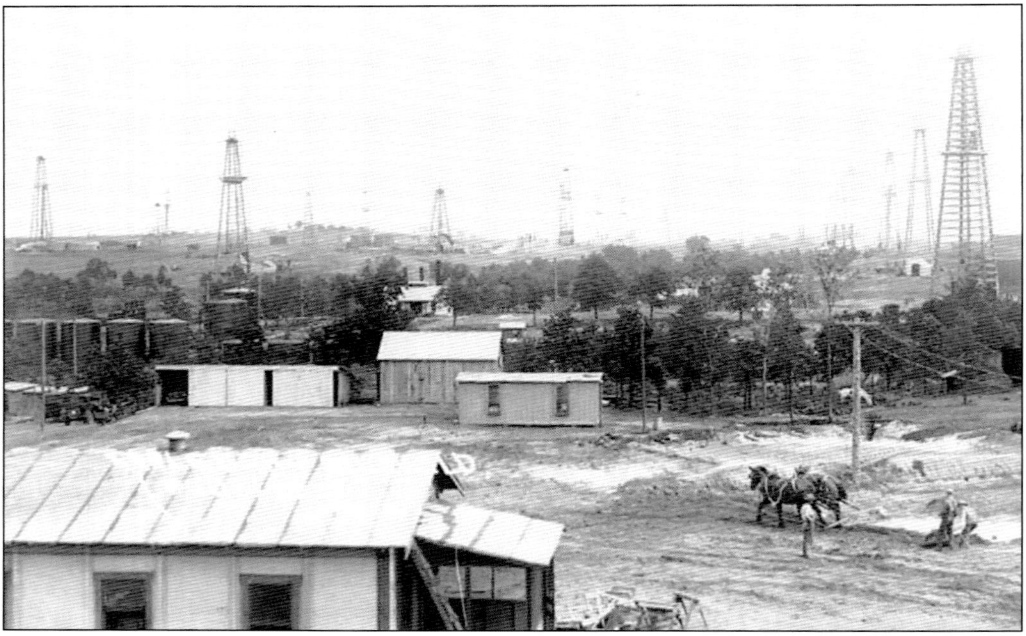

STRIKING OIL. Oil was big business in Pottawatomie County. St. Louis and Earlsboro had some of the largest oil pools, but Asher, Pearson, Maud, and Shawnee also had producing oil wells. Communities in south Pottawatomie County greatly grew to serve the needs of the oilfield workers when oil was struck nearby. Sometimes, the towns boomed in population by thousands of people. Hotels, restaurants, and stores sprang up quickly. Above, oil derricks are scattered on the horizon of Earlsboro's oilfields. Below, oil derricks can be seen behind the Saint Louis Cafe in St. Louis. (Above, courtesy of Pottawatomie County Historical Society; below, courtesy of Library of Congress.)

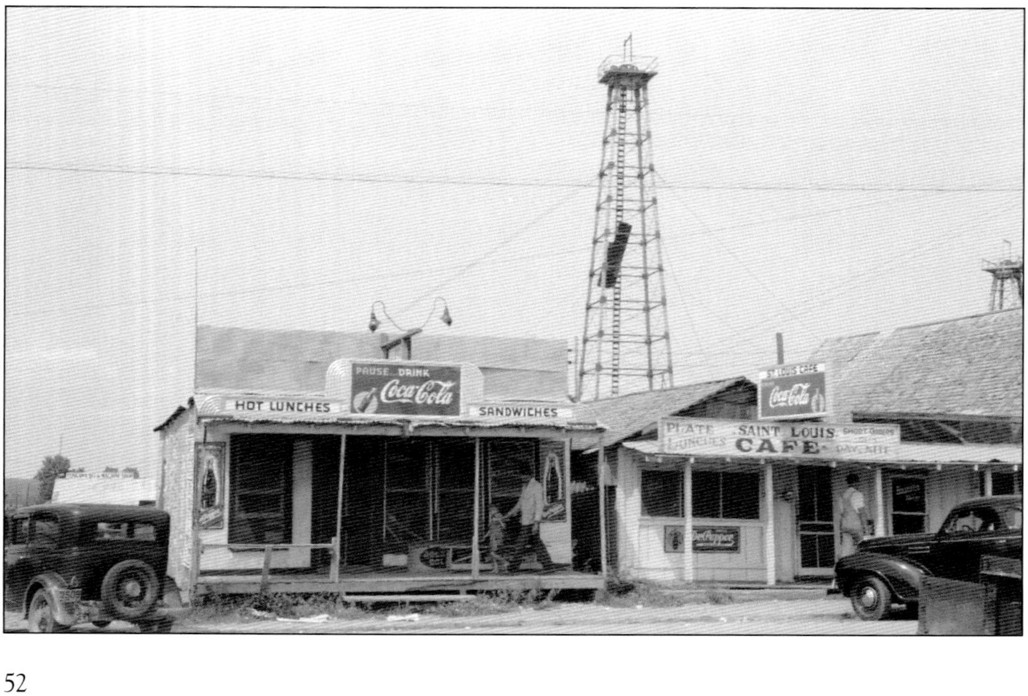

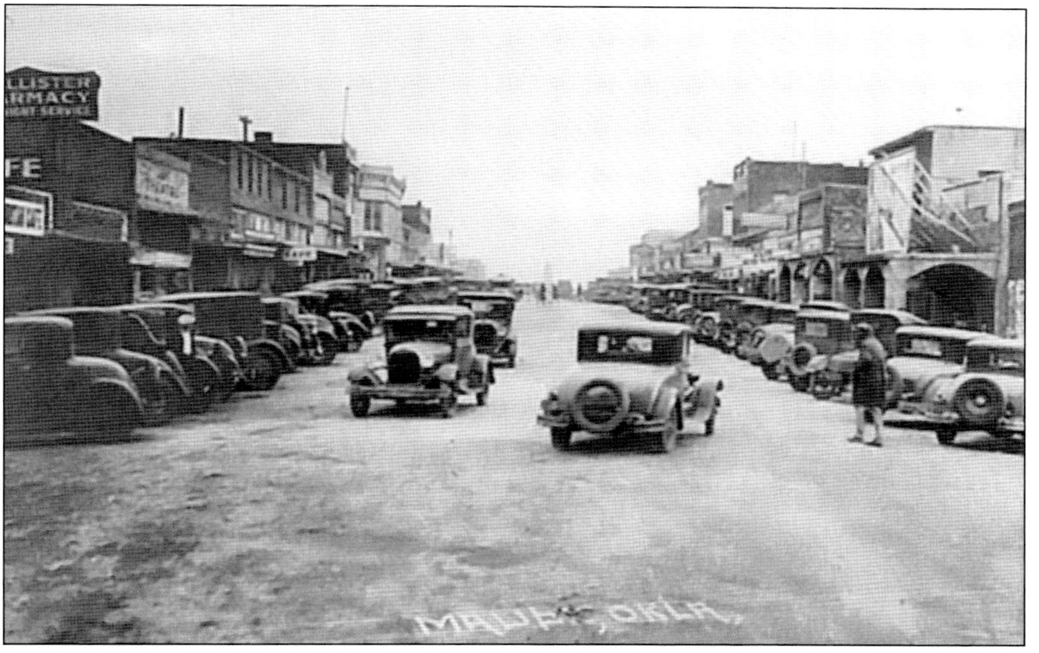

Maud Main Street. Main Street is full of cars in Maud. This picture was taken looking east in the late 1920s. Maud once had a population near 10,000 but quickly declined as the oil dried up. Maud still had an active Main Street through the 1950s. Rockabilly singer Wanda Jackson was born in Maud on October 20, 1937. Wanda Jackson Boulevard in the town is named for her. (Courtesy of Charles Villines.)

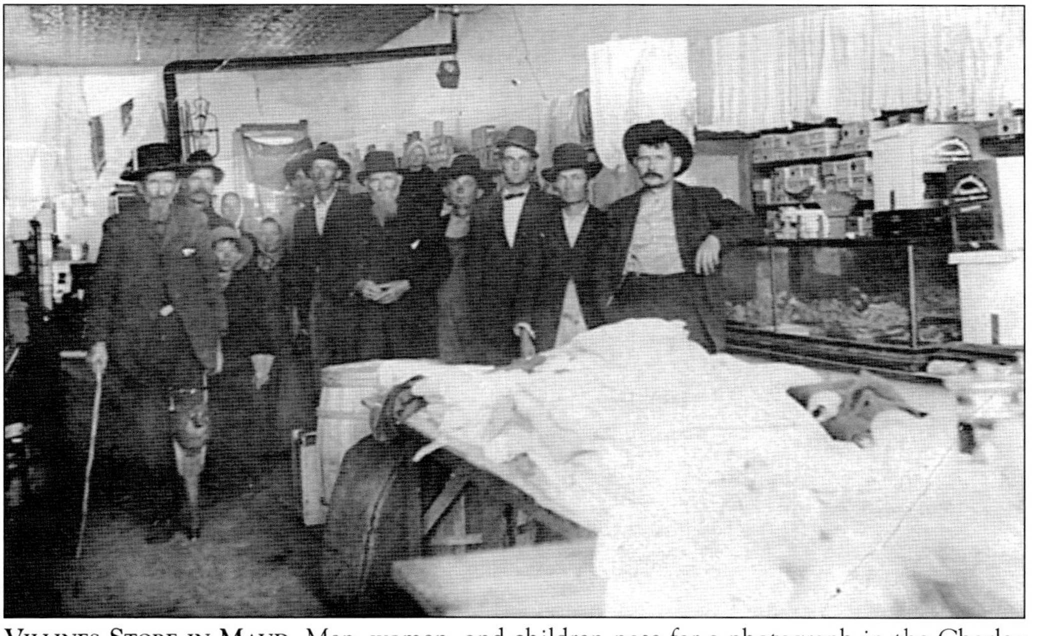

Villines Store in Maud. Men, women, and children pose for a photograph in the Charley Villines Store in Maud around 1900. Charles, on the far right with his arm on the counter, was one of Maud's early-day settlers. (Courtesy of Pottawatomie County Historical Society.)

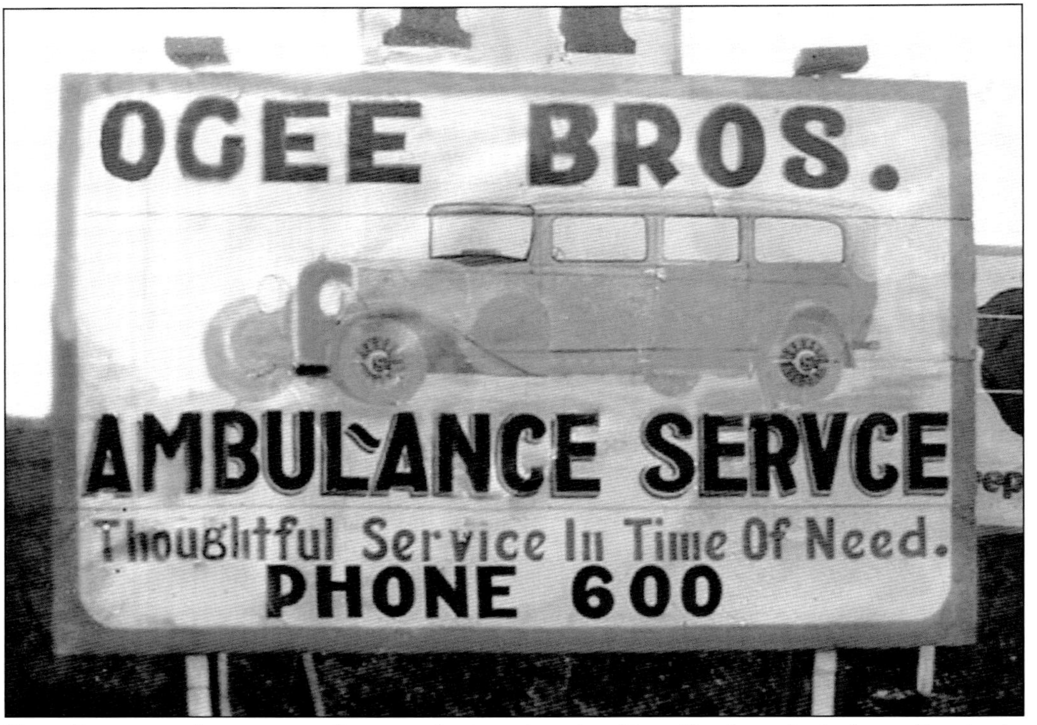

Ogee Brothers Ambulance Service. A sign advertises Ogee Brothers Ambulance Service in Maud. Lute Ogee was the owner. He is remembered by friends as a caring and respectful man who enjoyed playing the occasional practical joke. Lute's father made coffins and stored them in the family's barn. Lute inherited this business and later became Maud's first undertaker. (Courtesy of Charles Villines.)

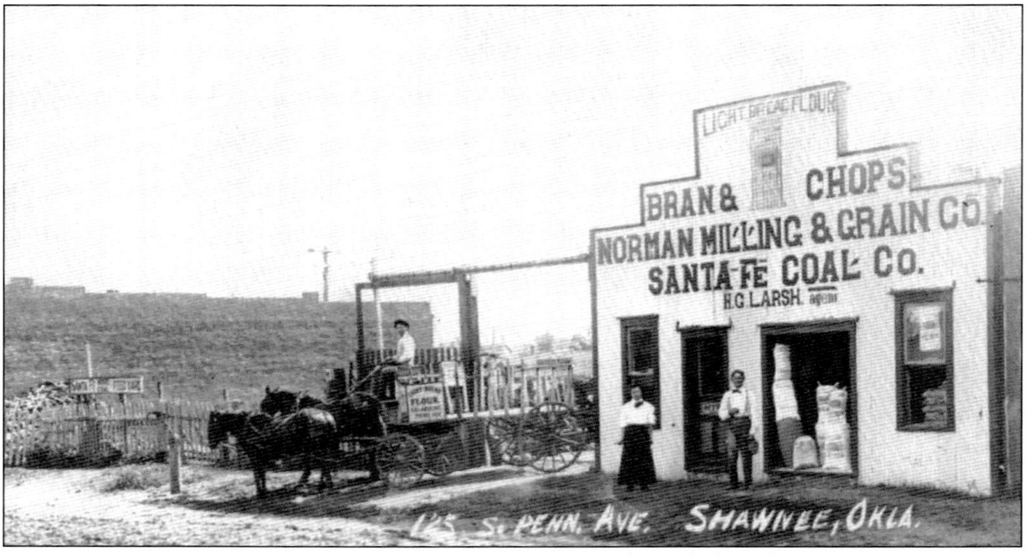

125 South Pennsylvania Avenue, Shawnee. Many goods, including flour, bran, chops, grain, and even coal, are offered at this early-day Shawnee store near the corner of Main Street and South Pennsylvania Avenue. (Courtesy of Pottawatomie County Historical Society.)

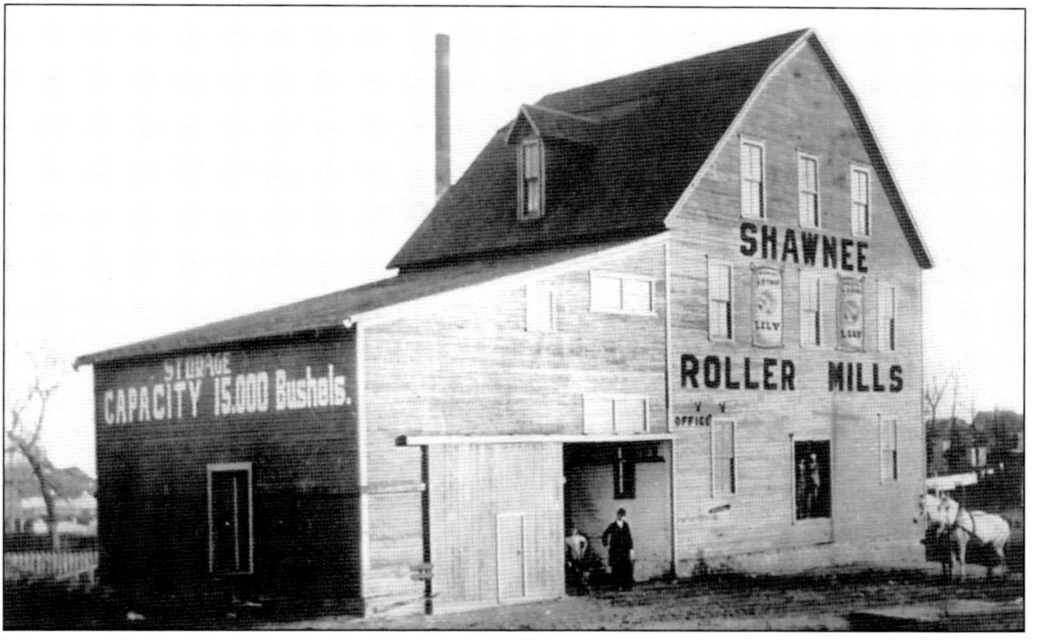

Made in Oklahoma Goodness. Shawnee Milling Company has been an establishment of Shawnee for over 100 years. The original flour mill was built in 1891 south of town. The mill was dragged across the North Canadian River using horses, ropes, and skids during a drought in 1895 and brought to its current site. The mill on that site gradually grew as the company expanded but burned in one of the worst fires in Shawnee's history in August 1934. A new facility was built the following year and still produces flour, gravy, and other mixes loved in the county and beyond. Above is the 1906 facility, when it was named Shawnee Roller Mills. Below is an aerial view of the current facility. (Both, courtesy of Shawnee Milling Company.)

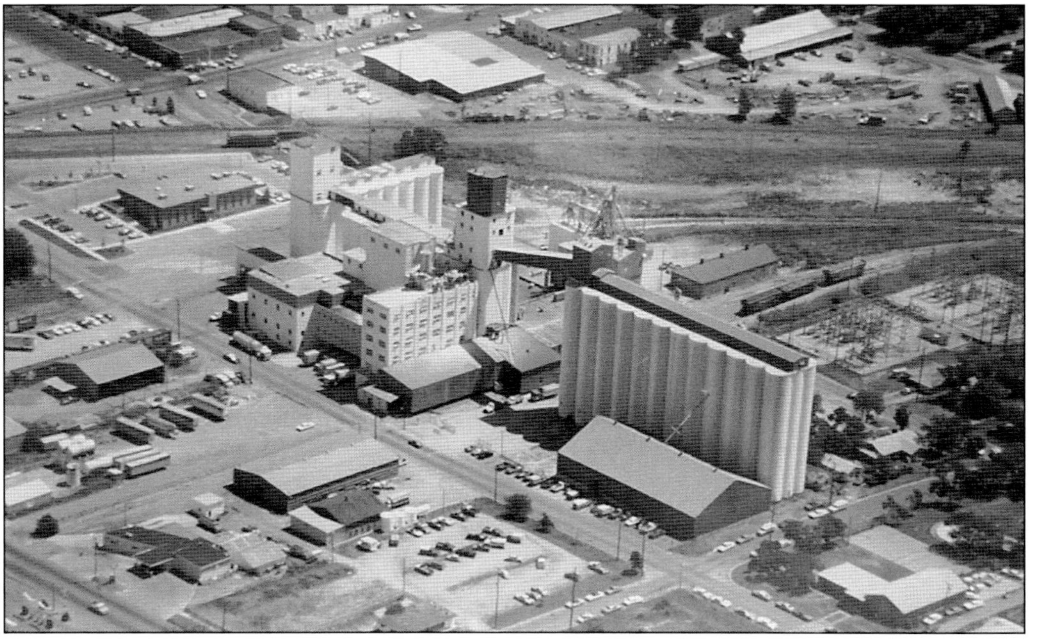

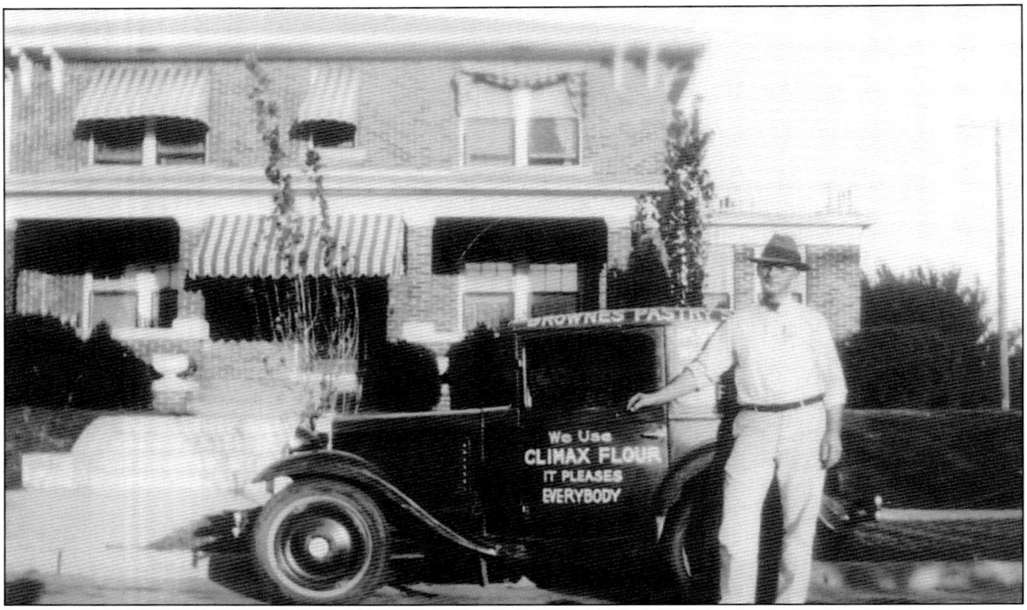

Making Deliveries. Harry Brown is pictured above making Shawnee deliveries in his bakery truck in the 1930s. Climax Flour, advertised on the door of his vehicle, was a product of Shawnee Mills and was promoted prominently on its building for some time (shown below in 1931). Climax Flour can still be purchased today, although it is now known by the name Shawnee's Best Flour. (Above, courtesy of Martin Schepers; below, courtesy of Shawnee Milling Company.)

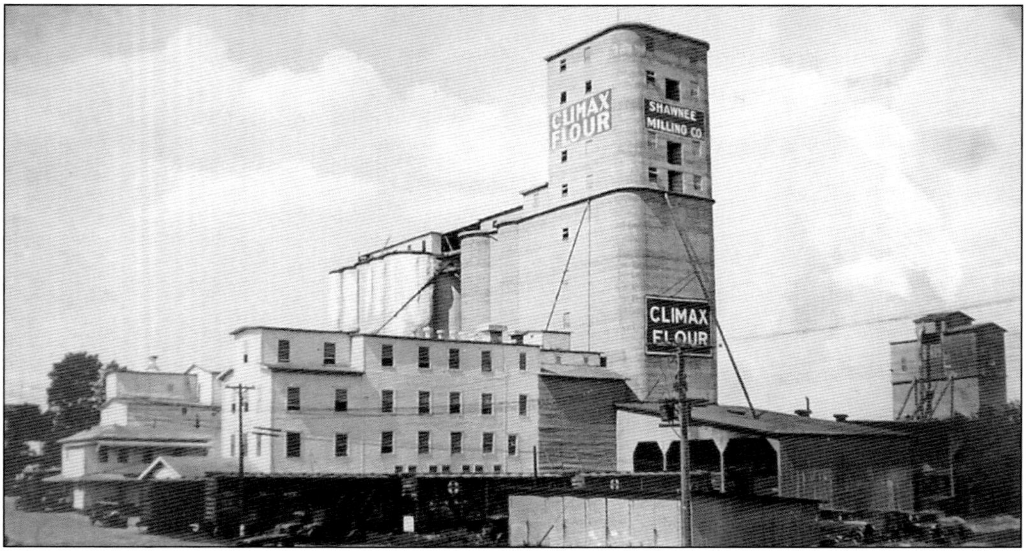

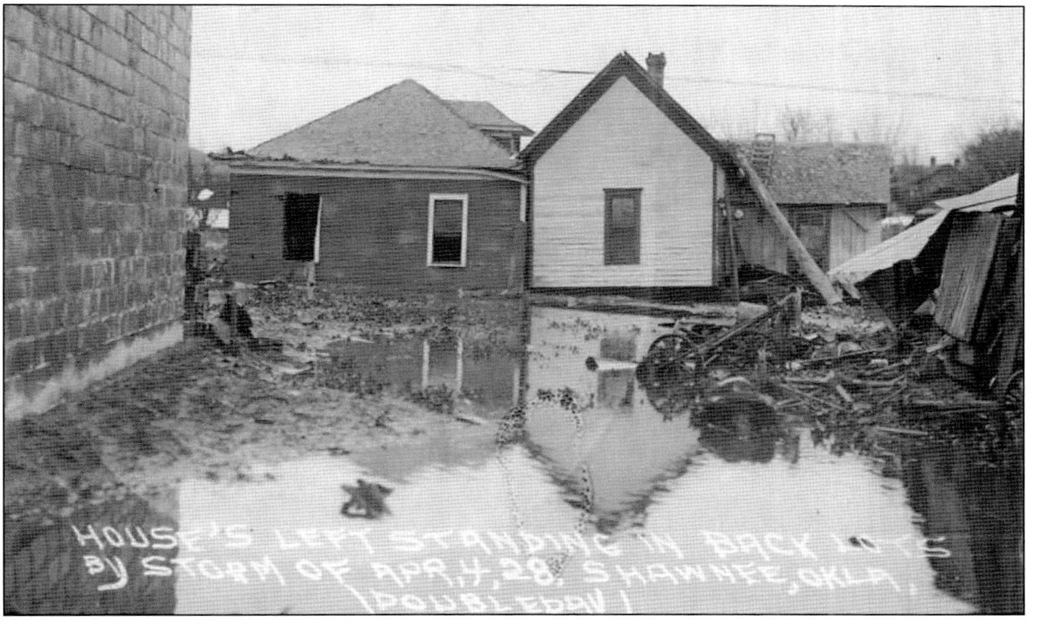

The 1928 Flood. Many people were asleep when this disastrous flood hit Shawnee on April 4, 1928. According to a newspaper article, six people drowned and property damage was more than a half-million dollars. A thousand people were made homeless, and 43 businesses received losses. Above, damaged houses are moved against each other in the background of a muddy mess. Below, water has carried off a two-story house and left it on the railroad tracks. (Both, courtesy of Pottawatomie County Historical Society.)

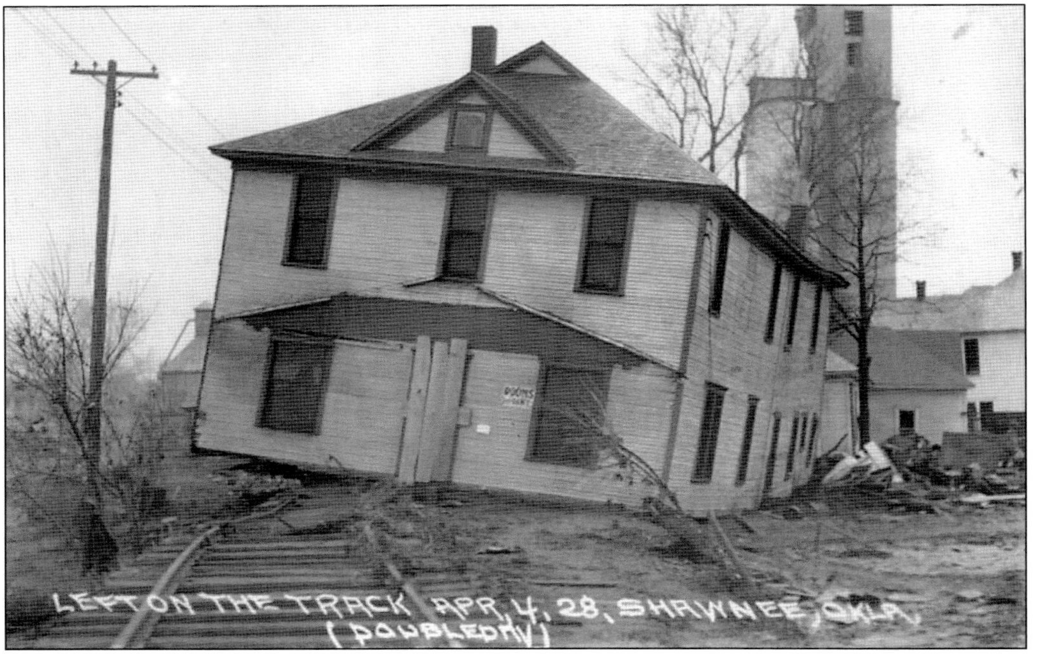

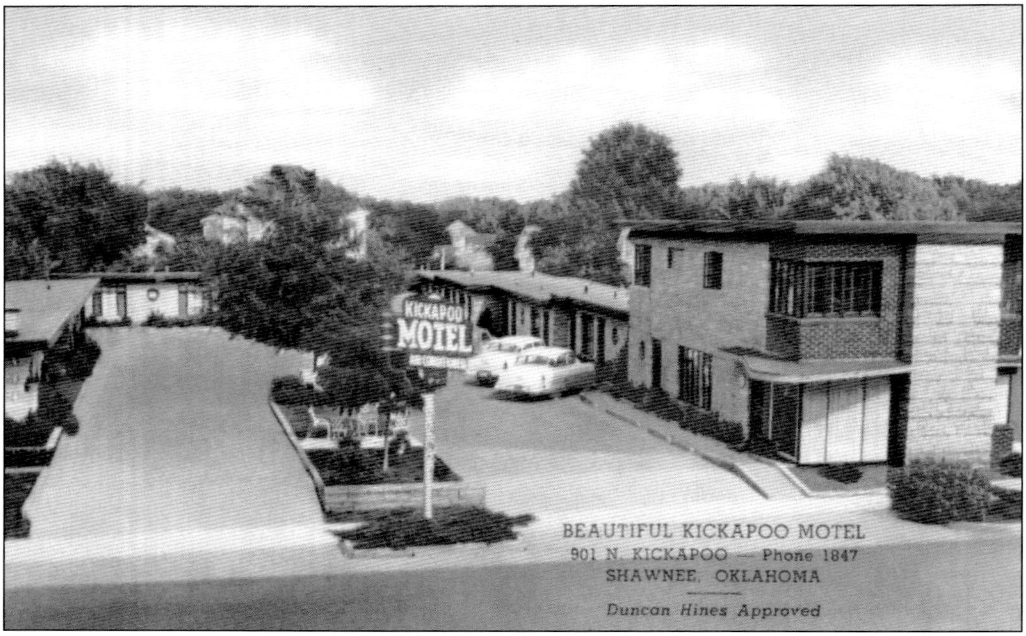

Kickapoo Motels. The postcard above of the Kickapoo Motel in Shawnee boasts it to be "the pride of Shawnee," with free radios, rooms with air-conditioning, carpet, and a television in the office. The Kickapoo Motel, located on North Kickapoo Avenue, still welcomes guests today. The Cinderella Motor Hotel, below, is shown in its more glamorous days. The hotel, on Kickapoo Spur, is known by many for the parties, reunions, and proms held there. Unfortunately, the hotel's condition and reputation gradually declined, and it closed in 2014. (Above, author's collection; below, courtesy of Pottawatomie County Historical Society.)

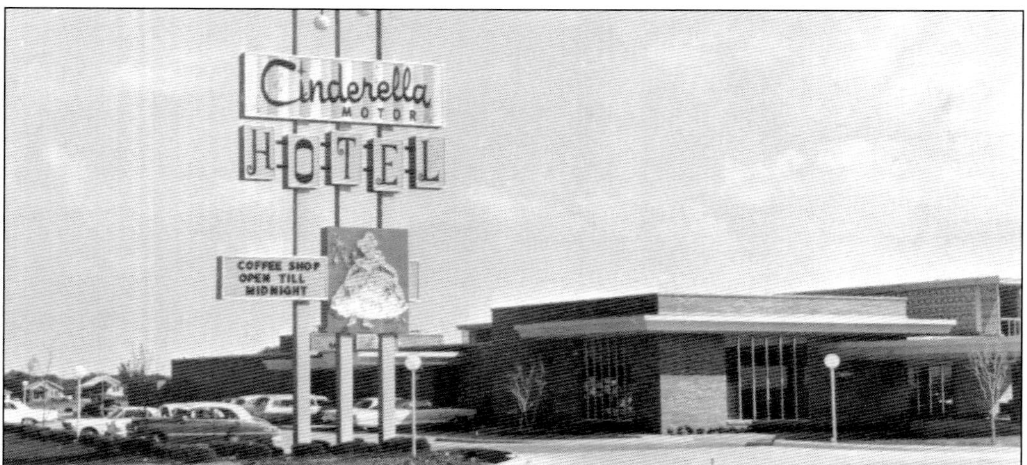

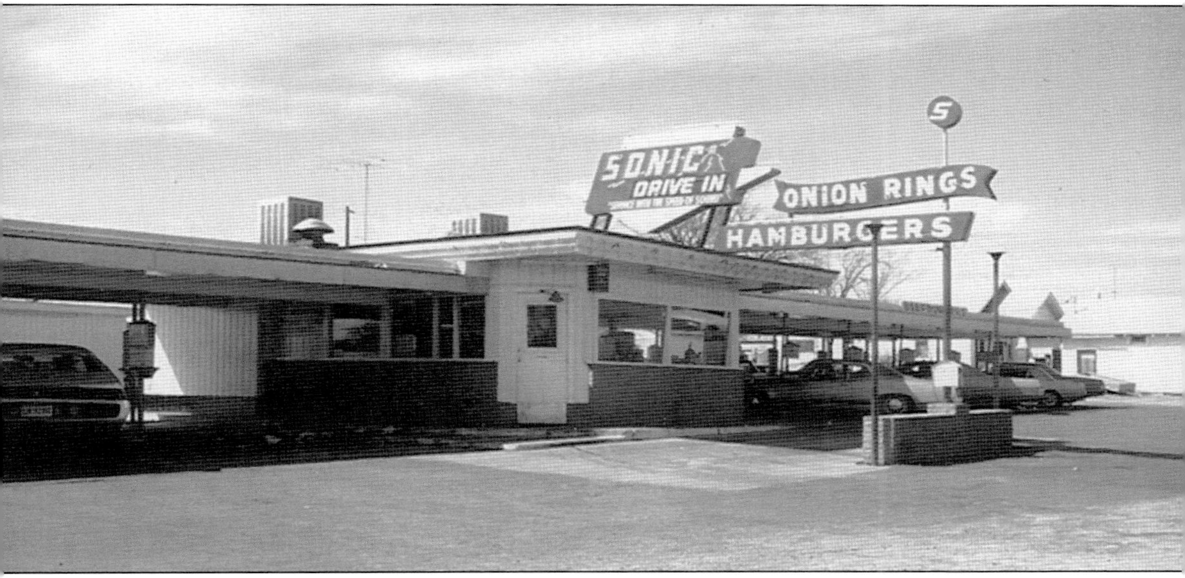

SONIC, AMERICA'S DRIVE-IN. In 1953, a small stand selling root beer, hamburgers, and hot dogs named Top Hat opened in Shawnee. Six years later, after operating a handful of Top Hat locations, partners Troy Smith and Charles Pappe renamed the locations SONIC, America's Drive-In. Today, there are more than 3,500 SONIC drive-ins across the country. Pictured about 1960 is the first SONIC in Shawnee at 1130 North Harrison Avenue. For a time, the SONIC restaurant coexisted with the still-operating Top Hat down the highway at 1814 North Harrison Avenue. (Courtesy of America's Drive-in Brand Properties, LLC.)

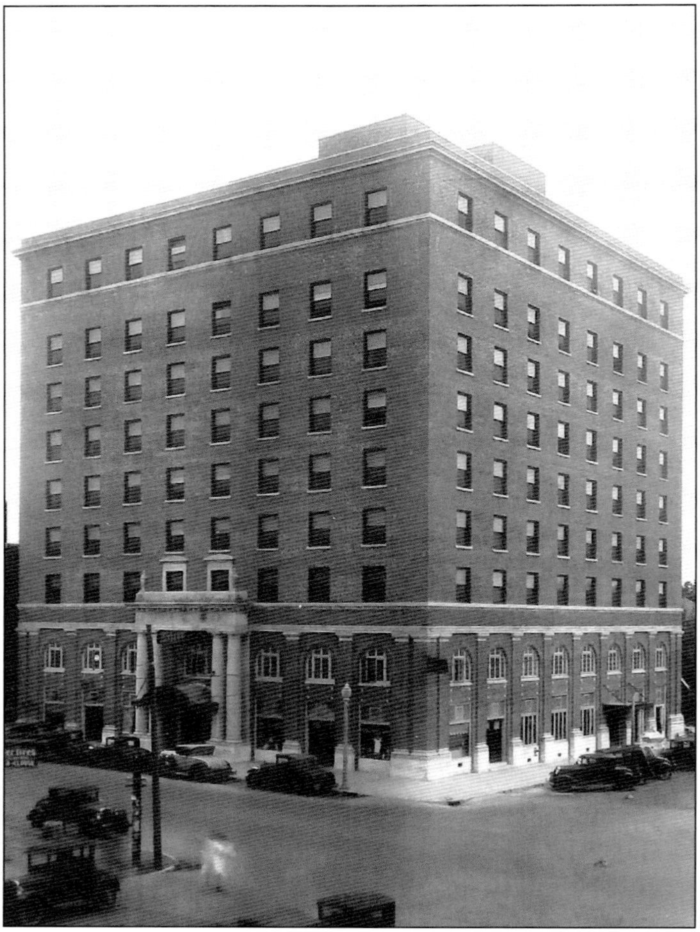

Aldridge Hotel, Shawnee. The Aldridge hotel (left) at the corner of East Ninth and North Bell Streets, is the tallest building in downtown Shawnee. The building, originally known as the Hilton Phillips Hotel, had its formal opening on February 26 and 27, 1929, and was Shawnee's leading hotel through the 1940s. The hotel opened with 200 rooms, all of which had "baths, ceiling fans, and circulating ice water," according to an advertisement. The interior of the hotel is shown below. The photograph was taken before it formally opened. The lower level housed several other businesses. The hotel closed in 1994, but in 2005, the building was restored for use as one- and two-bedroom apartments for senior adults. (Both, courtesy of Pottawatomie County Historical Society.)

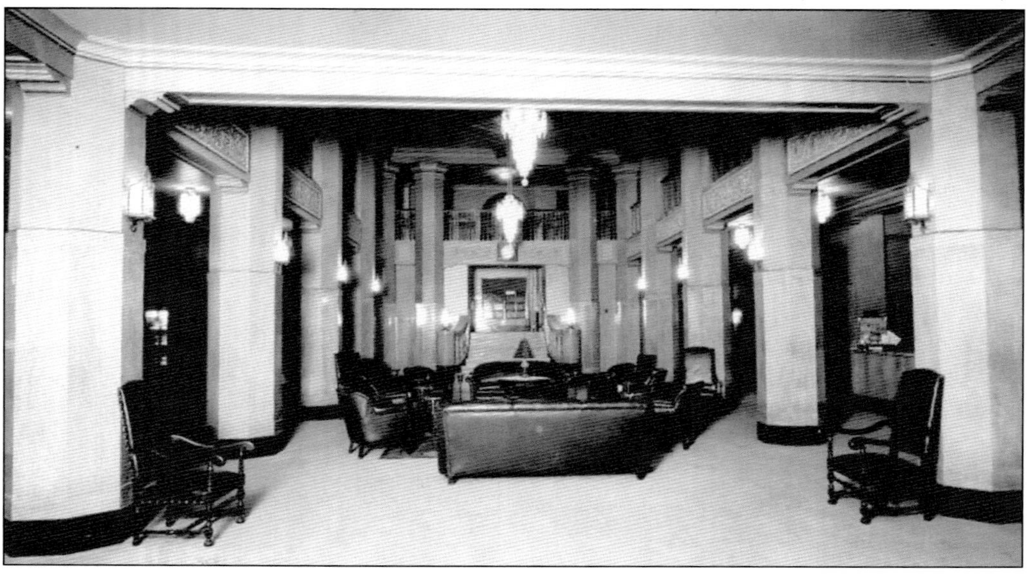

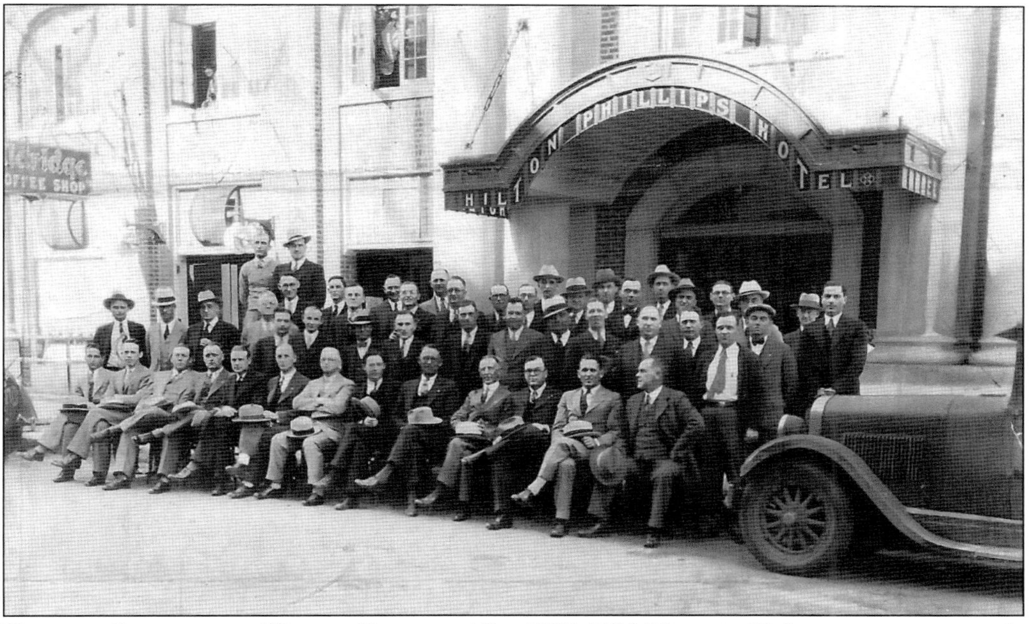

KIWANIS OUTSIDE THE HILTON PHILLIPS. The 1927–1928 Kiwanis Club group poses outside of the Hilton Phillips Hotel before it was renamed the Aldridge Hotel. The Aldridge Coffee Shop can be seen in the background. The Kiwanis Club remains active in Shawnee today by coordinating service projects to improve the community. (Courtesy of Pottawatomie County Historical Society.)

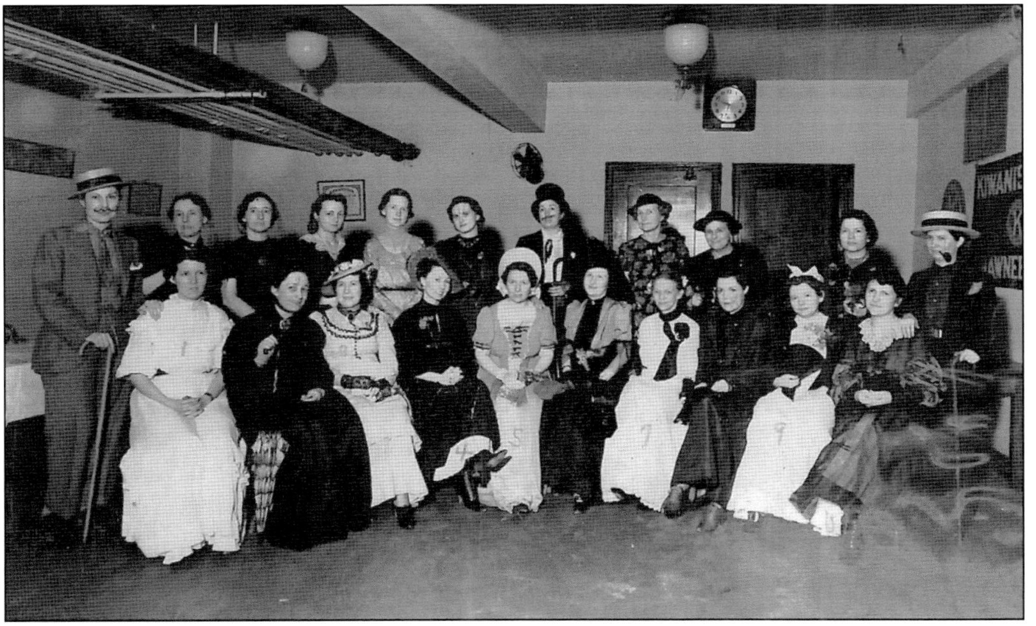

GAY NINETIES PARTY. These women, many of them teachers, are pictured at the Aldridge Hotel in 1937 for a Gay Nineties Party. These parties celebrated the perceived merriment and optimism of the 1890s. The party attendees are dressed in period clothing. (Courtesy of Pottawatomie County Historical Society.)

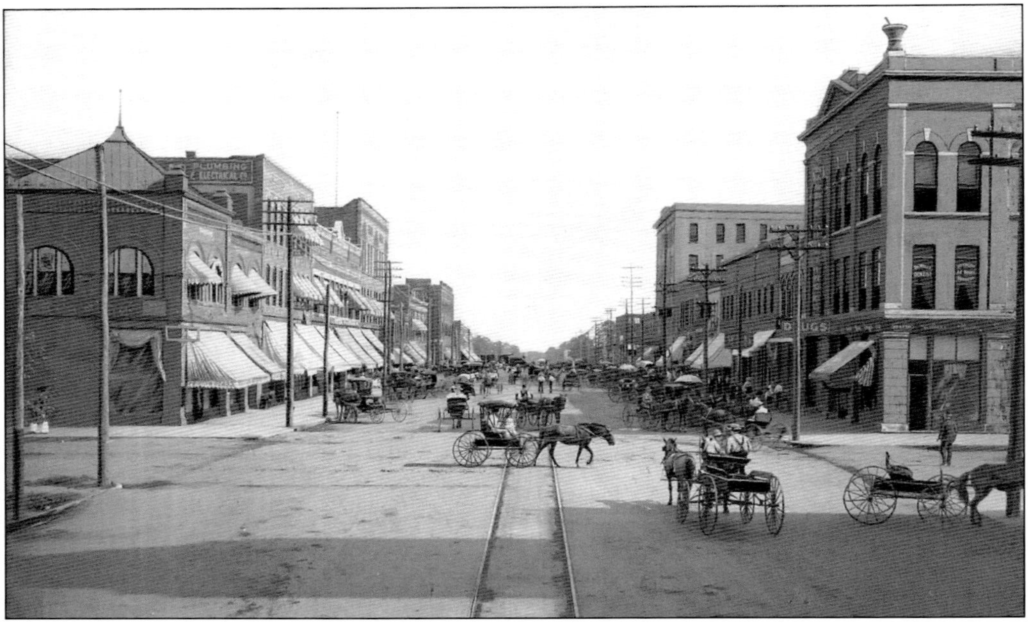

Broadway Avenue and Ninth Street. These two postcards, taken around the same time, show different views of Broadway Avenue and Ninth Street. The top picture was taken from a card postmarked in 1908. The drugstore on the right corner has an interesting feature—a large mortar and pestle rest on the top ledge. The taller building farther down the street on the right is the Norwood Hotel. Across the street, the post office building can be seen. Horses and carriages fill the street. The photograph below shows some of the same buildings, but it is taken from the opposite direction. On the left, the drugstore is again pictured along with city hall. (Above, courtesy of Pottawatomie County Historical Society; below, author's collection.)

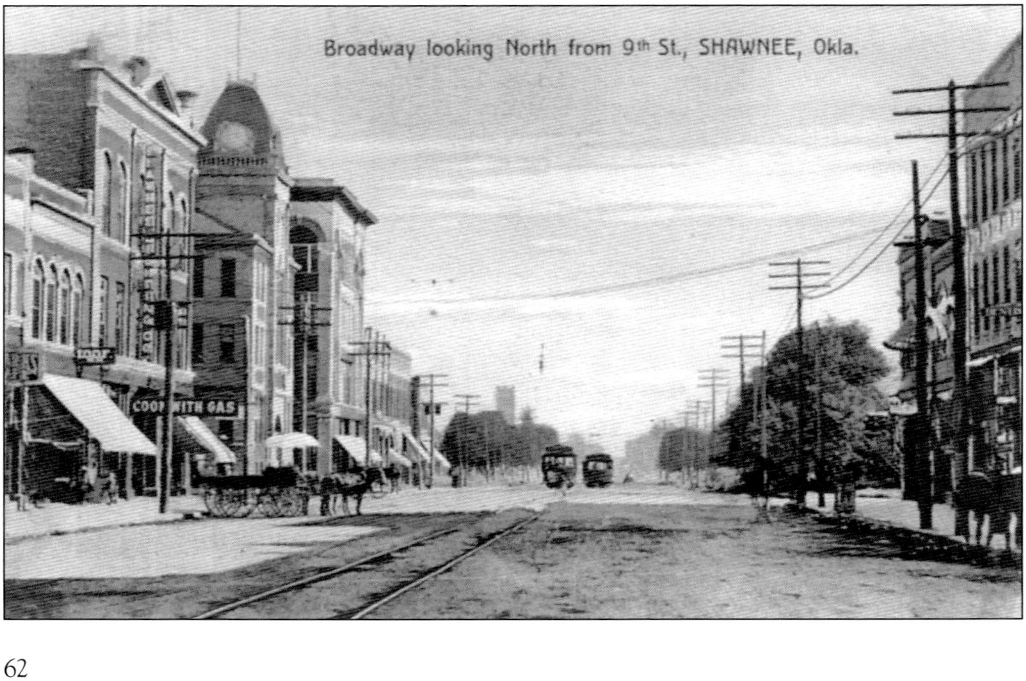

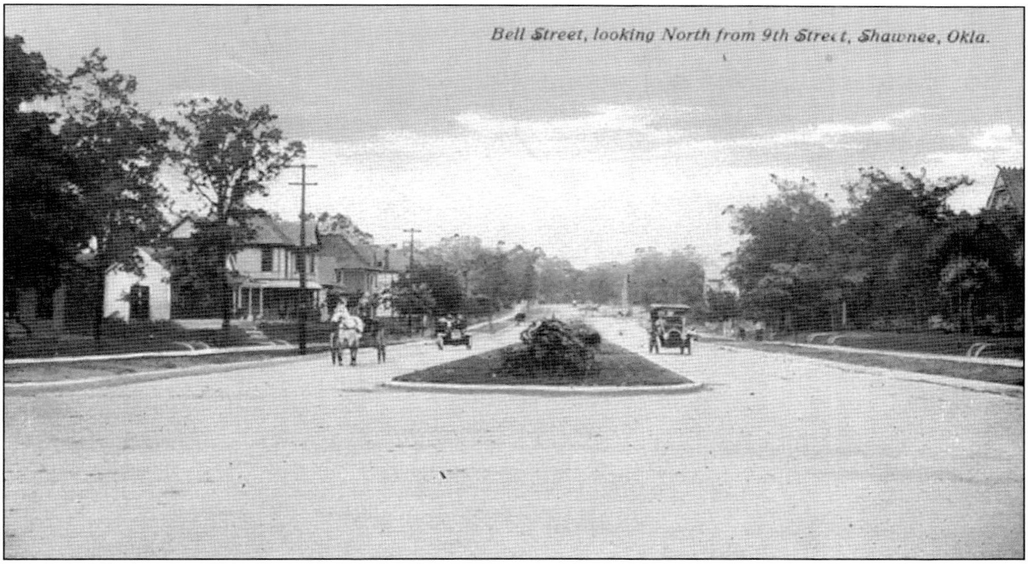

Bell and Ninth Streets. Only houses are present in this c. 1920s postcard view of Bell Street. This scene is looking north from Ninth Street in Shawnee. In only a few years, the Aldridge Hotel would be built here. A post office and the *Shawnee-News Star* offices also would be built in this area much later. (Author's collection.)

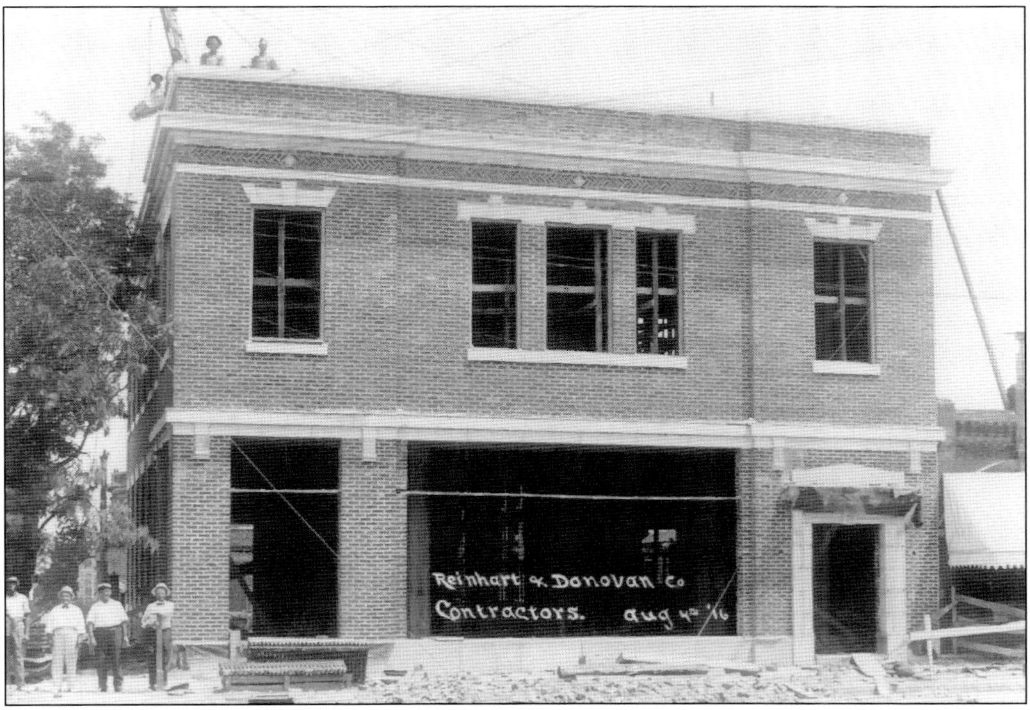

Bell Telephone. The Colonial Revival–style Bell Telephone building at the corner of Ninth and Bell Streets was built in two phases—1916 and 1927. In this August 4, 1916, photograph showing the Bell Street side of the building, construction is ongoing. The building is currently the home of the Shawnee Chamber of Commerce. (Author's collection.)

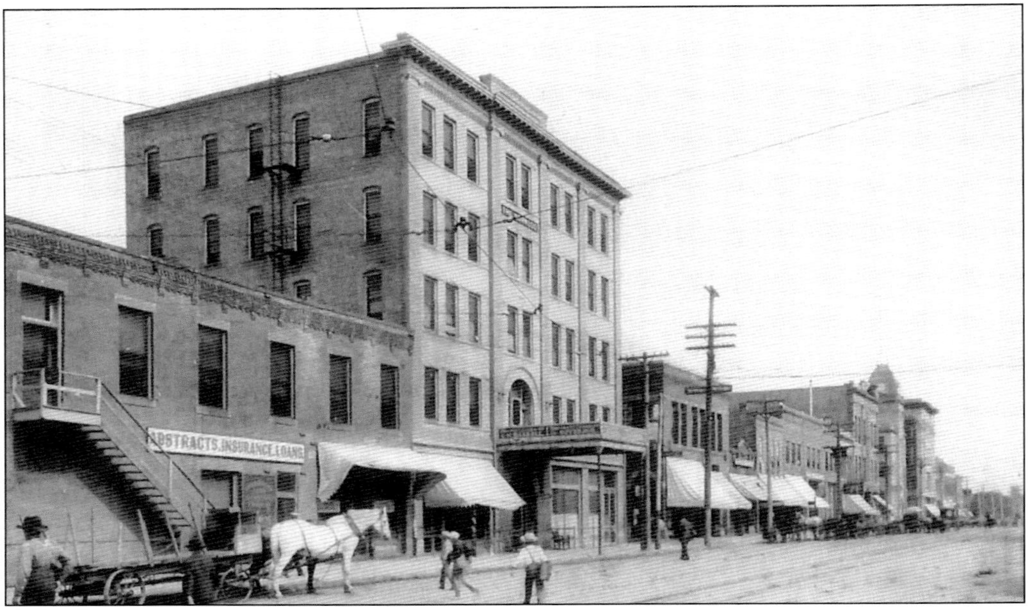

NORWOOD HOTEL. The Norwood Hotel, above, was built in 1903 at the corner of Broadway Avenue and Main Street. As one of two major downtown hotels, many people—both shoppers and salespeople—stayed here when they visited Shawnee. A 1910 advertisement in the *Shawnee News* boasted hot and cold running water, telephones, steam heat, gas, and electric lighting in every room. Rates were $2 to $3 per day. The photograph below shows the Norwood as it looked some years later. Cars have replaced horses in the street. The Elks Building and city hall can also be seen farther down. The Norwood building existed in almost unaltered condition until it was damaged in a 1999 tornado and subsequently torn down. The corner is now a green space. (Both, courtesy of Pottawatomie County Historical Society.)

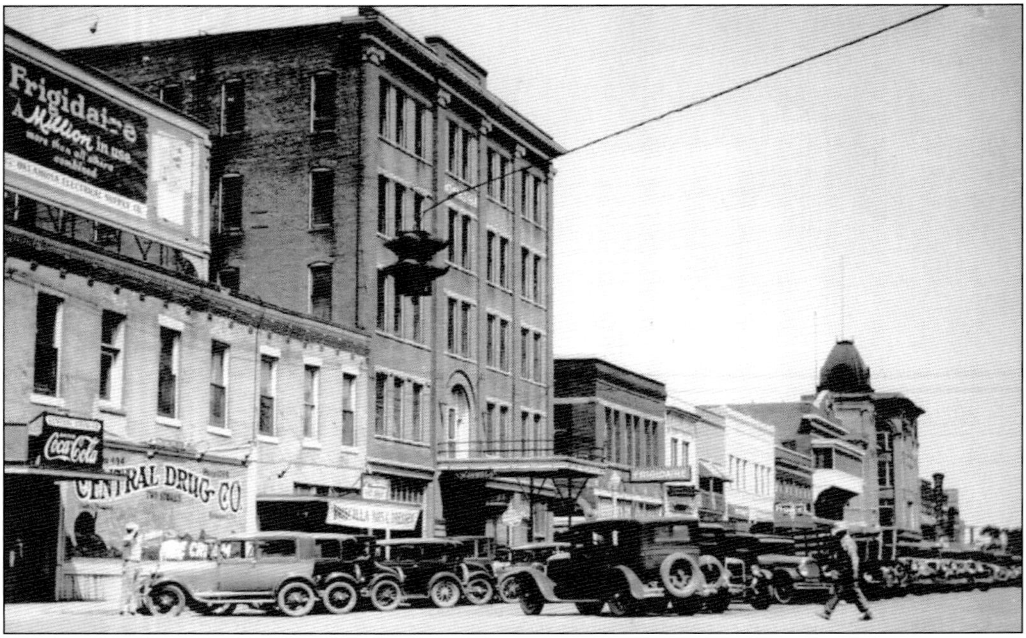

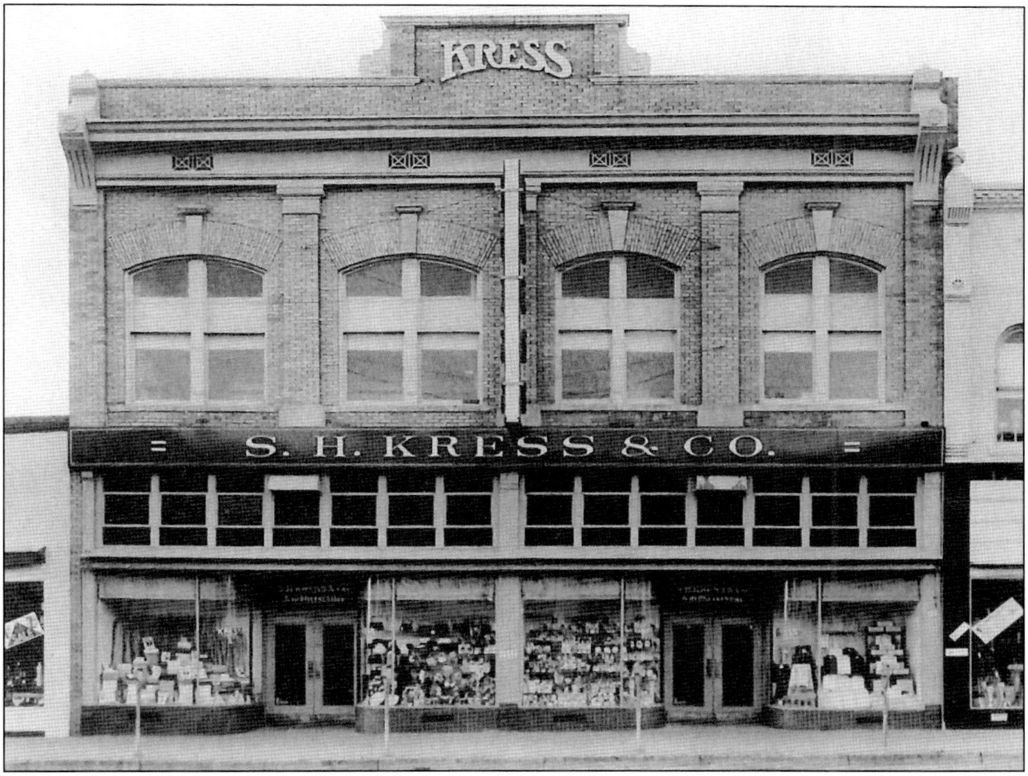

Kress Building, Shawnee. S.H. Kress & Company (photographed above) was located at 109 East Main Street in Shawnee. Kress was a chain of five-and-dime retail department stores that could be found in cities and towns across the country. Shawnee's store opened in 1907 and closed in 1980. The building still stands mostly unaltered on Main Street. Below, employees pose for a photograph inside the store on April 26, 1939. The store is packed with goods for sale. (Both, courtesy of Pottawatomie County Historical Society.)

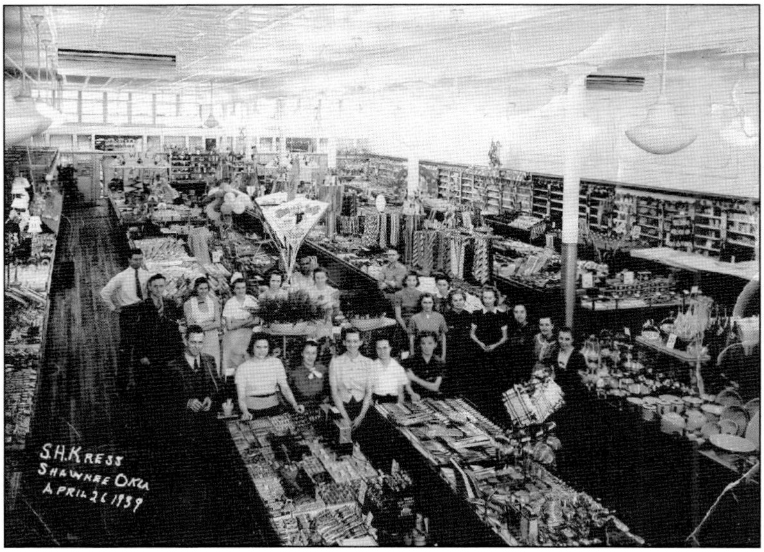

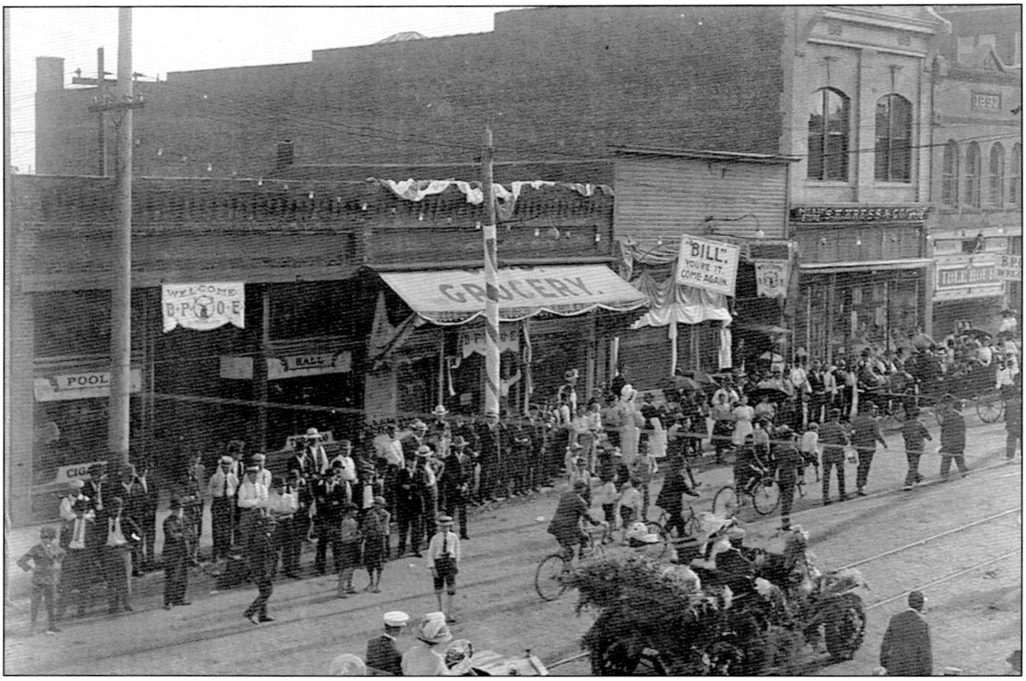

100 Block of East Main Street. Two views of the 100 block of East Main Street in Shawnee are shown here. In the older photograph above, a crowd has turned out to welcome the Benevolent and Protective Order of Elks. The Kress Building can be seen in this photograph at about half the size it is now. The later photograph below shows another busy Main Street. The Kress Building has taken over a neighboring lot and doubled in size. (Both, courtesy of Pottawatomie County Historical Society.)

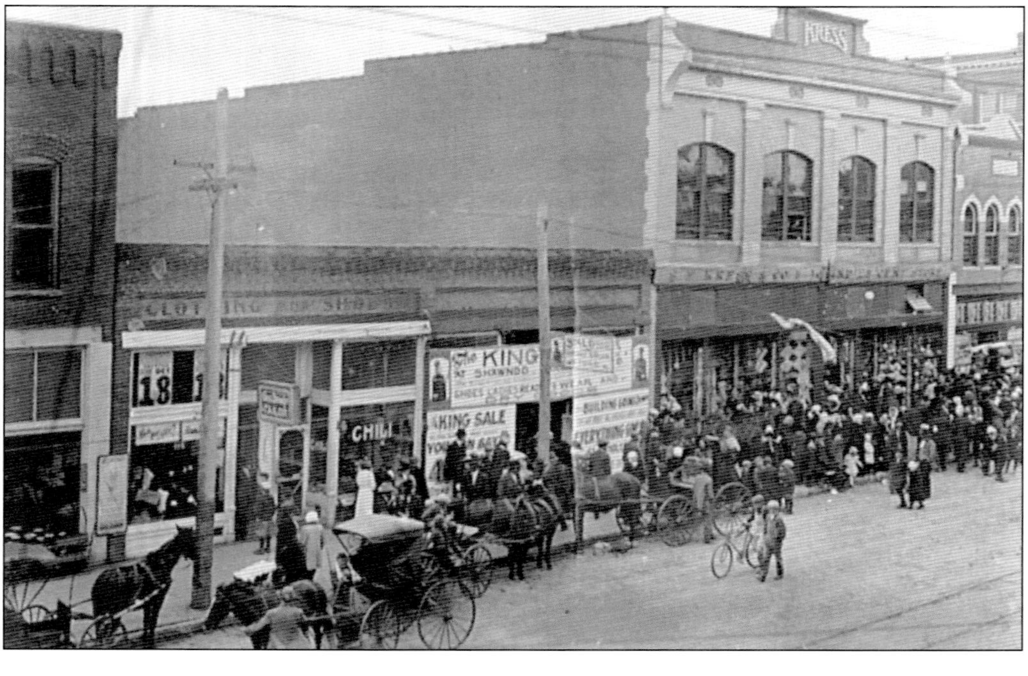

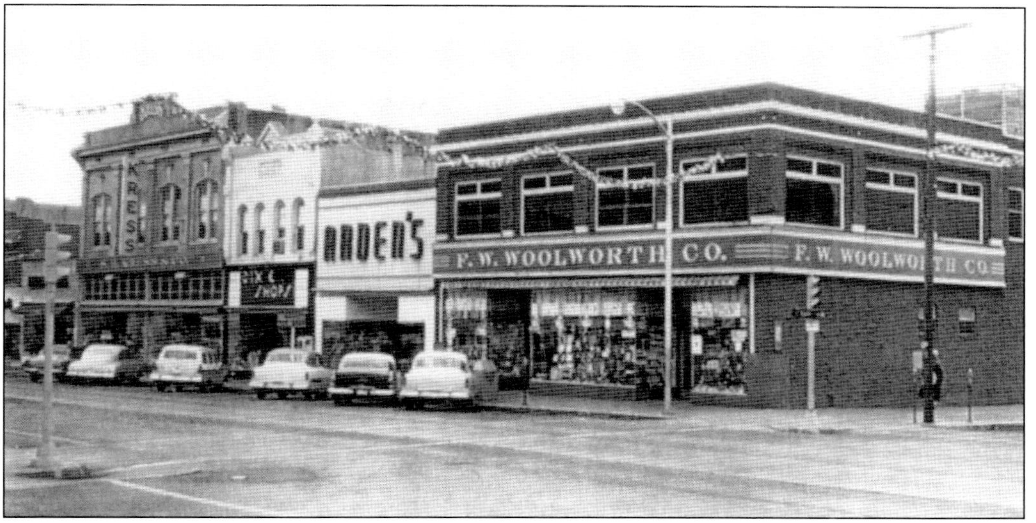

Main and Bell Streets. This postcard of Main and Bell Streets in Shawnee shows Kress, Arden's, and F.W. Woolworth. The Woolworth Building has been painted but still exists mostly unaltered otherwise. The Kress Building also still stands. (Author's collection.)

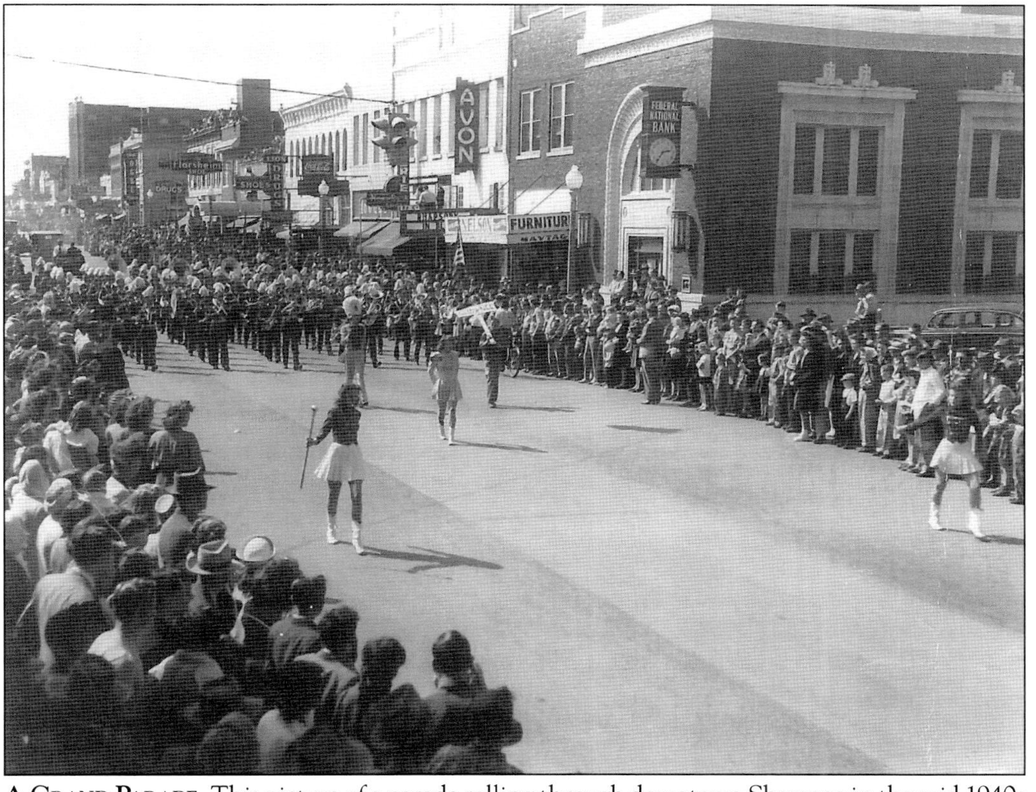

A Grand Parade. This picture of a parade rolling through downtown Shawnee in the mid-1940s features many businesses longtime locals still fondly remember, including Federal National Bank, the Avon Theater, Nelson's Furniture, Lion Drugs, and Moody's. (Courtesy of Pottawatomie County Historical Society.)

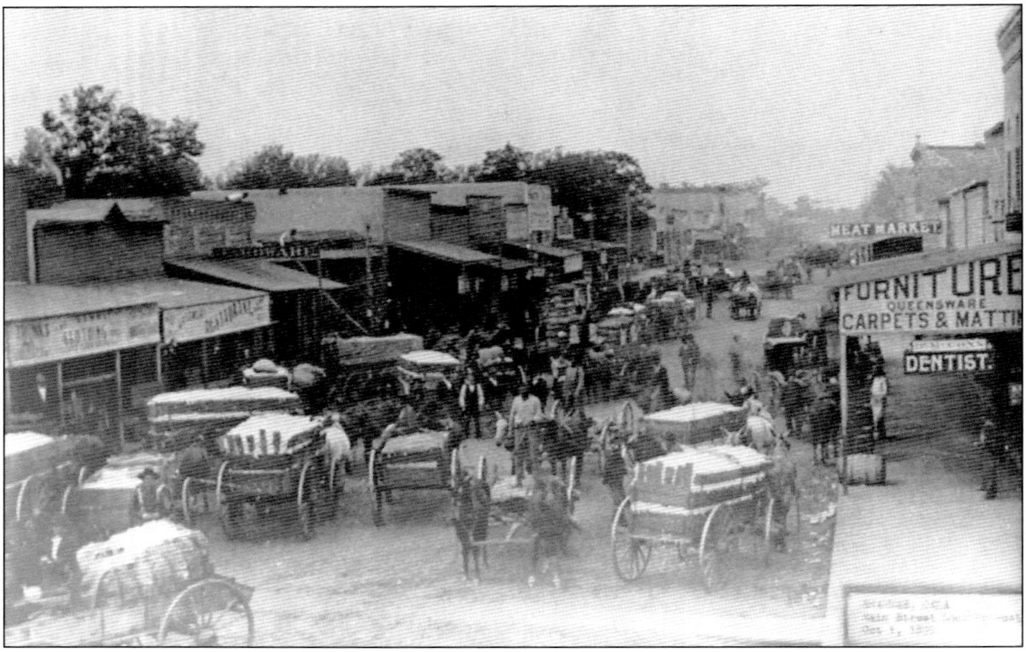

200 EAST MAIN STREET. The 200 block of East Main Street in Shawnee is shown looking west on October 1, 1899. A mercantile store, restaurant, hardware store, furniture store, meat market, and dentist are just a few of the businesses on this busy block. (Courtesy of Charles Villines.)

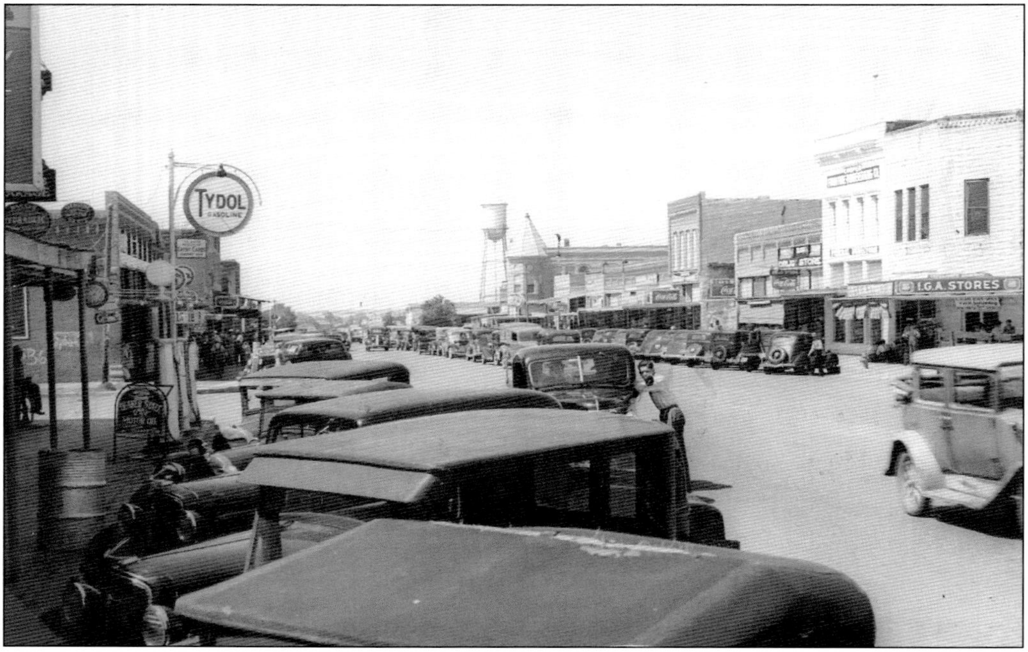

BROADWAY STREET IN TECUMSEH, 1940. Broadway Street in Tecumseh is lined with cars in this photograph from 1940. Many of these buildings, including the majority of the block on the right, still stand. The larger building with the steeple-type roof has been lost, unfortunately. (Courtesy of Pottawatomie County Historical Society.)

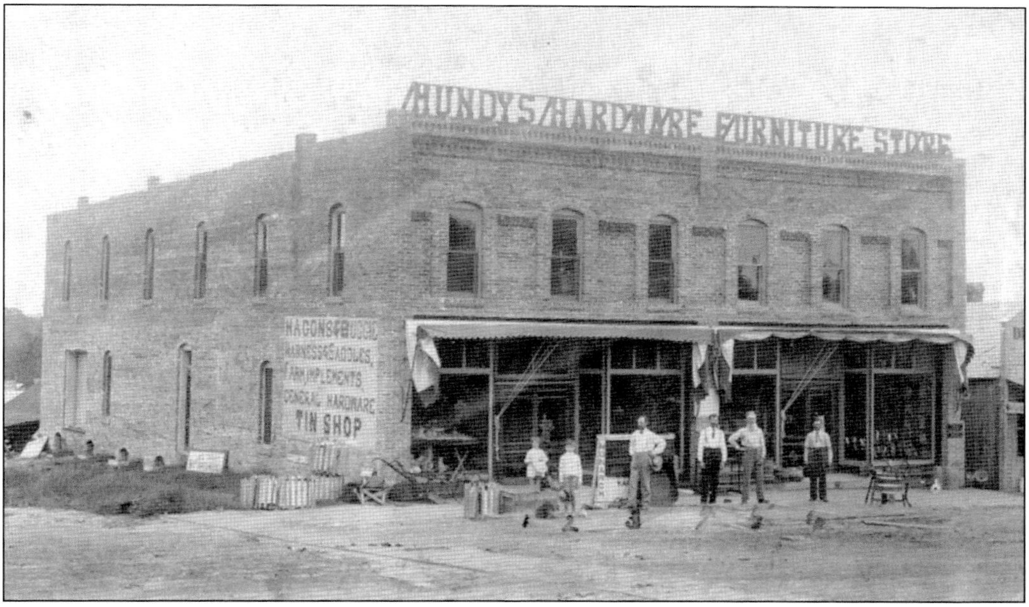

Mundy's Furniture. Mundy's Hardware and Furniture Store in Wanette is pictured above. This photograph was taken in 1904. Mundy's offered wagons, buggies, farm implements, and other general hardware. Standing outside the shop are, from left to right, Lillian Mundy, Lloyd Mundy, E.B. Mundy, Joe Mundy, unidentified, and Rolen ?. (Courtesy of Pottawatomie County Historical Society.)

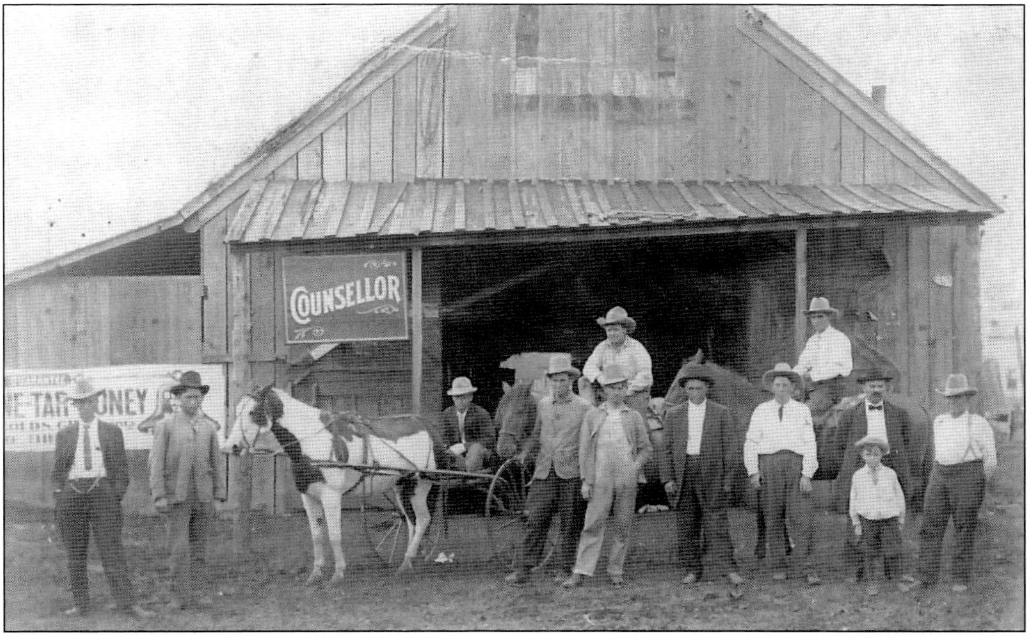

Blacksmith Shop. A group of people stands with a team of horses outside a Wanette blacksmith shop about 1910. Almost everyone in the early 20th century required the assistance of the local blacksmith. Not only would he offer horseshoeing services, but he also might repair machinery, wagons, and carriages and sharpen plows and other tools. (Courtesy of Melinda Pennington.)

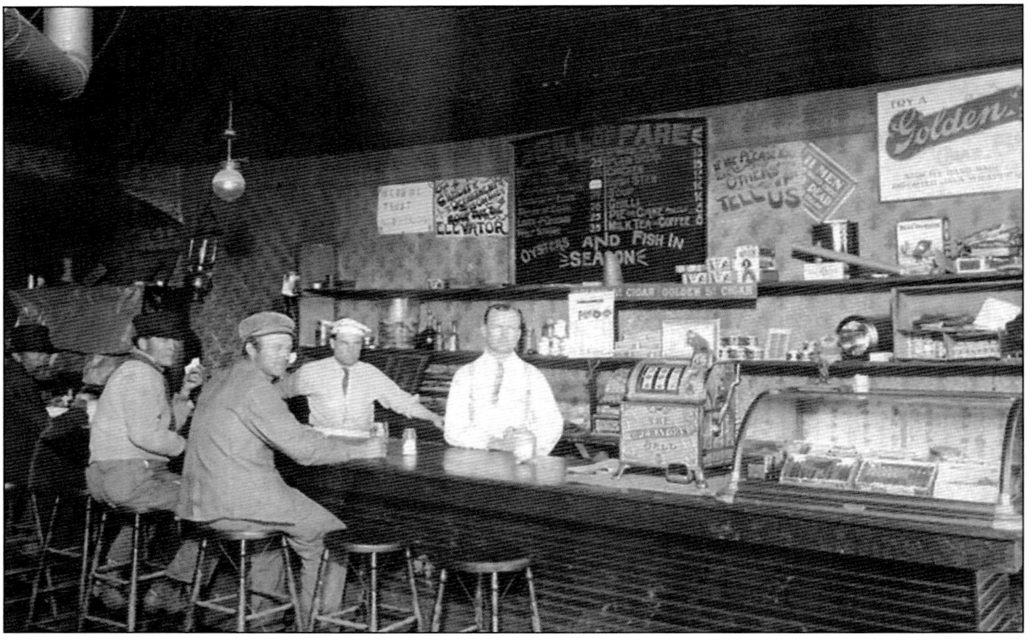

Wanette Restaurant. The Ivey Restaurant in Wanette served up bacon and eggs for 25¢ and soup for 10¢, among other menu items. The restaurant, which was owned by John and Lem Ivey, was open for business from 1905 to 1937. This photograph was taken in the 1930s. (Courtesy of Melinda Pennington.)

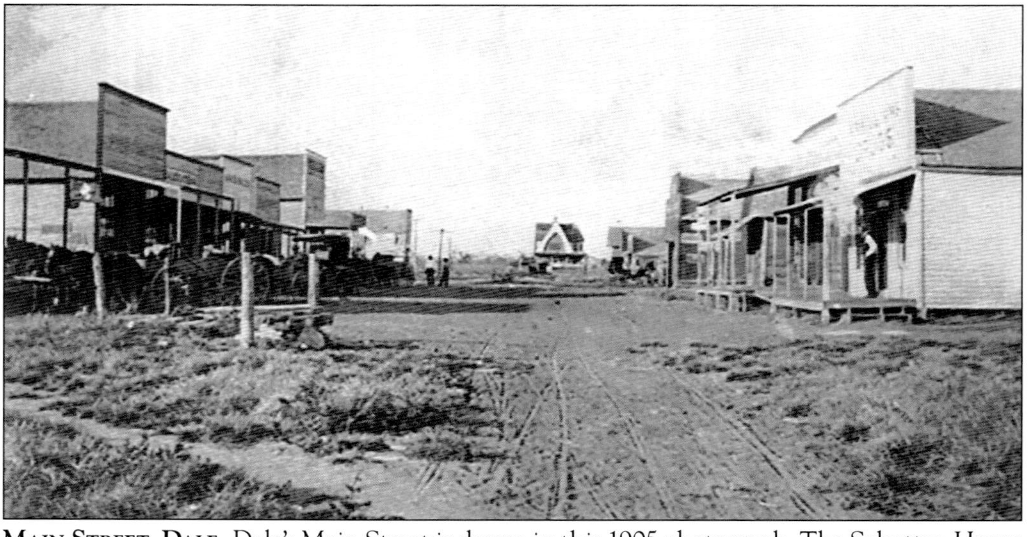

Main Street, Dale. Dale's Main Street is shown in this 1905 photograph. The Schutten House is visible at the end of the road. This house was built in 1905 by A.B. Jones and later sold to the Schutten family. While the home survived the disastrous 1907 fire that burned much of the town, the house burned down in 1962. (Courtesy of Pottawatomie County Historical Society.)

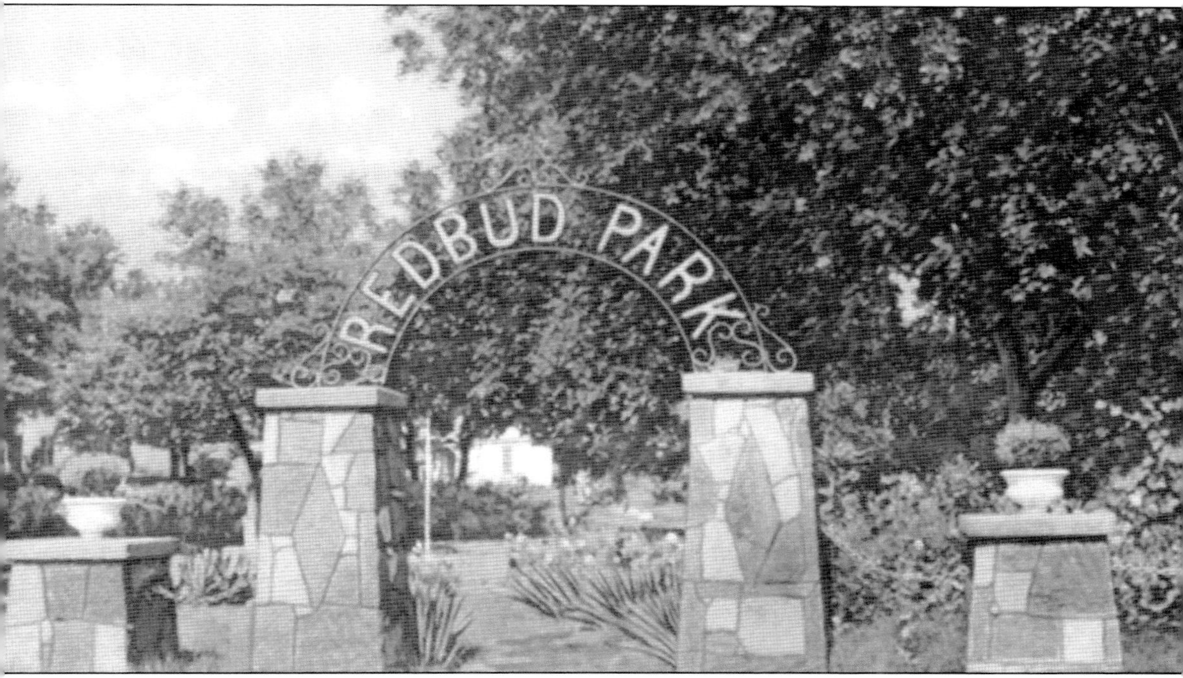

Redbud Park. Work began on Redbud Park on December 13, 1939. The park is located at North Broadway Avenue and West Dill Street in Shawnee. The Kellogg National Medal was awarded to the project in 1942. The designation of "Redbud City of Oklahoma" was adopted by the Shawnee City Council on April 9, 1940, and was confirmed by a resolution by the Oklahoma Legislature the following year. The Shawnee Council of Garden Clubs was responsible for this designation. Beginning in the 1930s, the council sold thousands of eastern redbud trees to the public for 25¢ each. Many were, of course, planted in Redbud Park. (Courtesy of Pottawatomie County Historical Society.)

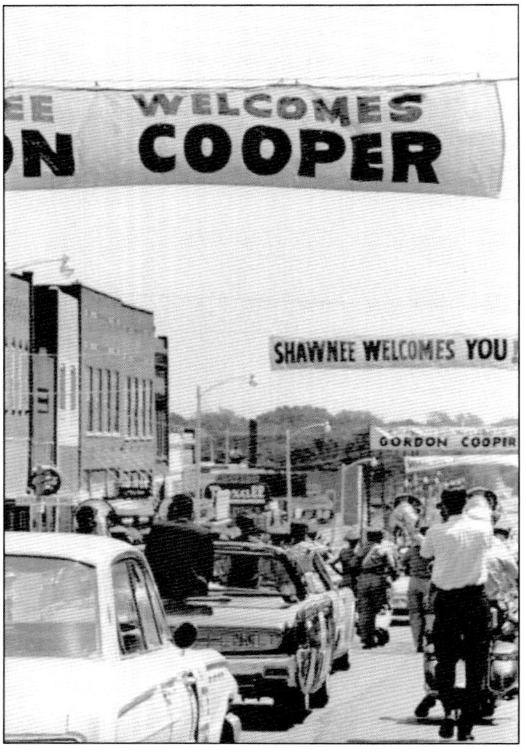

Astronaut Gordon Cooper. Gordon Cooper was born on March 5, 1927, in Shawnee and attended Shawnee schools before moving to Kentucky shortly prior to graduating from high school. Cooper would go on to become an aerospace engineer, Air Force pilot, and one of the seven original astronauts in Project Mercury, the first US manned space program. Cooper passed away in 2004. Gordon Cooper Technology Center in Shawnee is named for him. At left, a parade on Main Street welcomes Cooper on August 11, 1962. Below, a sign in Shawnee proudly claims Cooper to be one of their own. (Both, courtesy of Pottawatomie County Historical Society.)

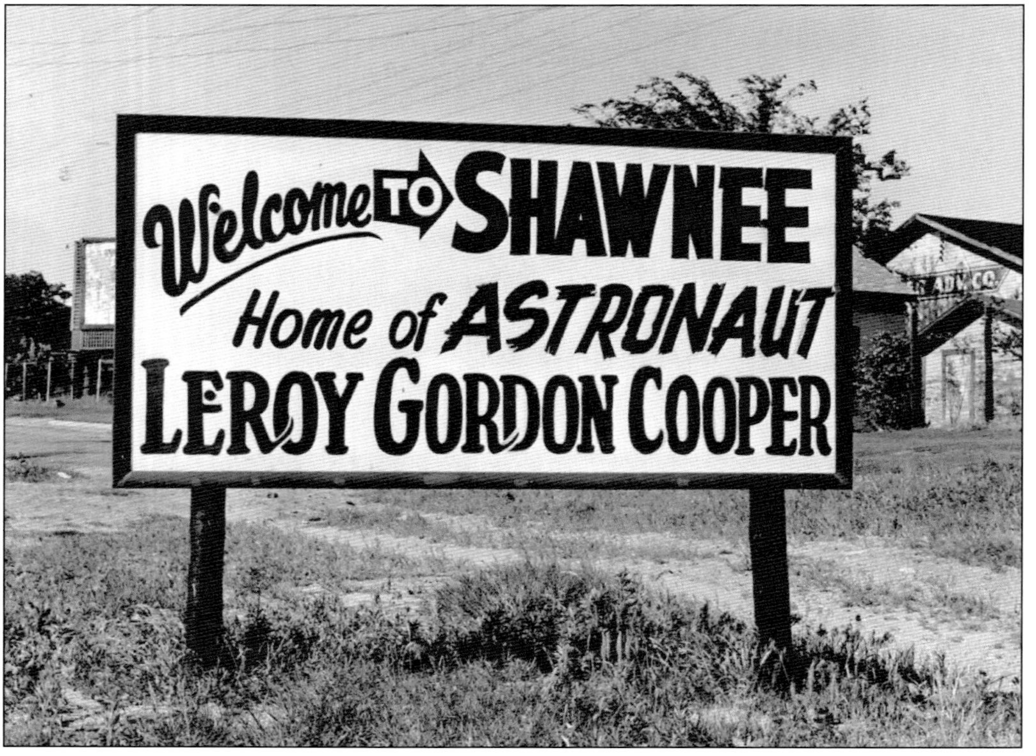

Four

THEATERS

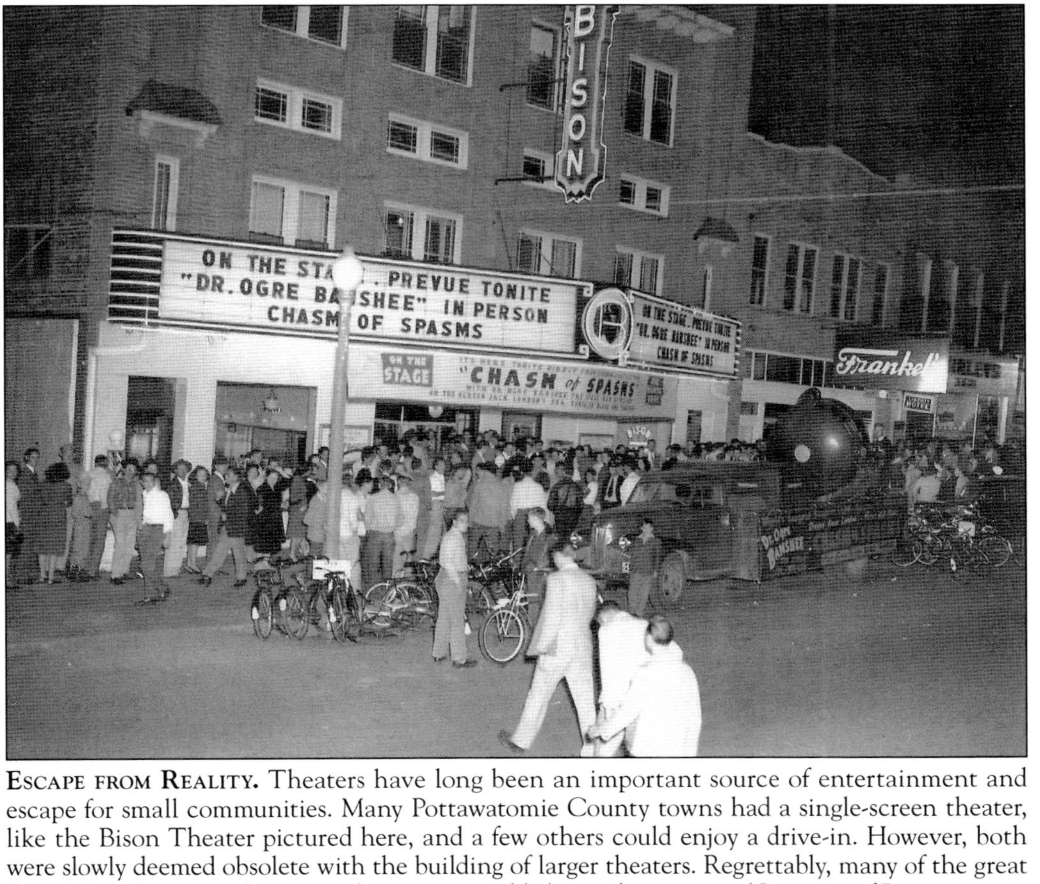

ESCAPE FROM REALITY. Theaters have long been an important source of entertainment and escape for small communities. Many Pottawatomie County towns had a single-screen theater, like the Bison Theater pictured here, and a few others could enjoy a drive-in. However, both were slowly deemed obsolete with the building of larger theaters. Regrettably, many of the great theater buildings were lost or made unrecognizable by modernization. (Courtesy of Pottawatomie County Historical Society.)

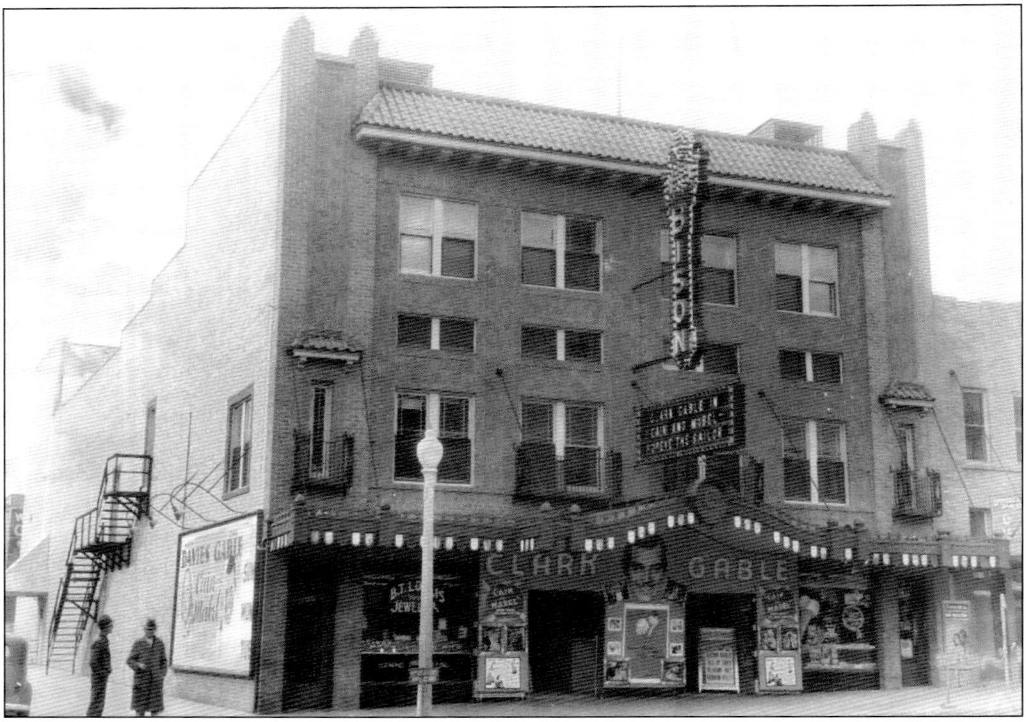

BISON THEATER. The Bison Theater, above, opened in October 1927 at Main Street and Philadelphia Avenue in Shawnee with seating for over 1,000 patrons. The art deco interior, below, featured a domed ceiling and included a complete working stage with a fly loft for scenery. The theater closed in the 1950s. The building still stands on Main Street, but the facade has been heavily modified. A newer marquee, added later, still exists and was moved to the Ritz Theater in 1966. (Both, courtesy of Jones Theatres.)

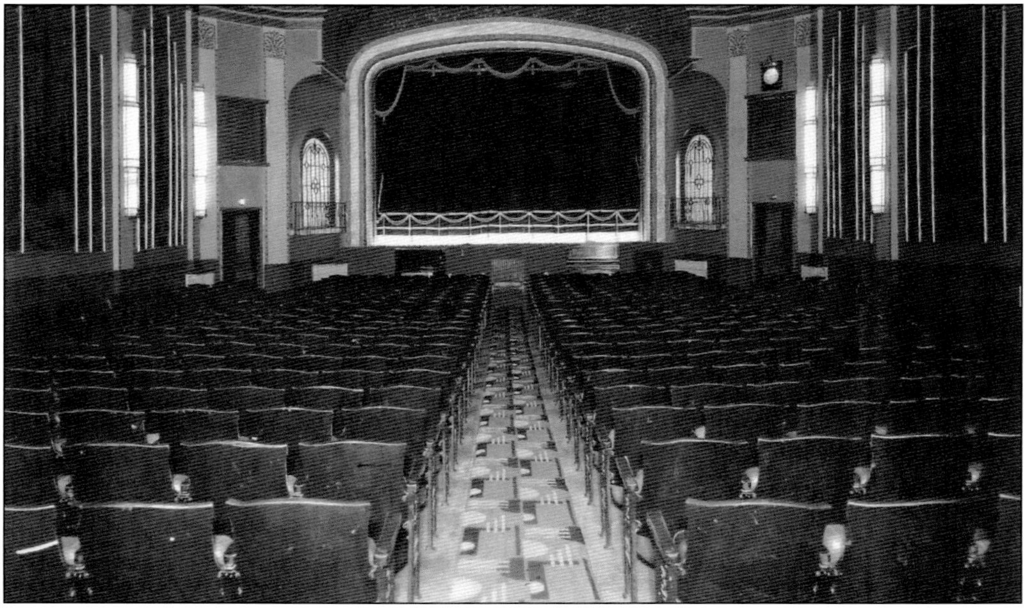

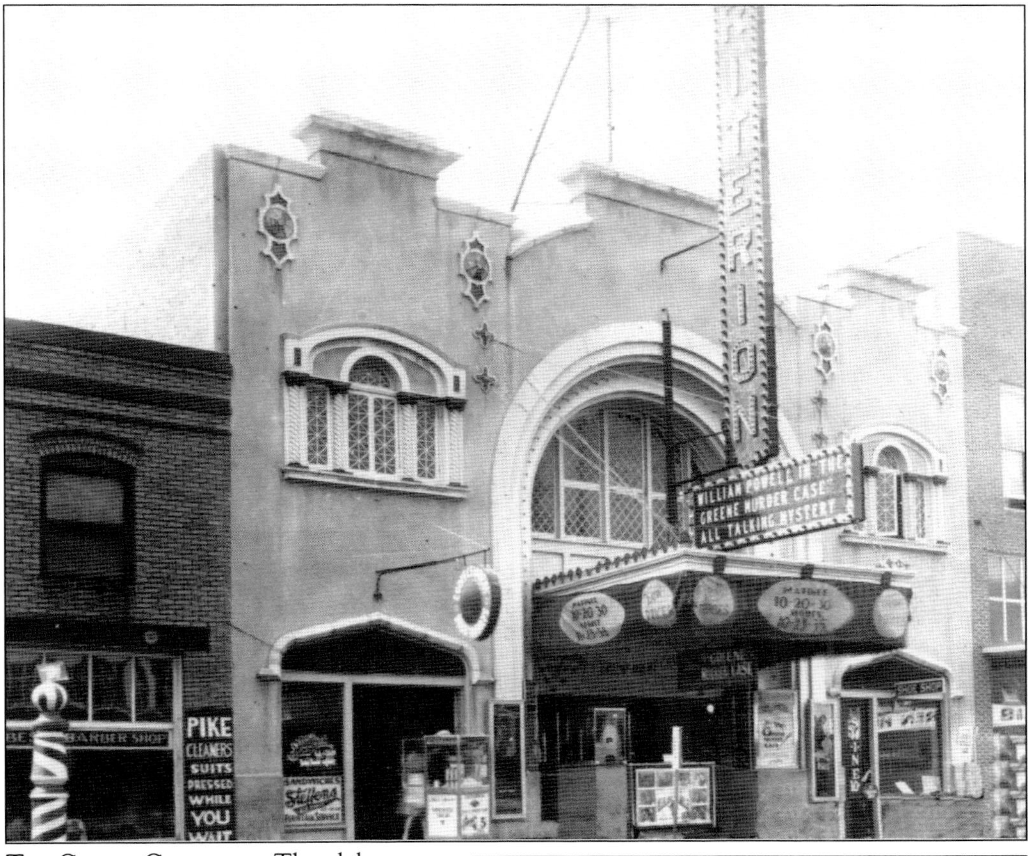

THE CLASSY CRITERION. The elaborate and classy Criterion Theater, above, was built in 1927 by Jake Jones. In addition to showing movies, the theater used its access to the railroad to bring in scenery, props, and other items from boxcars for use in live shows. John Phillip Sousa, known as the "March King," performed a show here in the 1920s. In the photograph above, *The Green Murder Case*, a 1929 "talking film," is being shown. At right, the Criterion is shown on December 16, 1939, after a remodel toned down the ornate windows and some decorative elements. A new marquee was also added. *Fast and Furious* is playing, although this 1939 movie about a crime-solving rare book dealer duo had little to do with illegal street racing. (Both, courtesy of Jones Theatres.)

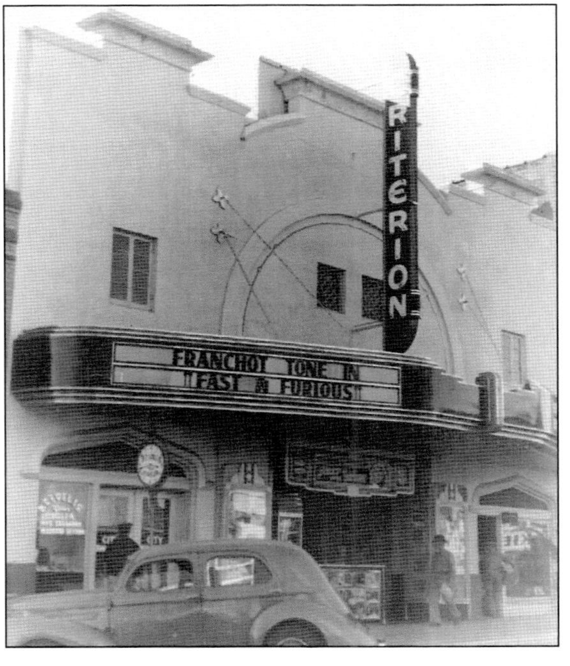

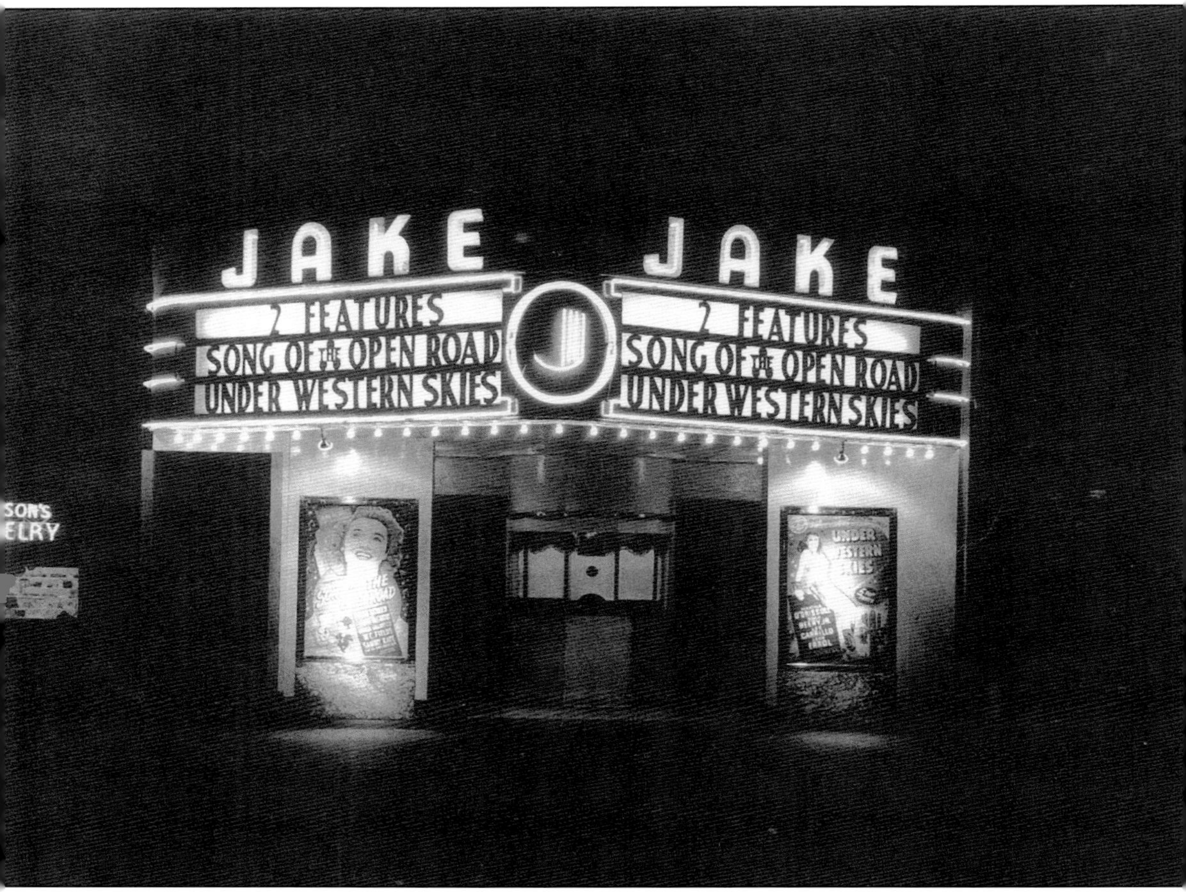

Odeon Becomes Jake. In 1943 Jake Jones's son and daughter, Johnny H. Jones Sr. and Ruby Jones, acquired the Odeon Theater, which was later renamed the Jake in their father's honor. This photograph of the Jake, which was located at 7 East Main Street, was taken about 1945. This building no longer exists. (Courtesy of Jones Theatres.)

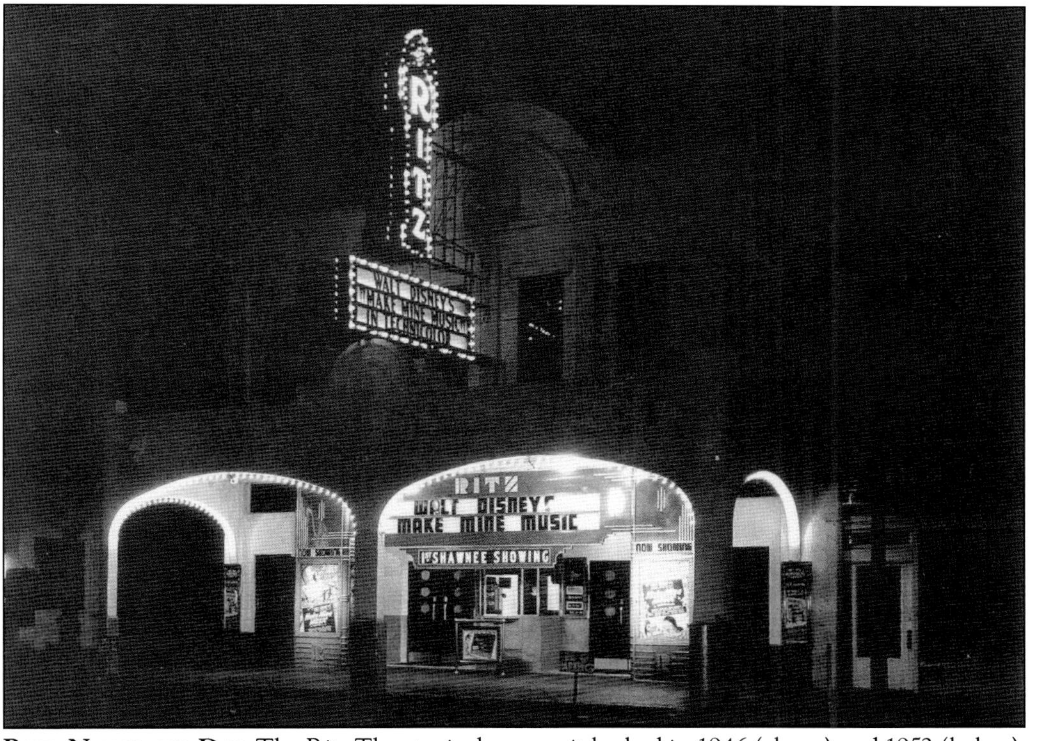

RITZ, NIGHT AND DAY. The Ritz Theater is shown as it looked in 1946 (above) and 1952 (below), with its arched front. The original name for the theater was the Cozy, but it was changed to the name most know now in 1926. The venue showed some of Shawnee's first talking motion pictures. The building housing the Ritz was constructed around 1899. The arched front was removed in a 1960s remodel and replaced with the marquee from the Bison Theater. The theater closed in 1988 but now operates as a live theater. (Both, courtesy of Jones Theatres.)

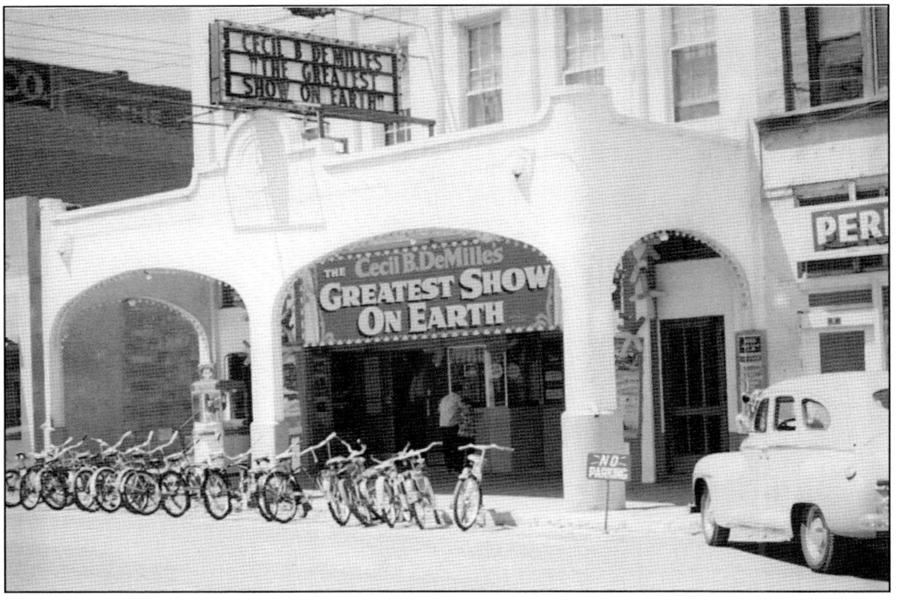

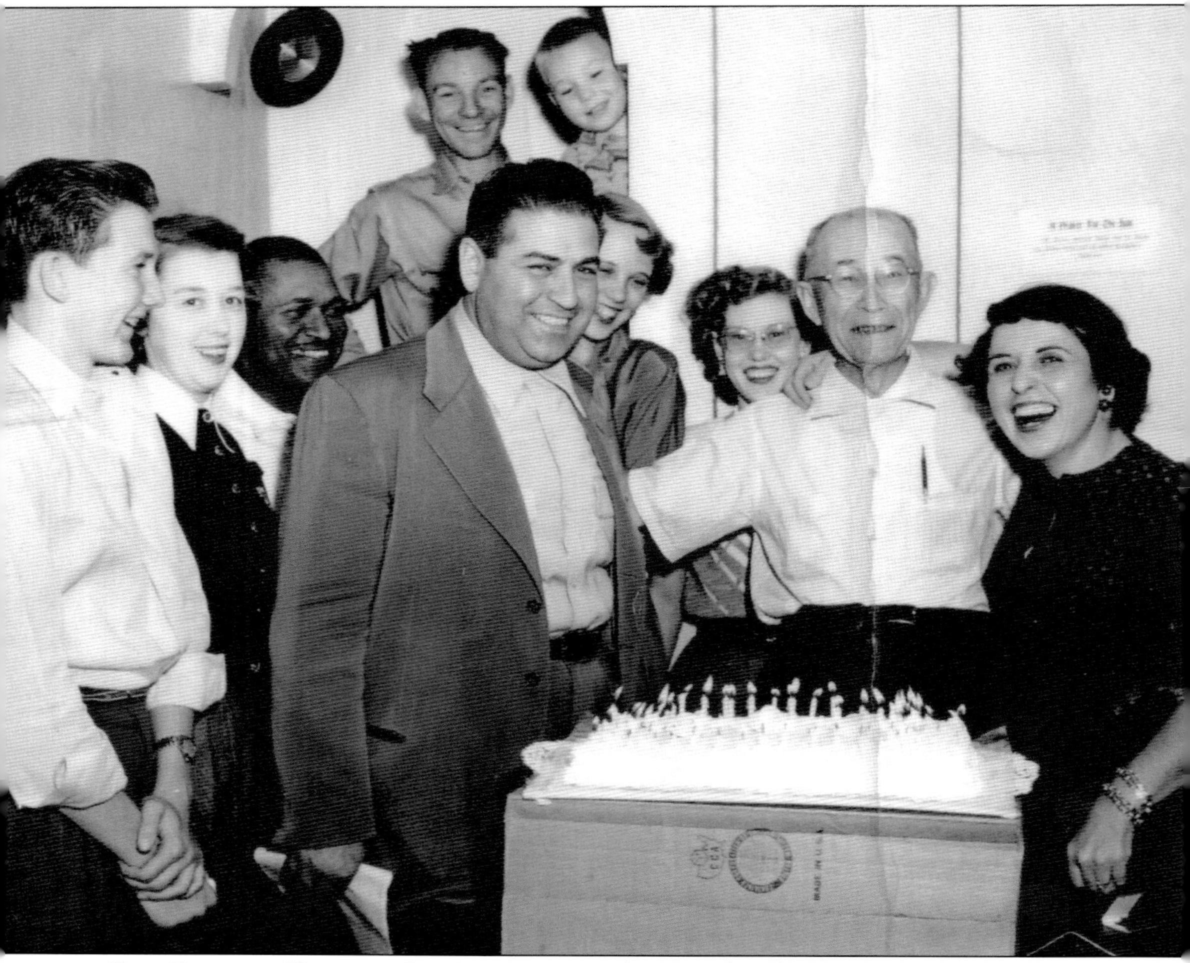

Ritz Employee Honored. Leo Montgomery, who started at the Ritz Theater when he was 31, celebrates his 70th birthday. Leo was working at the Ritz when Jake Jones purchased the theater from Leo's father. One condition of the sale was that Leo was to remain on staff. He worked at the Ritz for the remainder of his life. Pictured from left to right are Kenneth Gibson, Dorthea Bays, Emmett Young, Lee Estes, Johnny Jones, Mary Crownover, Virginia Long, Montgomery, and Ruby Jones. (Courtesy of Jones Theatres.)

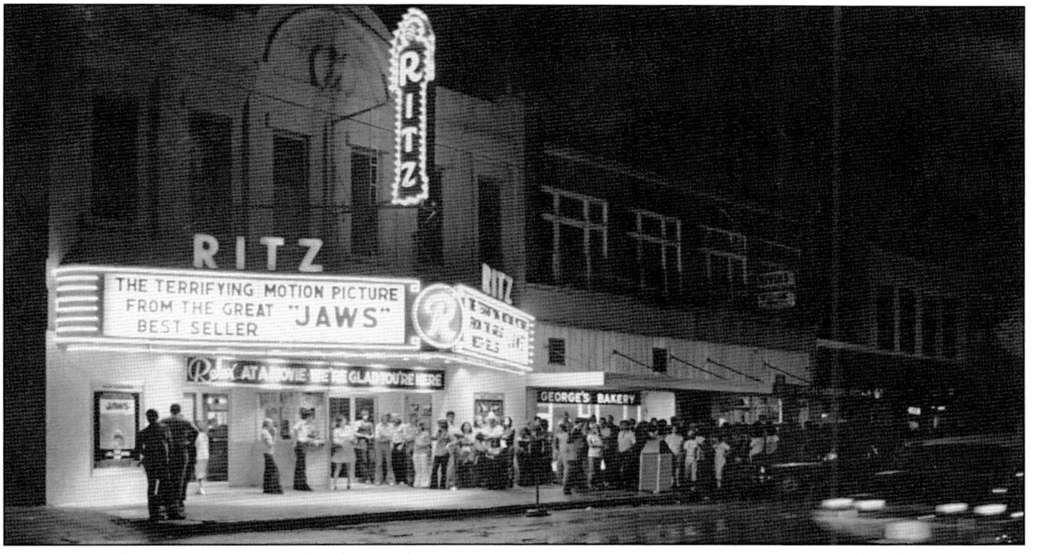

READY TO BE TERRIFIED. The line of anxious patrons waiting to see *Jaws* at the Ritz Theater flows down Main Street. Record-breaking crowds showed up to watch the movie in the summer of 1975. This photograph shows a Ritz Theater most people would recognize even today. The theater remained popular through the 1970s but had a hard time fighting off competition from larger theaters and closed in 1988. (Courtesy of Jones Theatres.)

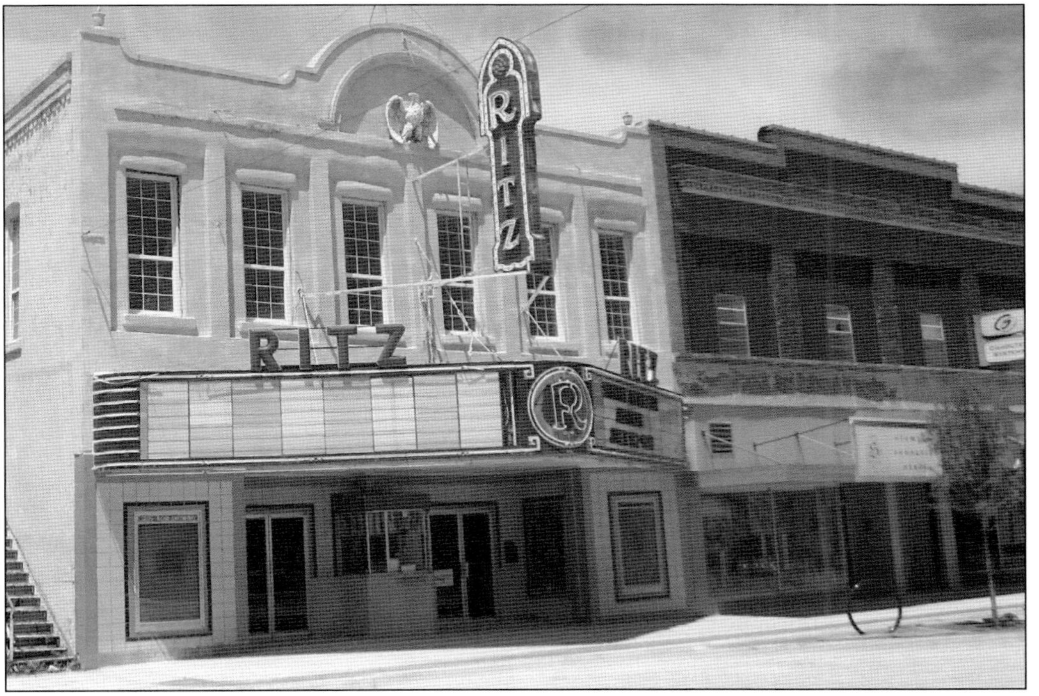

THE RITZ REBORN. This photograph of the Ritz as it looks today shows it has changed very little in the past 50 years. It is a historical landmark for the community. Although it closed as a motion picture theater in 1988, steady renovations began in 2000, and the building now operates as a live theater. (Author's collection.)

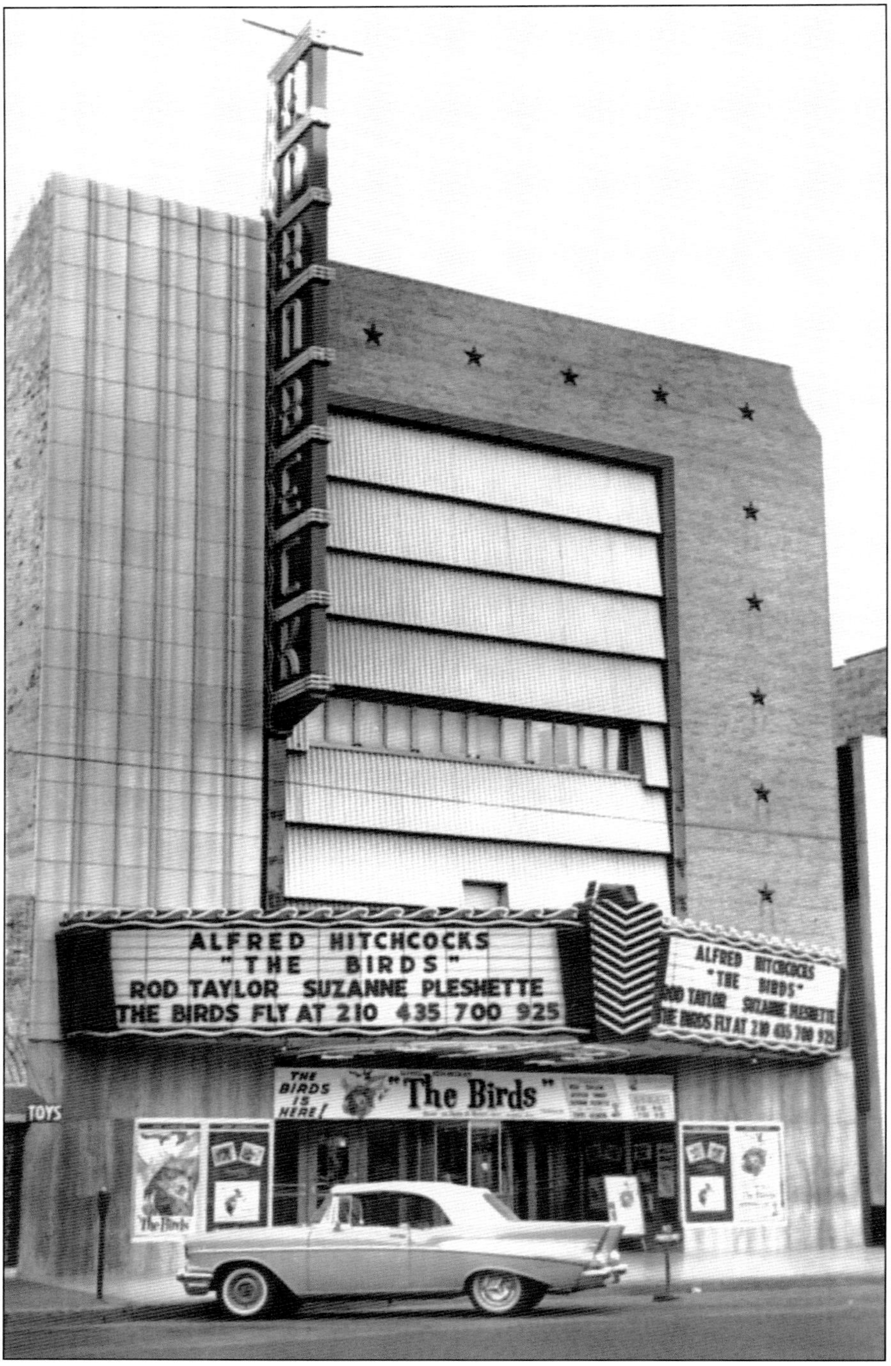

Birds Invade the Hornbeck. The Hornbeck Theater on North Bell Street in Shawnee opened in 1947 as a single-screen movie house. Streamlined modern lines and lots of neon set this theater apart. In this 1966 photograph, *The Birds* is playing. In 1973, the balcony was remodeled into a piggyback twin. The upper theater is known as the Penthouse. (Courtesy of Pottawatomie County Historical Society.)

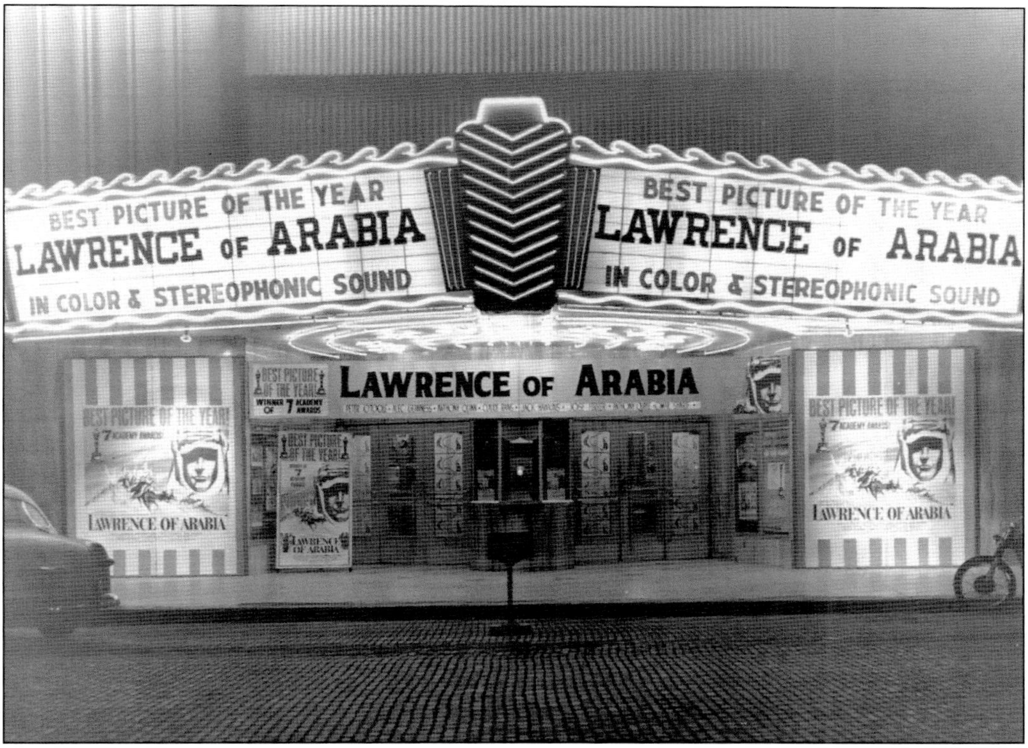

Hornbeck Marquee, c. 1962. *Lawrence of Arabia* plays at the Hornbeck Theater about 1962. Theaters of this time often adorned the outside of their establishments with advertisements to publicize certain films. The advertisements in this particular photograph were installed by a young Ronny Jones of the Jones Theatres family. (Courtesy of Jones Theatres.)

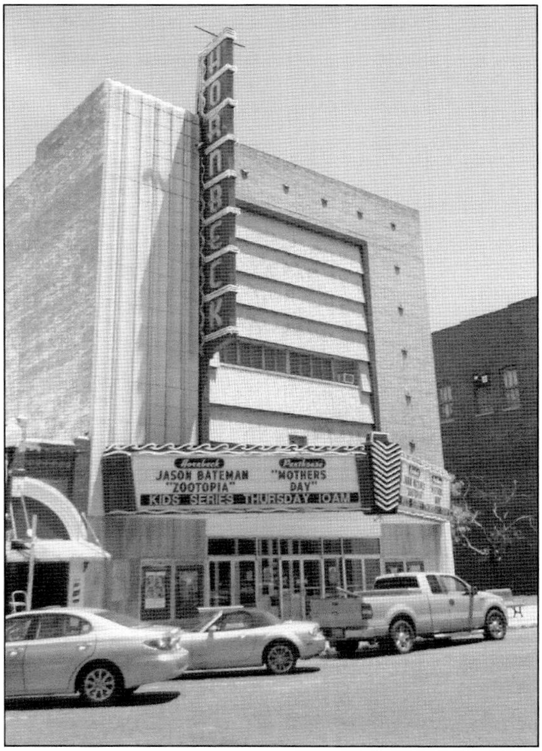

The Hornbeck Today. The Hornbeck has changed very little from when it opened over 60 years before. The theater still operates with its balcony reconfigured into a second theater, the Penthouse. The interior has been remodeled and retains much of the original look of the movie house. The theater shows recent movies at a reduced price. It is pictured as it looks today. (Author's collection.)

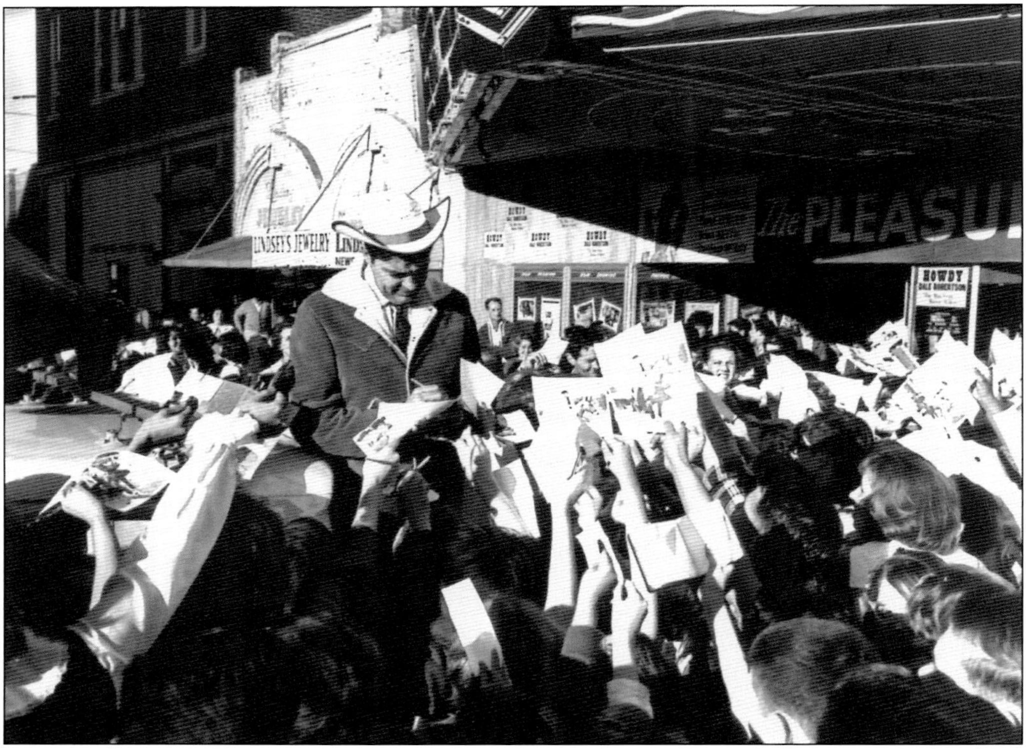

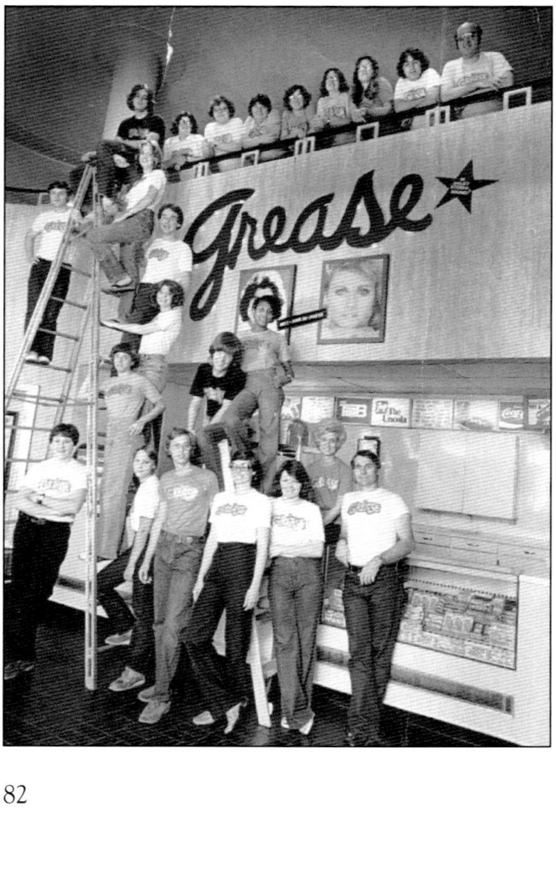

DALE ROBERTSON AUTOGRAPH PARTY. Dale Robertson signs autographs for a group of fans outside the Hornbeck Theater in 1965. Robertson was born in Harrah, Oklahoma, and is best known for his roles on television's *Tales of Wells Fargo* and *The Iron Horse*. He also starred in many Westerns. (Courtesy of Jones Theatres.)

CRUISIN' FOR A BRUISIN'. Employees wearing *Grease* T-shirts gather for a photograph in front of the concession area of the Hornbeck Theater. The theater is promoting the movie, which ran at the Ritz during June and July 1978 and became a critical and financial success. (Courtesy of Jones Theatres.)

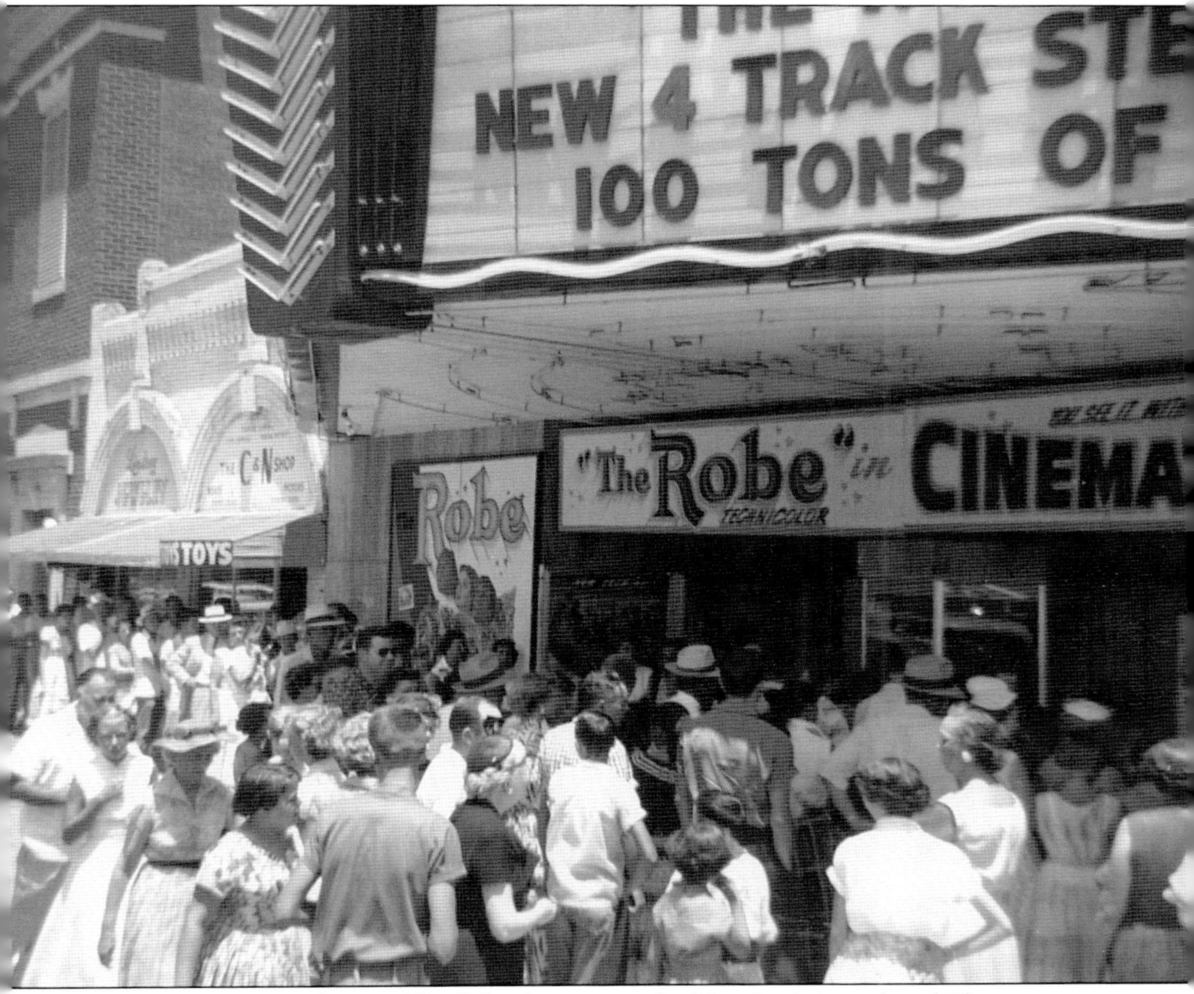

Introducing CinemaScope. *The Robe* showing at the Hornbeck introduced Shawnee to CinemaScope in July 1954. The technology allowed the showing of wide-screen movies, almost twice as wide as the previous technology. Other Shawnee theaters and even the Starlite Drive-In upgraded to this new equipment. (Courtesy of Jones Theatres.)

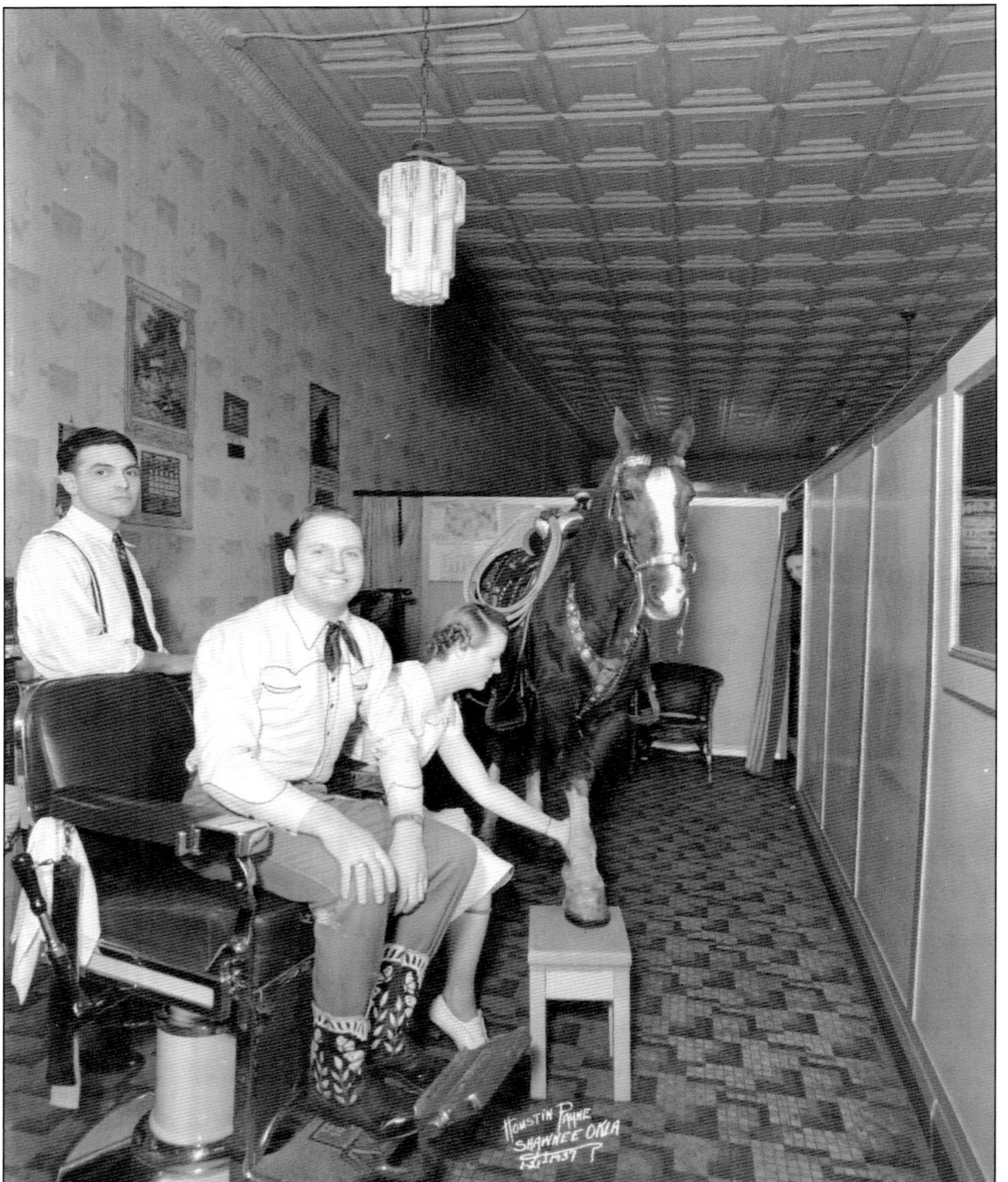

CUT AND A QUICK SHINE. Gene Autry (seated in chair) visits a Shawnee barbershop in January 1937 while promoting a movie. Autry gets a cut while his horse, Champion, has his hooves examined. Autry gained fame as a singing cowboy on the radio, in movies, and on television. He was also an important figure in country music. Although he was born in Texas, Autry lived in Oklahoma in the 1920s. The town of Gene Autry, Oklahoma, is named in his honor. (Courtesy of Jones Theatres.)

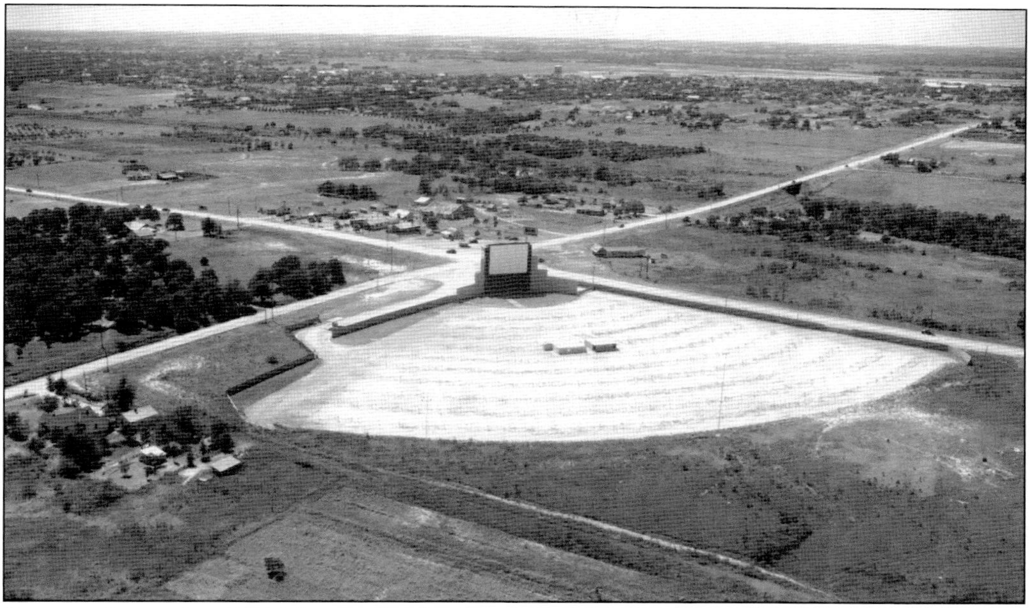

STARLITE DRIVE-IN, 1947. The new Starlite Drive-In in Shawnee is shown in this 1947 photograph. In 1980, a twin indoor theater was built next to the drive-in, and the two shared a common lobby and concession area. In 1987, the drive-in was closed, and the twin theater was expanded to an eight-screen complex, now known as the Cinema Centre 8, which is still operating at this site today. (Courtesy of Jones Theatres.)

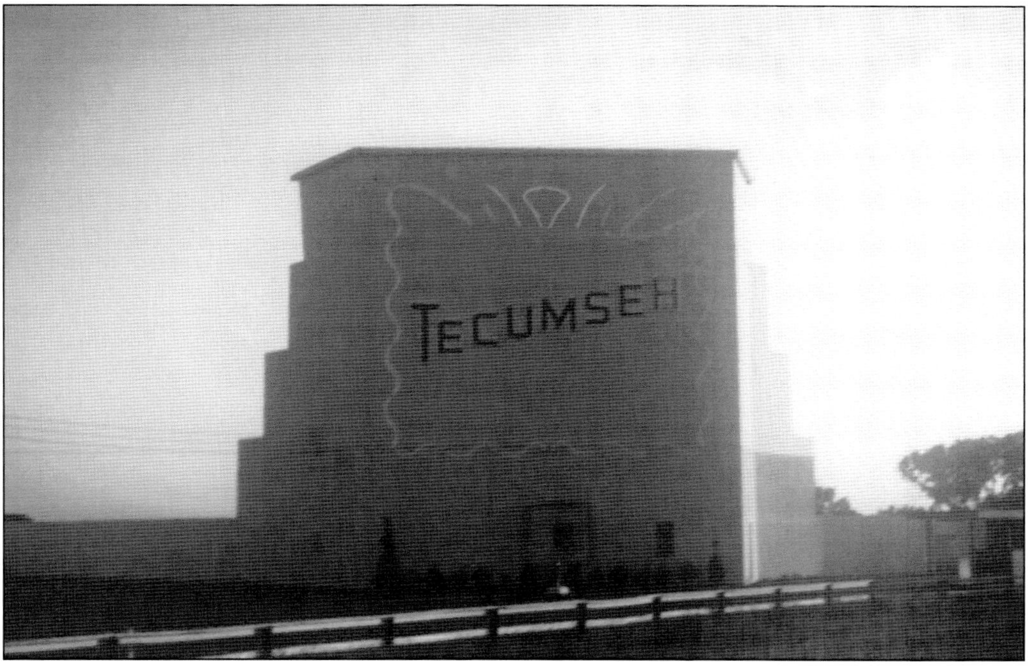

TECUMSEH DRIVE-IN. The Tecumseh Drive-In, located just south of the North Canadian River, was a typically simple design accented by a large butterfly lit in neon on the reverse of the screen structure. It was destroyed by a tornado in the early 1960s. (Courtesy of Jones Theatres.)

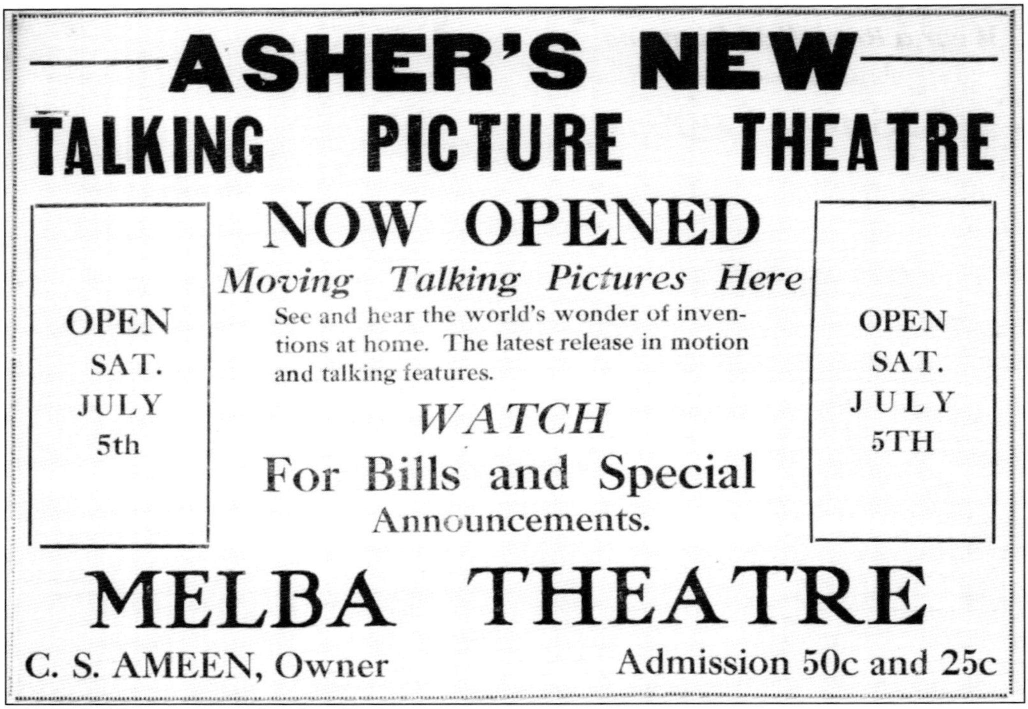

ASHER'S TALKING PICTURE THEATER. This July 4, 1929, advertisement in the *Tecumseh Oil Record* promotes Asher's new "talking picture" theater, which opened the next day. An accompanying article suggests the theater would draw in business from neighboring towns, specifically Wanette. (Courtesy of the Gateway to Oklahoma History.)

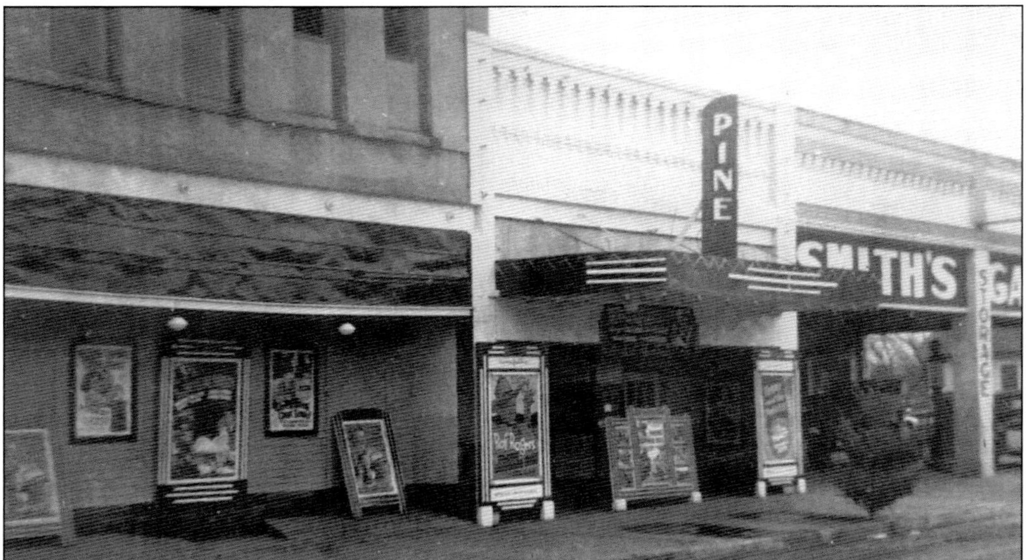

TECUMSEH'S PINE THEATER. Roy Rogers stars in *Wild Buffalo Bill* at the Pine Theater in Tecumseh about 1940. The building that housed the theater still stands on Broadway Street. (Author's collection.)

Five

Churches and Community

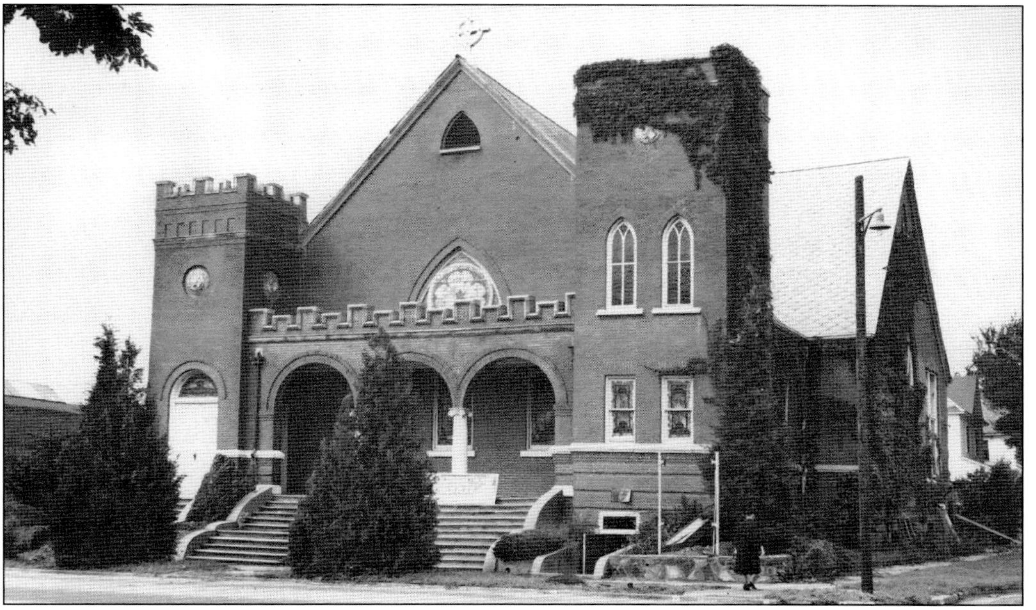

Importance of Community. Churches, such as the Christian church pictured here, have always played a crucial role in the community. Many people turn to church in times of tragedy and adversity. As communities were formed over the county, church buildings were some of the first to be constructed along with public buildings. Churches and community buildings are, therefore, some of the most historic buildings in the county. (Courtesy of Pottawatomie County Historical Society.)

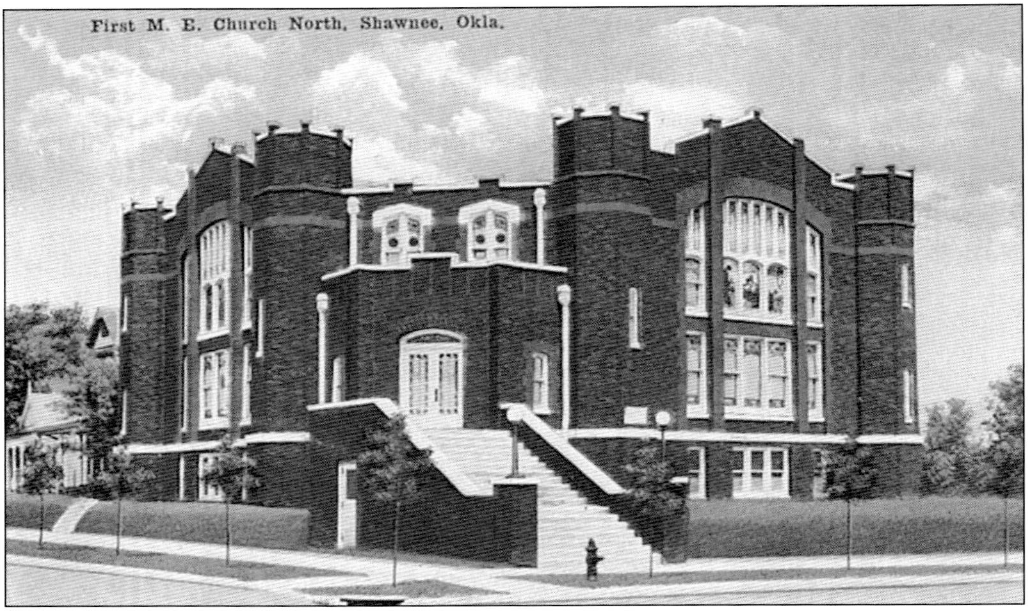

METHODIST BEAUTIES. Both of these Methodist churches in Shawnee were stunning buildings. The First Methodist North building (above) still stands at Philadelphia Avenue and Ninth Street. The Methodist South building (below, from a c. 1919 postcard) was located at Tenth and Beard Streets. While St. Paul's United Methodist still holds services on the site, the church has been replaced with a modern building. (Both, author's collection.)

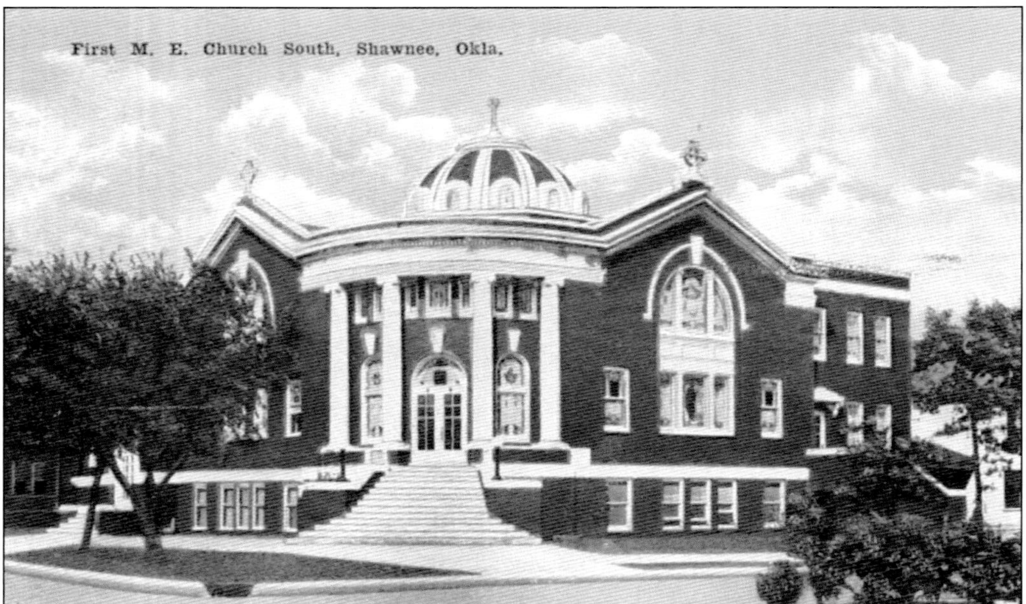

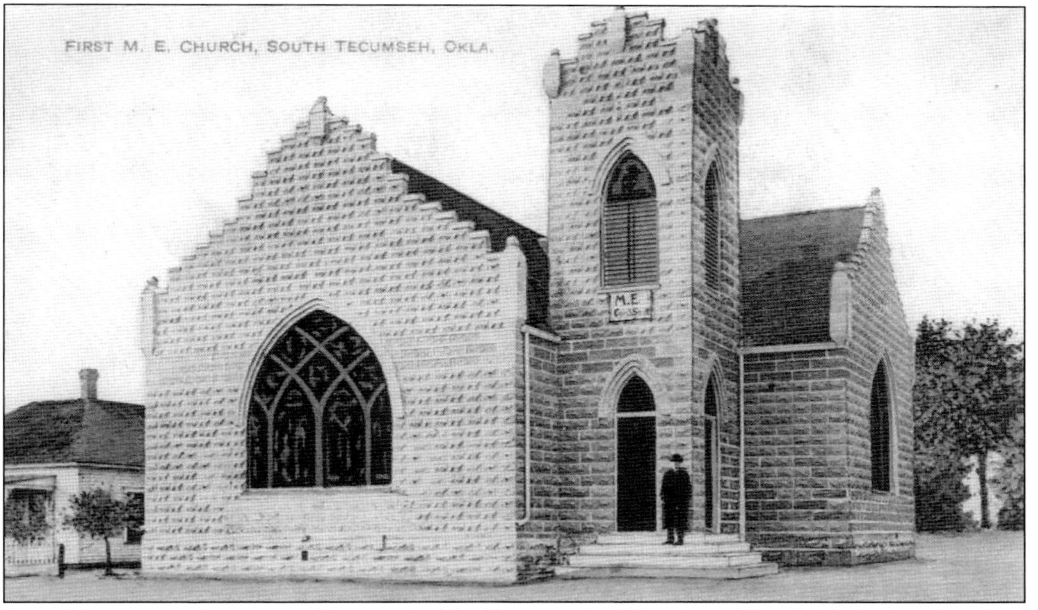

First Methodist, Tecumseh. Tecumseh, like Shawnee, had North and South Methodist churches. In this postcard, a man stands on the steps of the First Methodist Church South. At some point, the two churches merged. The building pictured no longer stands, but Tecumseh continues to have a United Methodist church on Broadway Street. (Author's collection.)

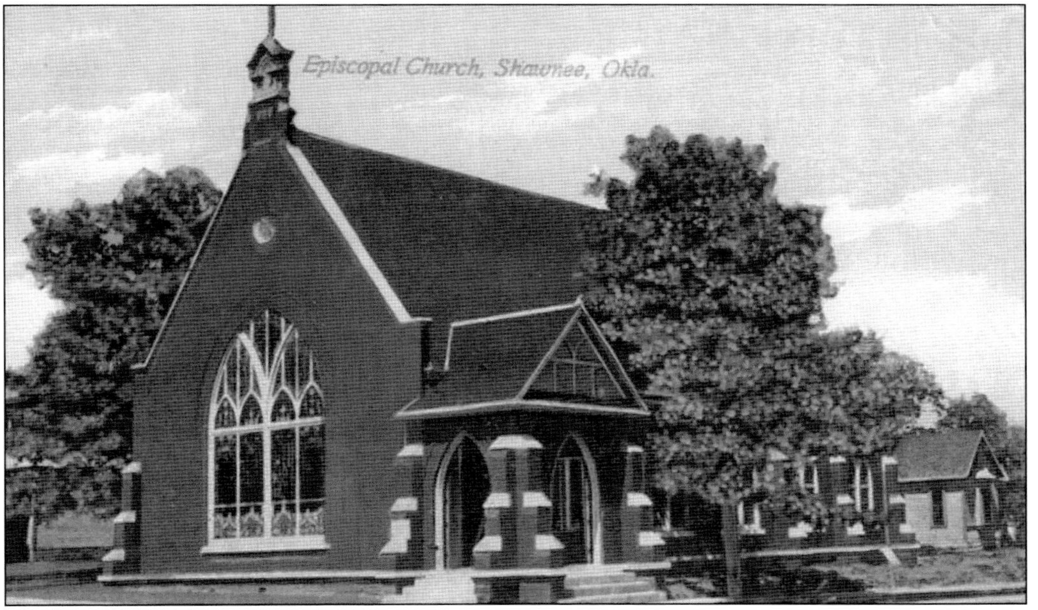

Episcopal Church, Shawnee. The Emmanuel Episcopal Church was established in 1897 at the corner of Broadway Avenue and Tenth Street. The building pictured was the church's second home and was completed by 1909 at the corner of Broadway Avenue and Highland Street. The original building was moved and integrated into the new building's parish hall. A main feature of the church building is the beautiful 12-by-26-foot window on the west side of the structure. (Courtesy of Pottawatomie County Historical Society.)

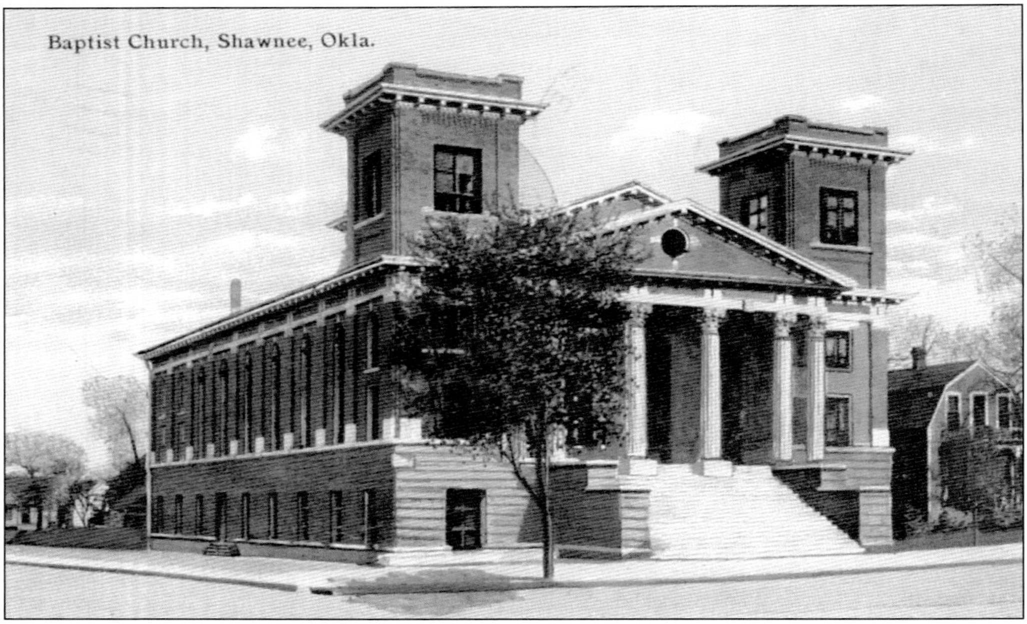

FIRST BAPTIST CHURCH, SHAWNEE. Shawnee's First Baptist Church, above, has seen a lot of changes over the years, but still stands prominently at Tenth and Union Streets. This church, which was dedicated on Sunday, June 27, 1909, was originally built with a dome and two bell towers. The dome and towers were removed during a remodel of the building. Below is the church building as it appears today. (Both, author's collection.)

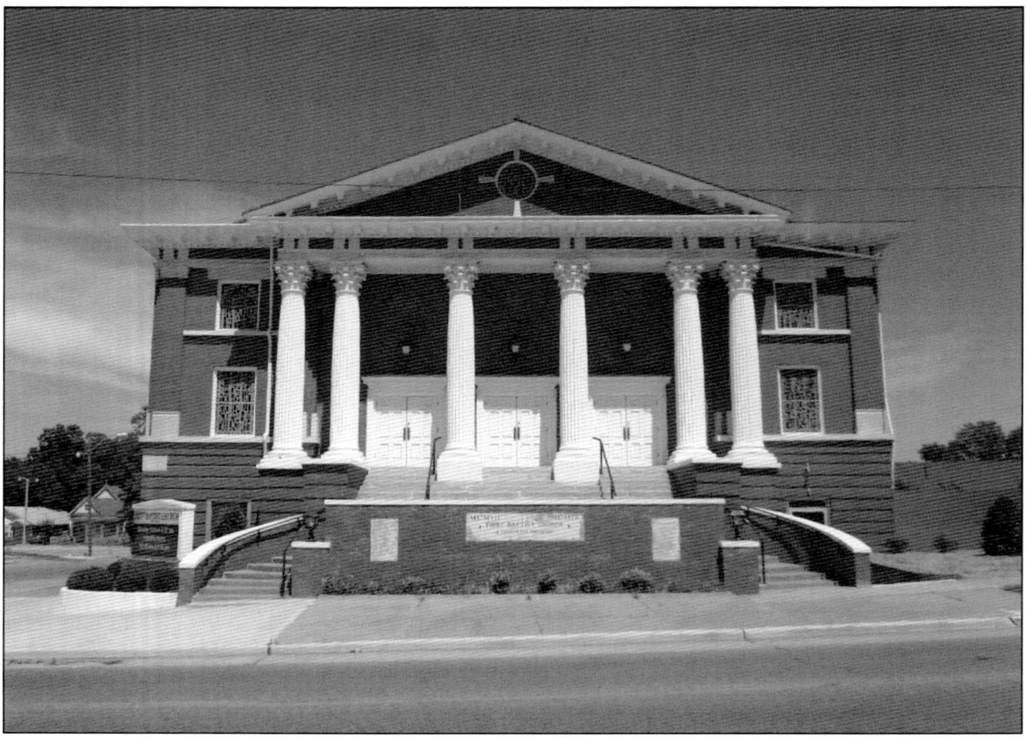

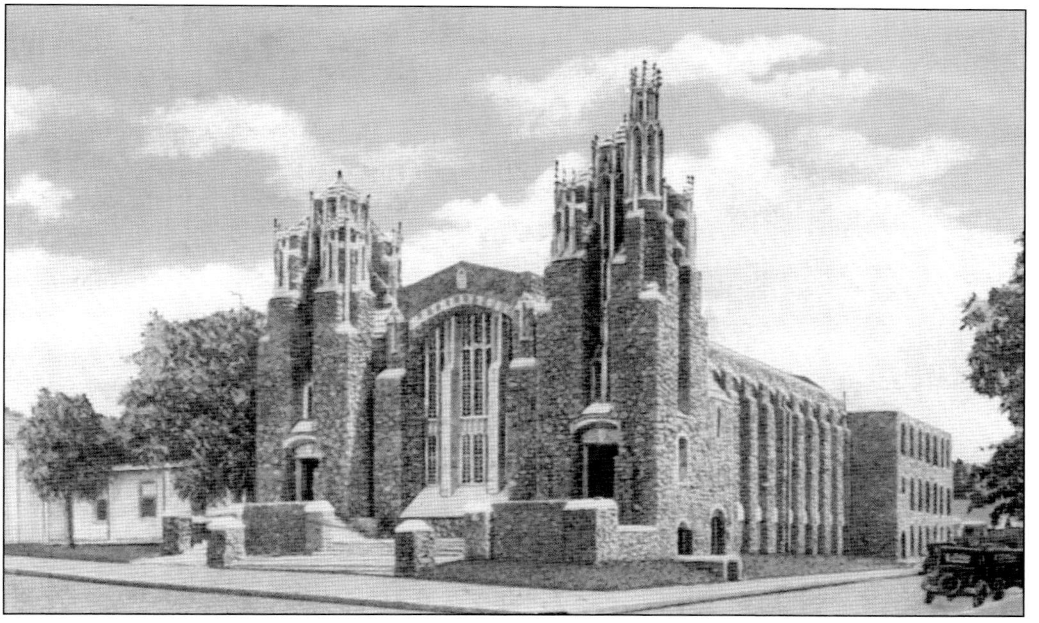

IMMANUEL BAPTIST CHURCH. The Immanuel Baptist Church in Shawnee was built in 1929 at a cost of $100,000. The stonework and elaborate detail of the church caused many who grew up near it to remember it as a castle. The building, at the corner of East Main Street and South Eden Avenue, serves as a nondenominational Christian outreach center today. (Author's collection.)

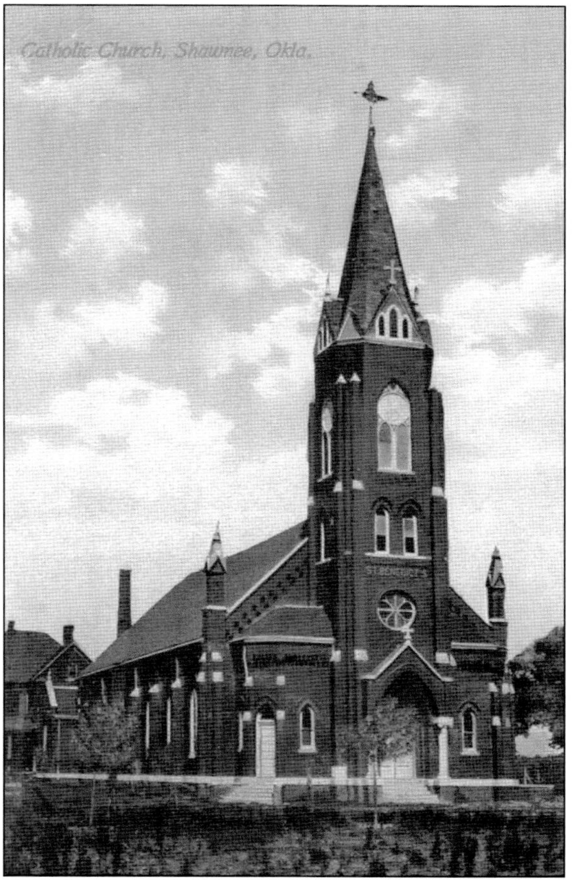

ST. BENEDICT'S CATHOLIC CHURCH. St. Benedict's Catholic Church, at Benedict and Kickapoo Streets, has been a landmark in Shawnee since it was completed in 1907. Many generations were educated at the elementary and high school there. The church building was extensively remodeled in 1962, and in 2006, the stained-glass windows were refurbished. (Courtesy of Pottawatomie County Historical Society.)

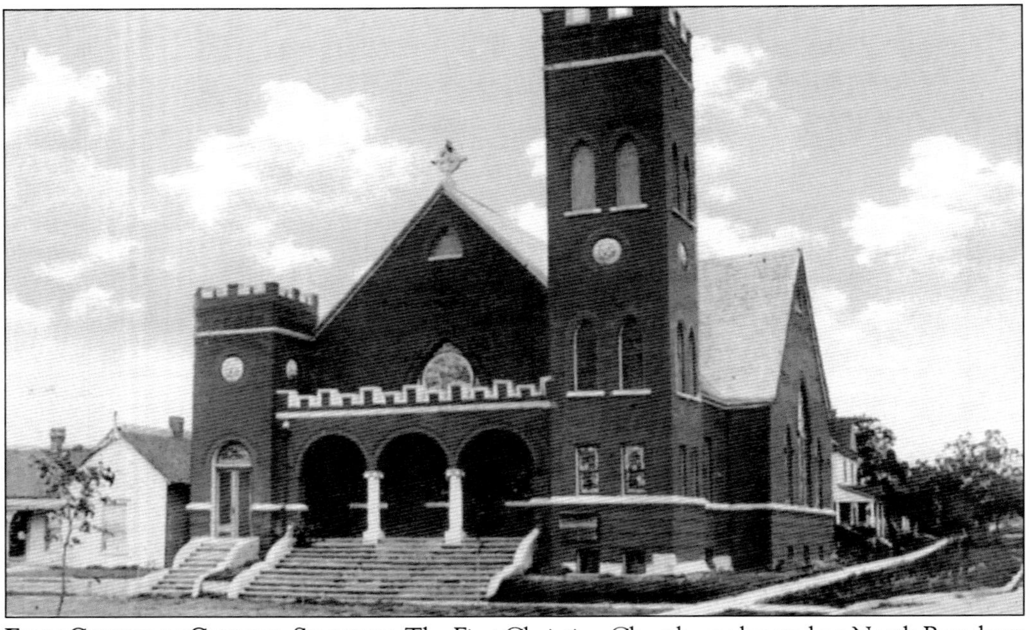

FIRST CHRISTIAN CHURCH, SHAWNEE. The First Christian Church was located on North Broadway Avenue and Eleventh Street in Shawnee across from the Carnegie Library. The cornerstone was laid in 1907, and the church building was in use until 1948, when the building was determined to be unsafe due to trusses found to be bowing. The property was sold, and the building was torn down. The church constructed a new building at North Broadway Avenue and Elizabeth Street in 1950 where it continues to meet today. (Courtesy of Pottawatomie County Historical Society.)

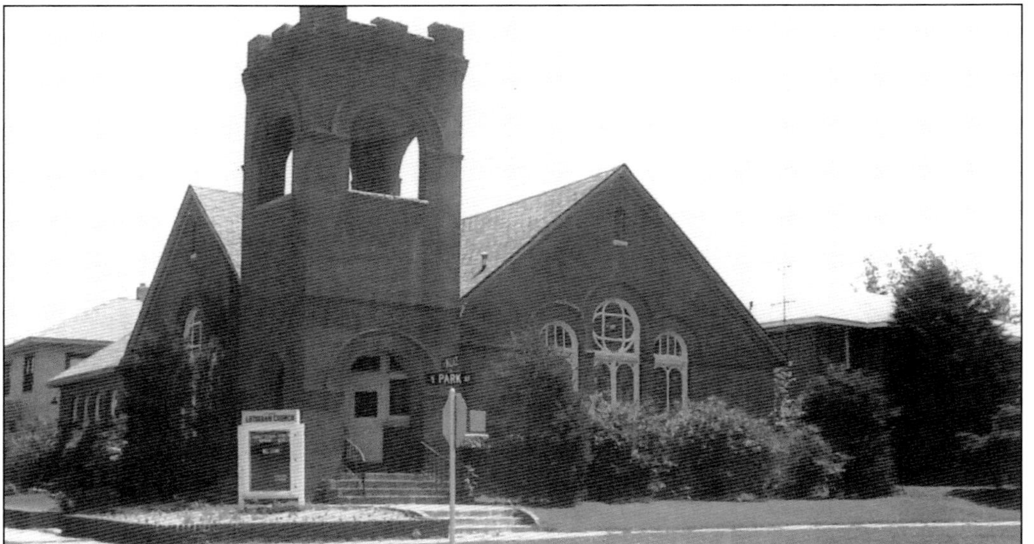

ST. JOHN'S LUTHERAN CHURCH. St. John's Lutheran Church was built at the corner of Park Avenue and Wallace Street in Shawnee in 1906. The building was originally a Dutch Reform worship center. The first Lutheran services were held on Easter Sunday, 1916. The church moved to a new location in 2009, and the building now serves as a private residence. (Courtesy of Pottawatomie County Historical Society.)

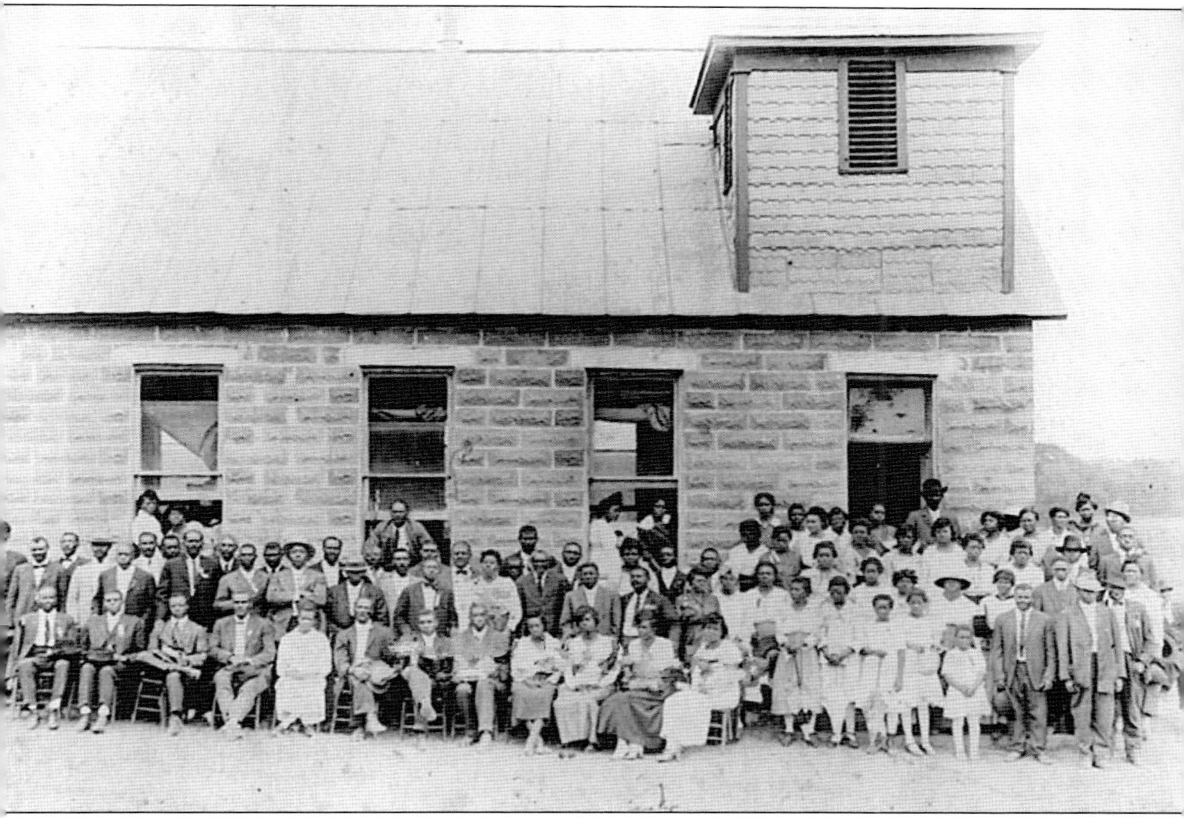

Brooksville. There were once 50 all-black communities in Oklahoma. Brooksville is one of only 13 that still exist. This photograph shows a group outside St. John's Baptist Church. The church was built about 1907 and still stands today. (Author's collection.)

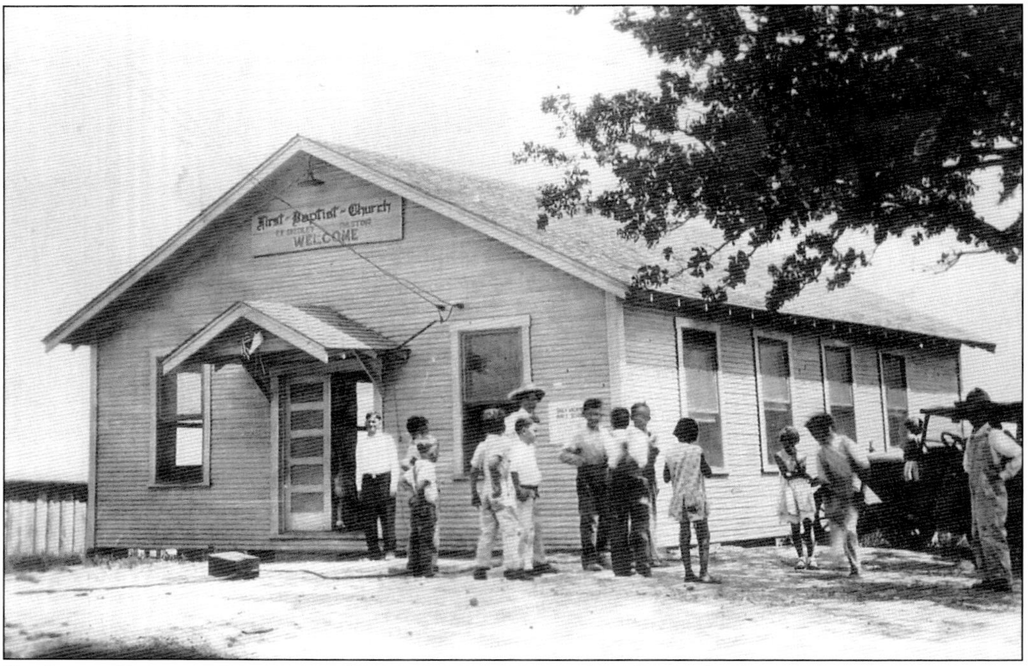

St. Louis Baptist Church. The St. Louis Baptist Church was built in 1929. Above, a group of children and a few adults stand outside the building. The pastor, E.E. Smedley, stands near the doorway. Below, the first group of vacation Bible school students poses for a photograph in 1930. The church continues to meet in this building. (Both, courtesy of Pottawatomie County Historical Society.)

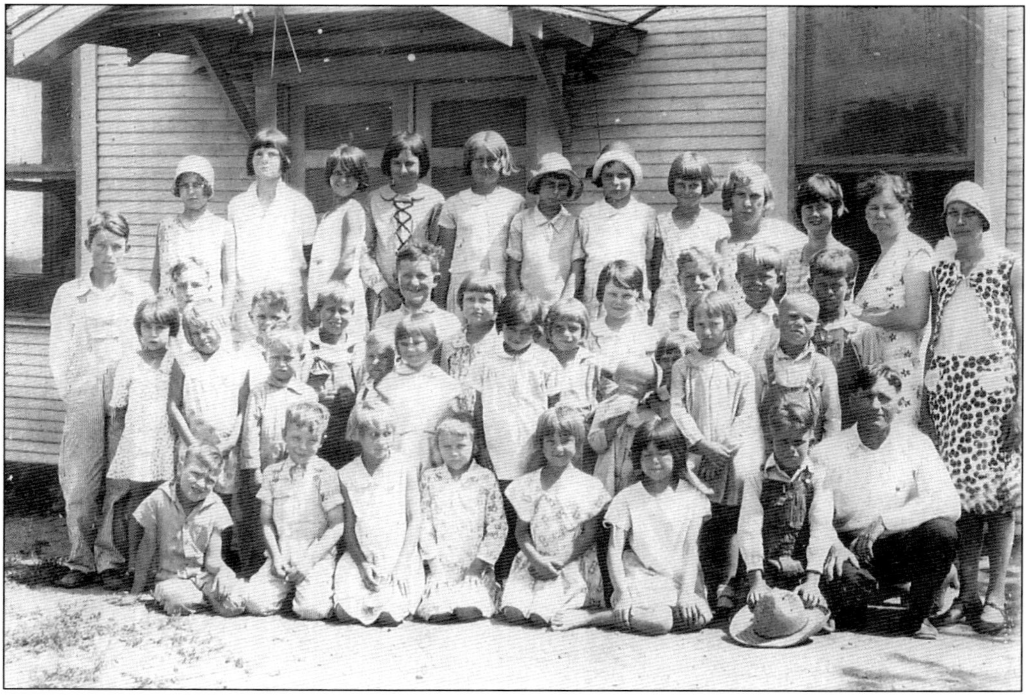

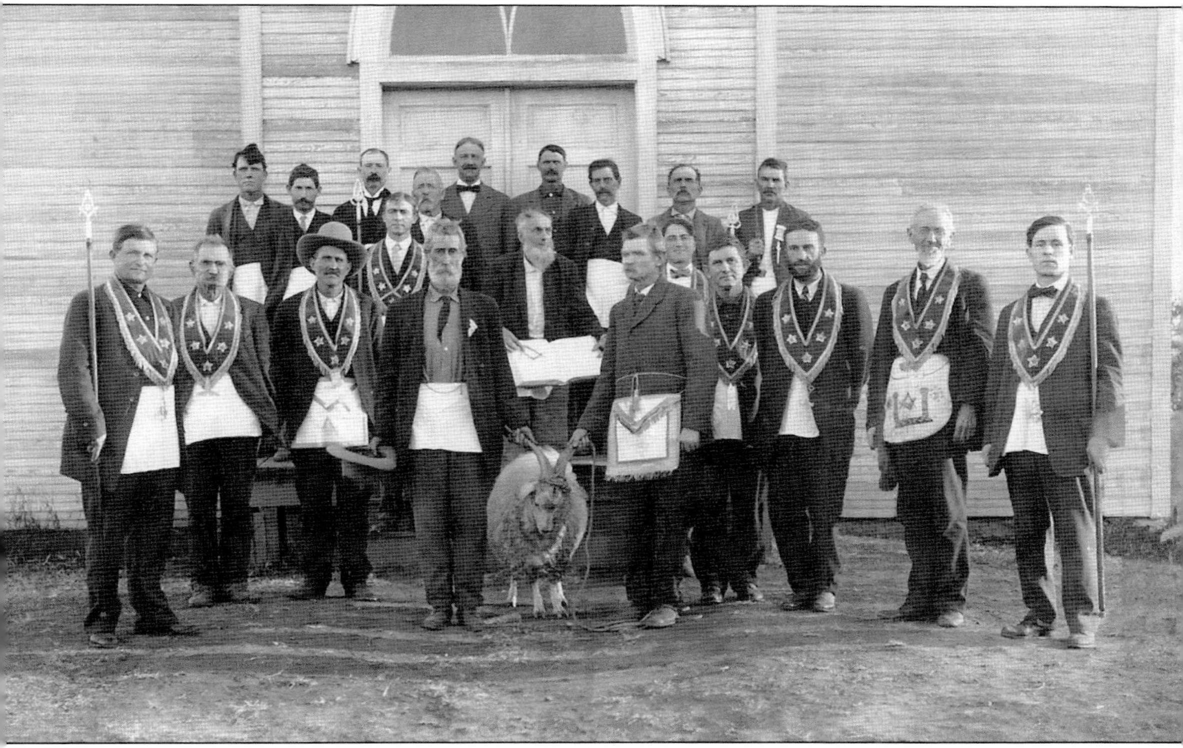

Asher Masons. This photograph features the Asher Masons and was taken on the steps of the original First Baptist Church in 1918. Independent Masonic lodges were established around the country, and Freemasons like these often included leaders of the community. From left to right are (first row) Noah Butts, Johnnie Hoover, Mr. Pierce (in hat), Grandpa Hill, G.B. Bailey, John Kirk, John Brandenburg, Mr. Rawlings, and David White; (second row) Jay Herndon, Mr. Sanders (with book), and Terrill Lassiter. In the third row, listed in no particular order, are John McCully, Dr. Martin, C.B. Kidd, John Bennett, and Millard Hoover. (Author's collection.)

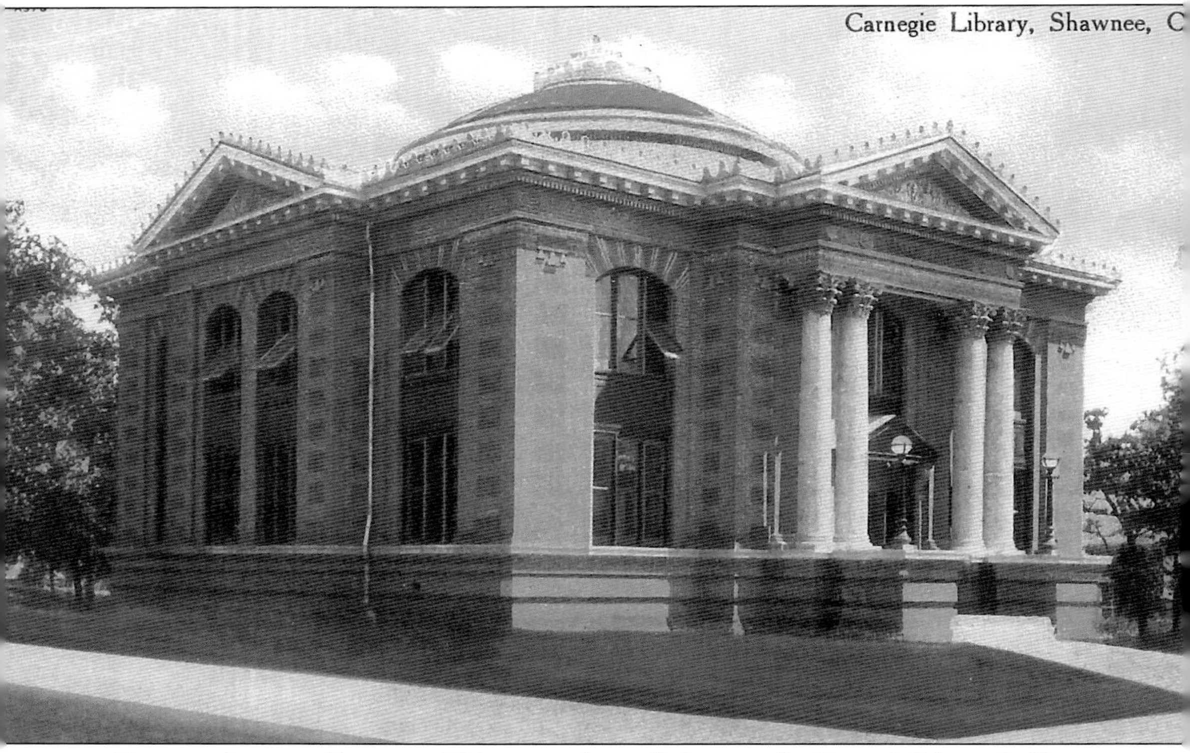

Carnegie Library, Shawnee. This postcard proudly features the Carnegie Library in Shawnee. Granted in 1904, the library was built in 1905 on Broadway Avenue. It was badly damaged in a fire in 1929 and lost its dome and ornate trim. The building continued to serve as a library until 1989, when the library moved and the building was remodeled for the district attorney's office. Its future neighbor, the Pottawatomie County Courthouse, would not be built until three decades later. (Courtesy of Pottawatomie County Historical Society.)

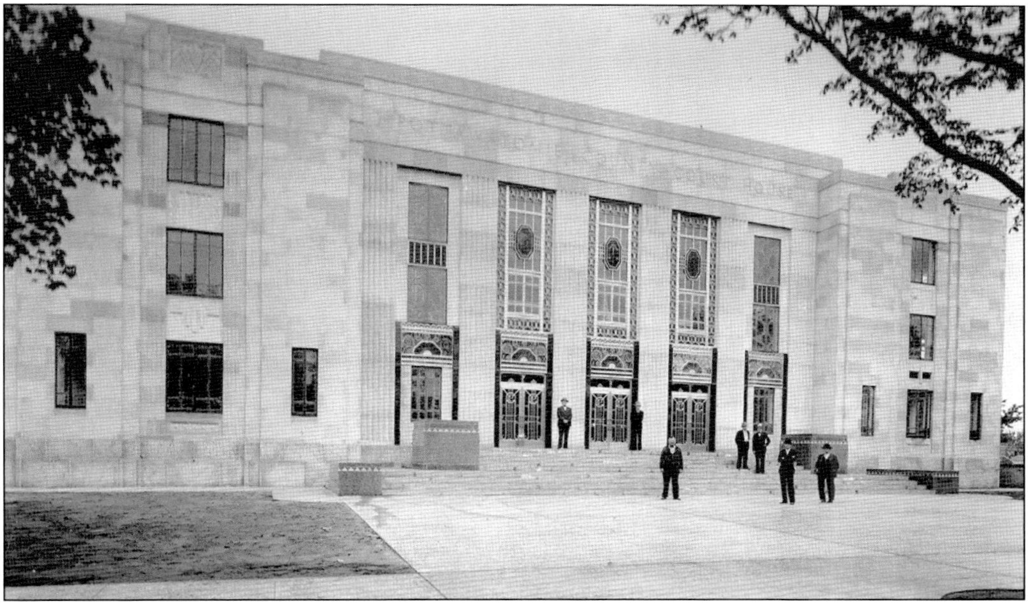

Pottawatomie County Courthouse. The Pottawatomie County Courthouse (above), at North Broadway and Tenth Street in Shawnee, was built in 1934. It features art deco styling, one of the few courthouses in the state to do so. The elaborately carved granite panels above each doorway and metal decorating the doors and windows further set it apart. The photograph below shows the building under construction. The courthouse is listed in the National Register of Historic Places. (Courtesy of Pottawatomie County Historical Society.)

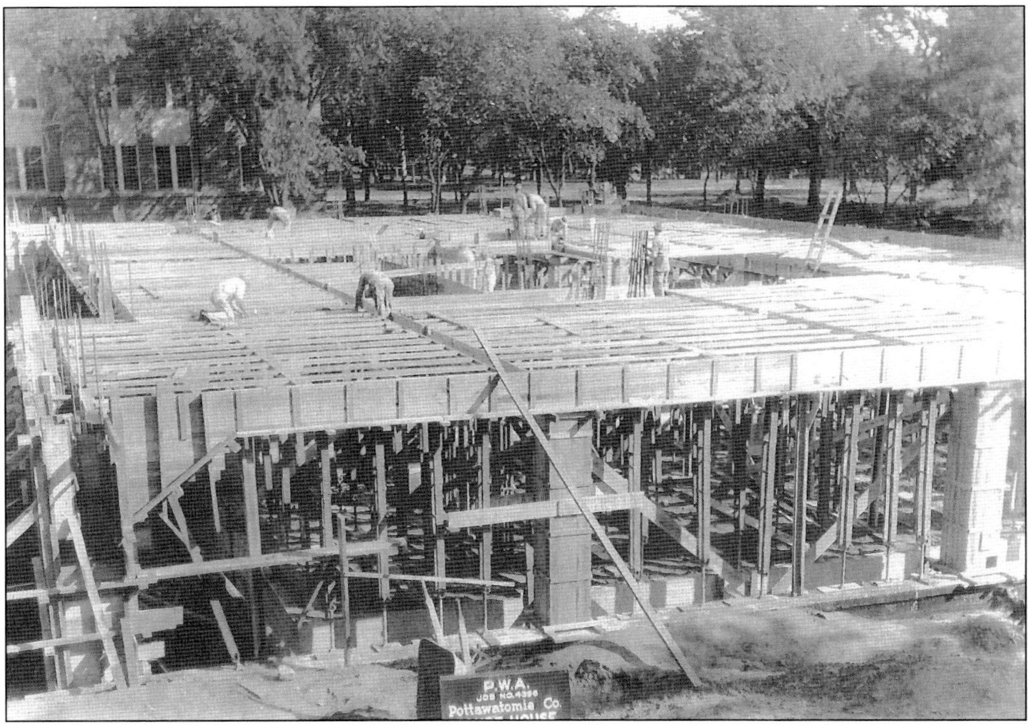

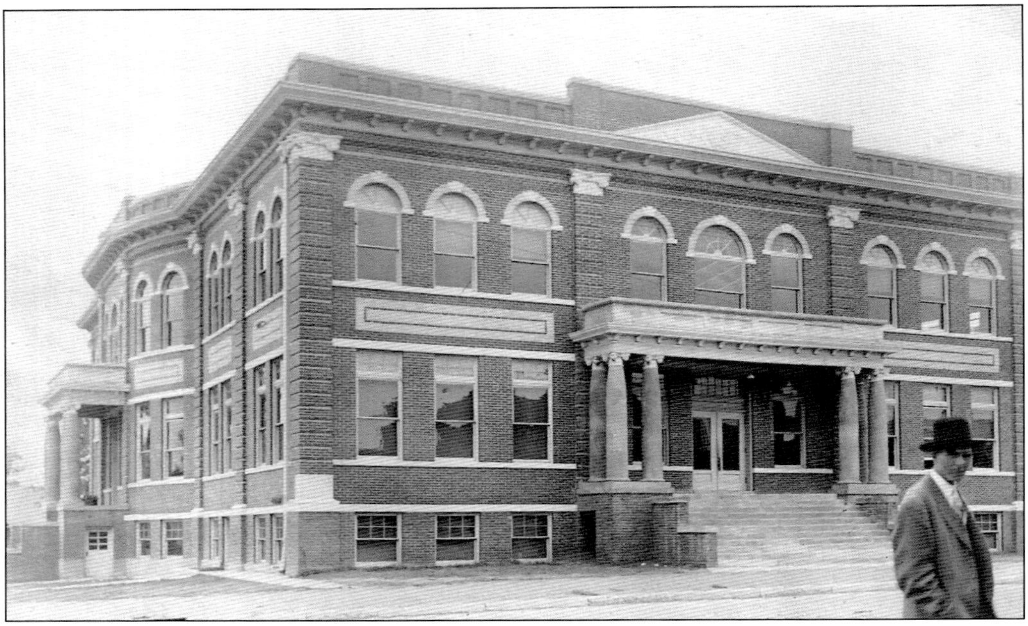

Lost Convention Hall. The Shawnee Convention Hall was a large building at the corner of Ninth and Union Streets. The hall (above) was built sometime in the early 1900s. Like many great Shawnee buildings, the hall burned down in the late 1920s. Below, several groups pose for a photograph outside the Shawnee Convention Hall. (Both, courtesy of Pottawatomie County Historical Society.)

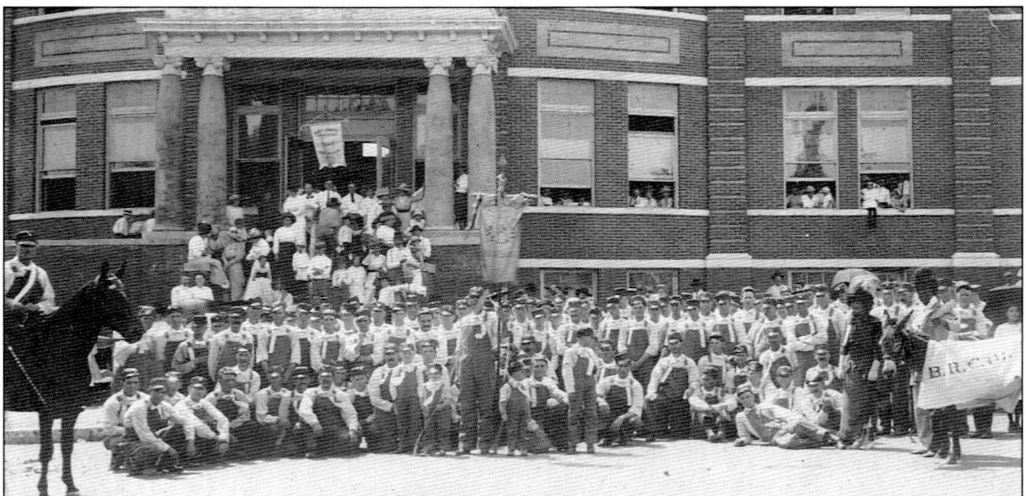

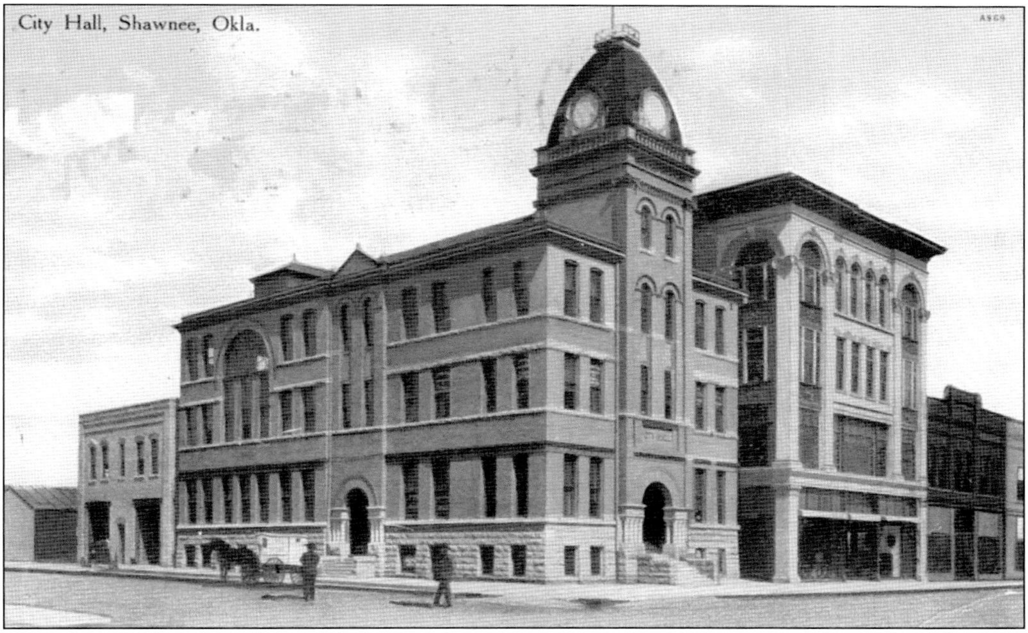

City Hall Stands Tall. This impressive structure is the Shawnee City Hall and Central Fire Station as it looked shortly after completion in the mid-1900s. It was located at Ninth Street and Broadway Avenue. The building was badly damaged in a tornado in the 1970s and replaced with a much less formidable building. (Author's collection.)

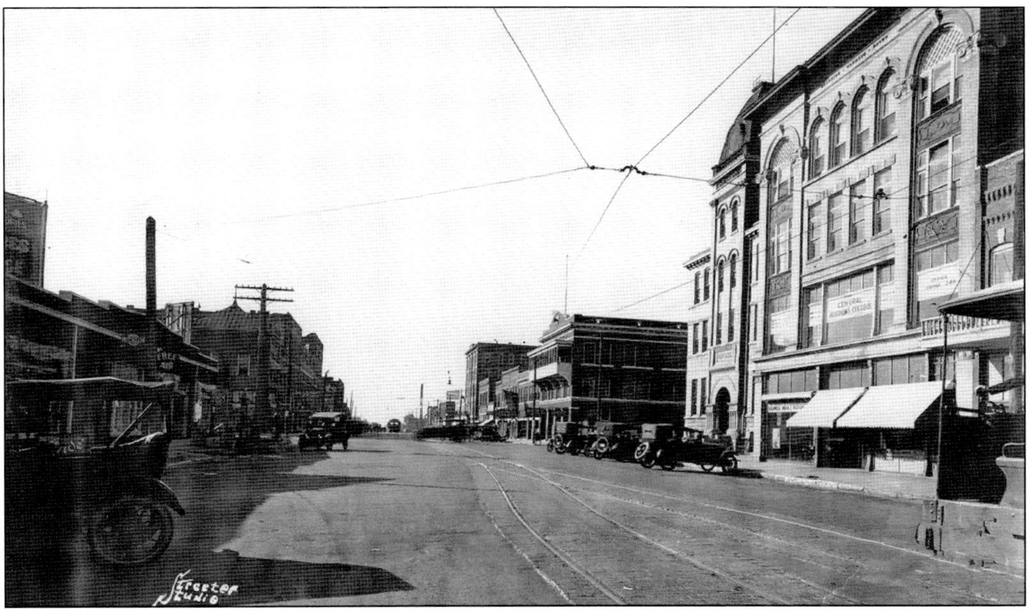

Business College. This photograph, taken from the opposite end of Broadway Avenue, gives a better view of the building next to city hall. At this time, it was the Central Business College. Neither the city hall nor the business college building still stands, but the former Elks building, seen farther down Broadway Avenue, exists today as an office building. (Courtesy of Pottawatomie County Historical Society.)

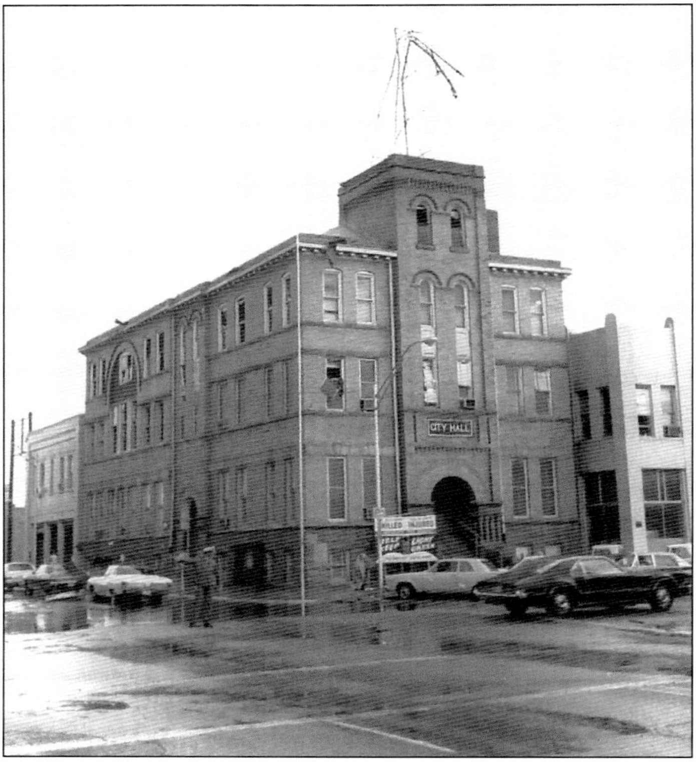

Tornado Damage. This photograph shows the Shawnee City Hall after the 1970s tornado that damaged it and multiple other buildings. It was later torn down and replaced with a new city hall on the same site. (Courtesy of Pottawatomie County Historical Society.)

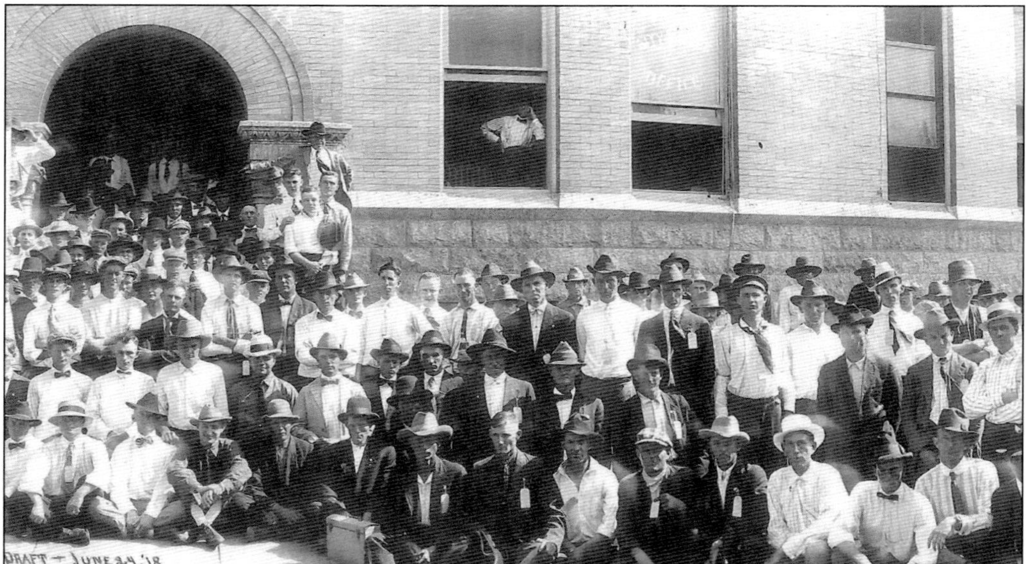

Reporting for Basic Training. A group of men poses for a photograph outside the Shawnee City Hall on June 29, 1918, before heading out for basic training. All men ages 20 to 40 were required to register. Numbers were then drawn to determine who would report. A group was sent off nearly every month from Pottawatomie County until the war ended. (Courtesy of Pottawatomie County Historical Society.)

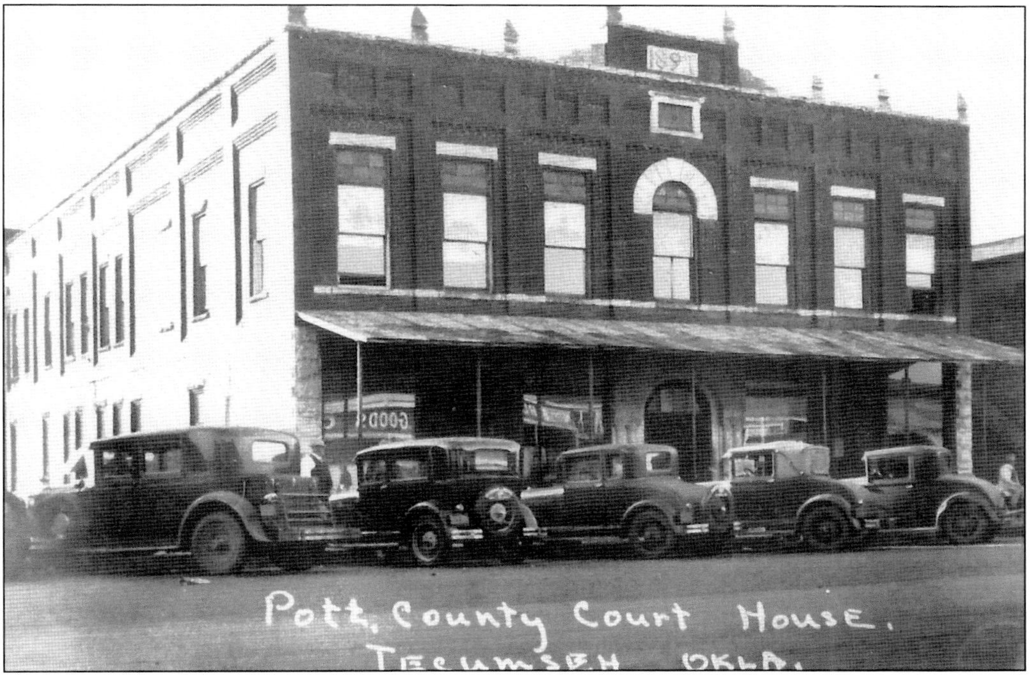

First Pottawatomie County Courthouse. Tecumseh, the original county seat of Pottawatomie County, was home to the first county courthouse. It was built in 1897 on Broadway Street. In 1930, Tecumseh lost the county seat, and a new courthouse was built in Shawnee on land offered in Woodland Park. The original courthouse no longer stands, and Tecumseh City Hall is now on this site. (Courtesy of Pottawatomie County Historical Society.)

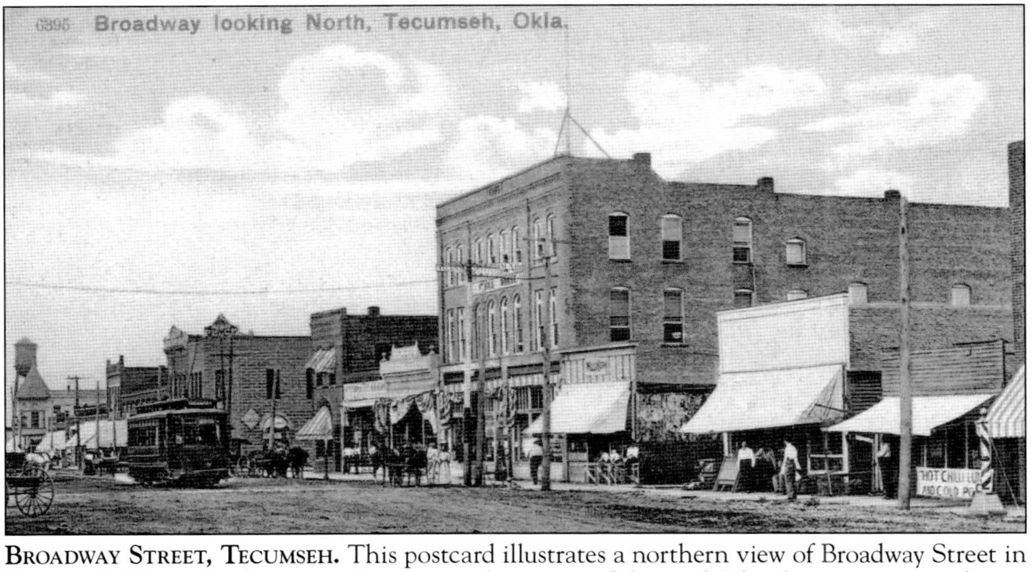

Broadway Street, Tecumseh. This postcard illustrates a northern view of Broadway Street in Tecumseh. The opera house can be seen in the center of the card. The three-story opera house was erected around 1905. Although not in great condition, it still stands. Some other buildings in this scene also still exist, including the corner building with the awnings, a beautiful 1920s building that has been restored. (Author's collection.)

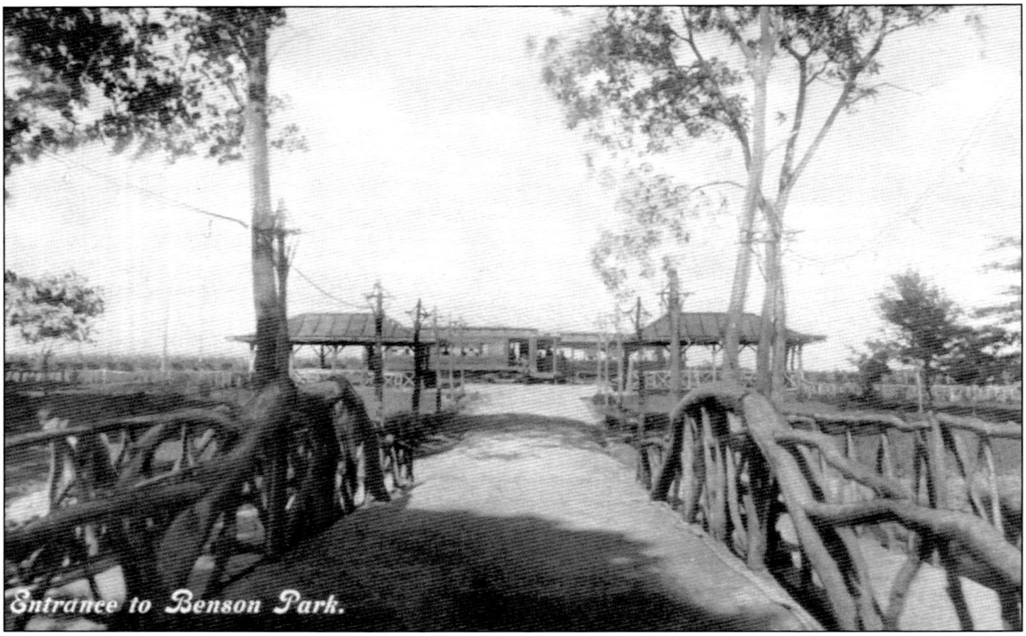

FUN IN BENSON PARK. Benson Park was located on over 20 acres between Shawnee and Tecumseh on what is now Benson Park Road. Construction of the park began in 1907. Two views of the park are shown in these postcards. The above photograph features the entrance with the rustic bridge. The photograph below shows the skating rink and another view of the bridge, crowded with many people. The park was a gathering place for entertainment and amusement and also featured an amphitheater, a swimming pool, and a roller coaster, the Circle Dip. The interurban trolley running between Shawnee and Tecumseh made Benson Park an easy getaway. Benson Park closed in 1932. (Both, author's collection.)

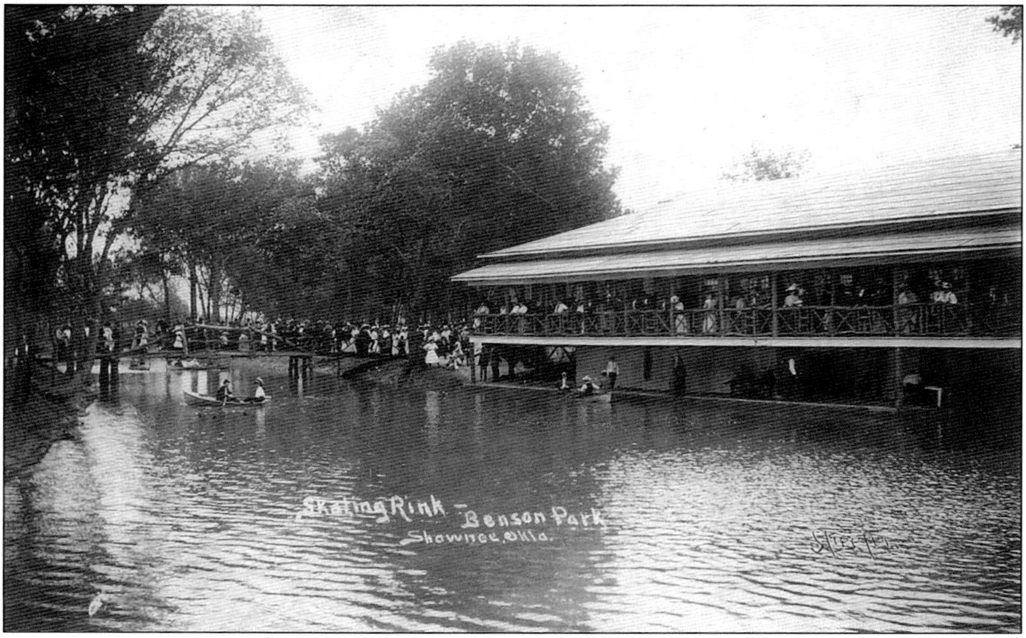

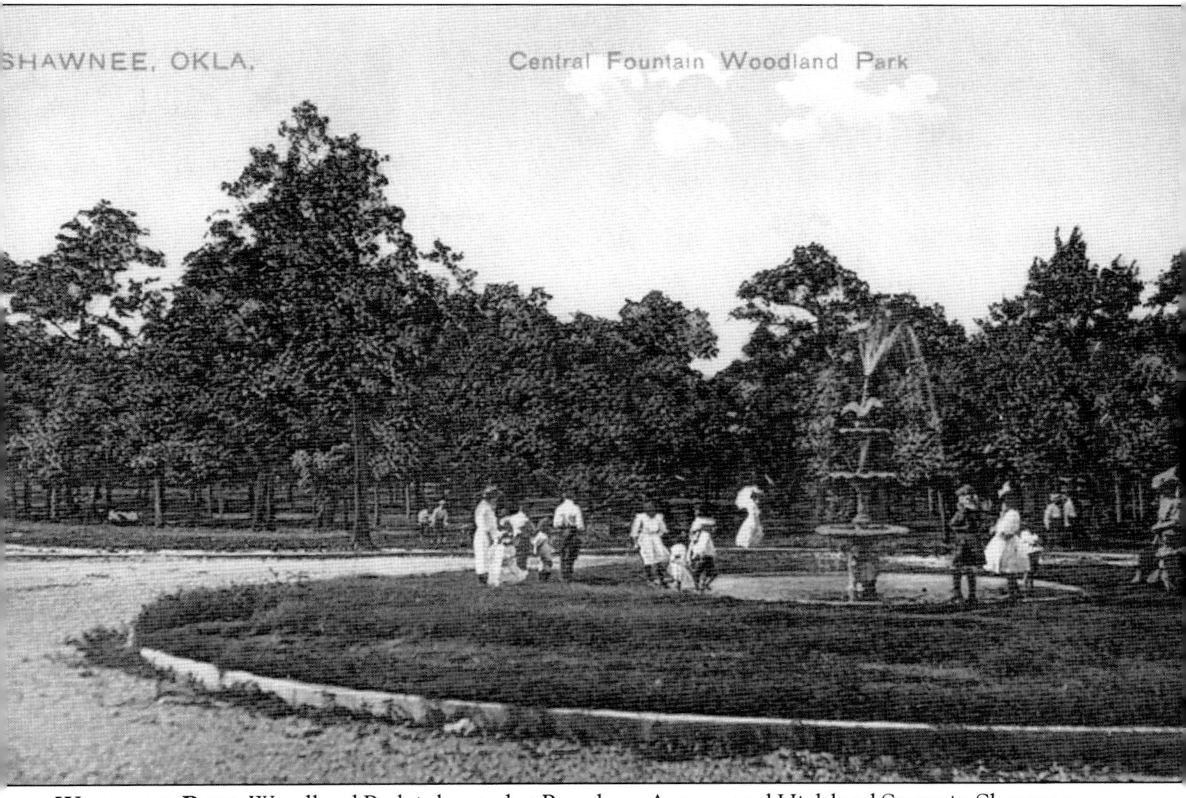

Woodland Park. Woodland Park is located at Broadway Avenue and Highland Street in Shawnee. It was built in 1905 and included a sunken garden and fountains. This postcard gives a glimpse of how the park used to look and features the Central Fountain. One section of this fountain is now at the Santa Fe Depot. Today, the park features many activities, the municipal pool, and an aquatic center. (Courtesy of Pottawatomie County Historical Society.)

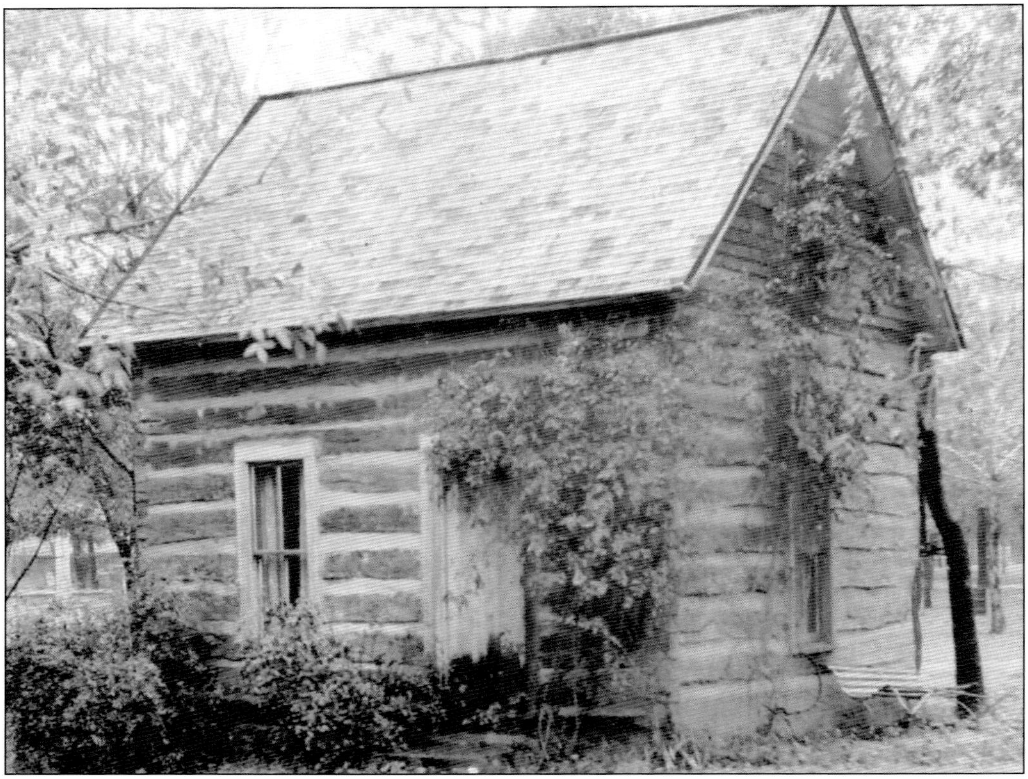

Shawnee's First Home. The Beard Cabin (above) is an approximately 15-by-20-foot log structure erected in about 1892 at Kickapoo and Highland Streets. Built by Henry Beard, it is widely considered the first home constructed in Shawnee. It was moved to the historic Woodland Park area in 1928. For a time, the cabin was used by the Camp Fire Girls as an office. In the early 1950s, it was restored. Much of the cabin with the exception of the roof is original. The cabin has a main room, a loft above, and a small room under the stairway. In 1990, the cabin was moved to the Santa Fe Depot property, where it stands today (below). The cabin is in the National Register of Historic Places. (Both, courtesy of Pottawatomie County Historical Society.)

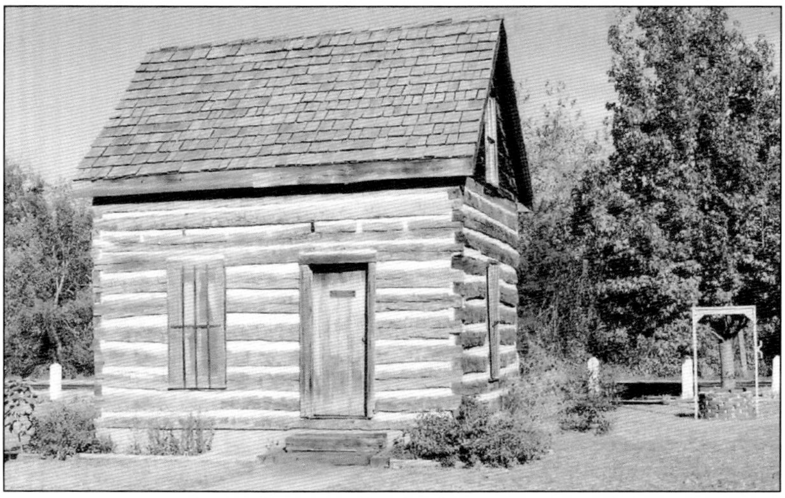

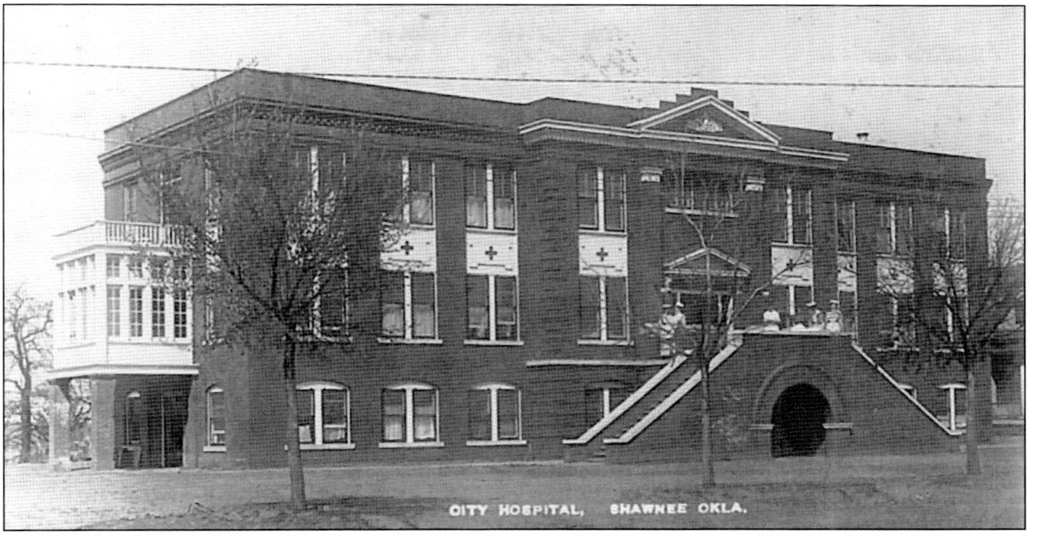

SHAWNEE CITY HOSPITAL. Generations of Pottawatomie County residents were born at Shawnee City Hospital in the 1940s, 1950s, and 1960s. The hospital was located at Center Avenue and Walnut Street in Shawnee. It closed in the 1960s, when Mission Hill Hospital was built. The building was demolished at some point afterward. (Courtesy of Pottawatomie County Historical Society.)

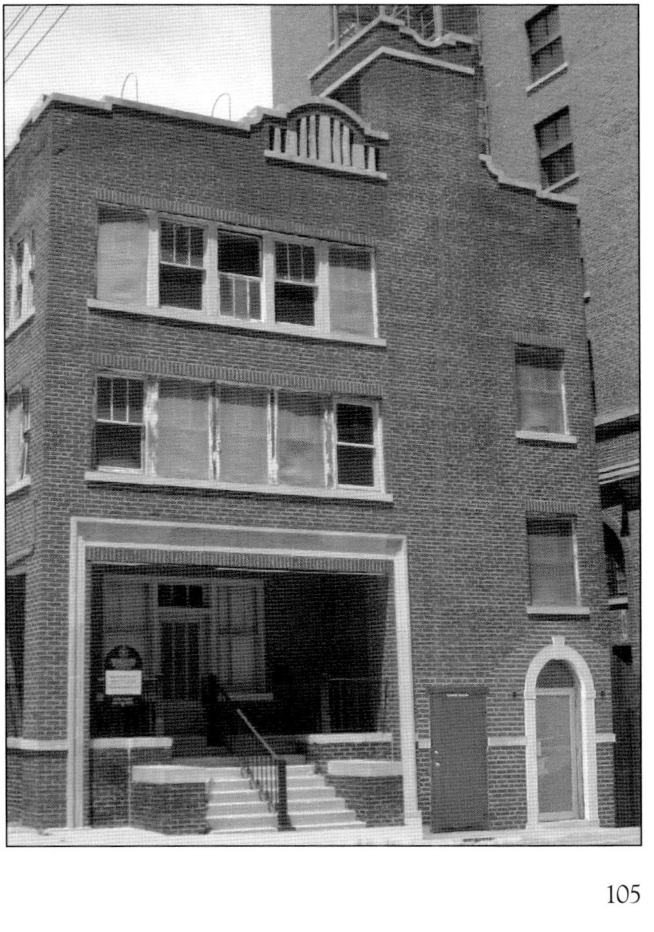

A.C.H. HOSPITAL. Many county citizens also were born at A.C.H., but probably none more famous than actor Brad Pitt, who was delivered here on December 18, 1963. The hospital, which stands next door to the Aldridge Hotel, was built during Shawnee's oil boom by three physicians—Anderson, Carson, and Hughes—for whom the hospital is named. It served as the core hospital in Shawnee from 1929 to 1967. (Author's collection.)

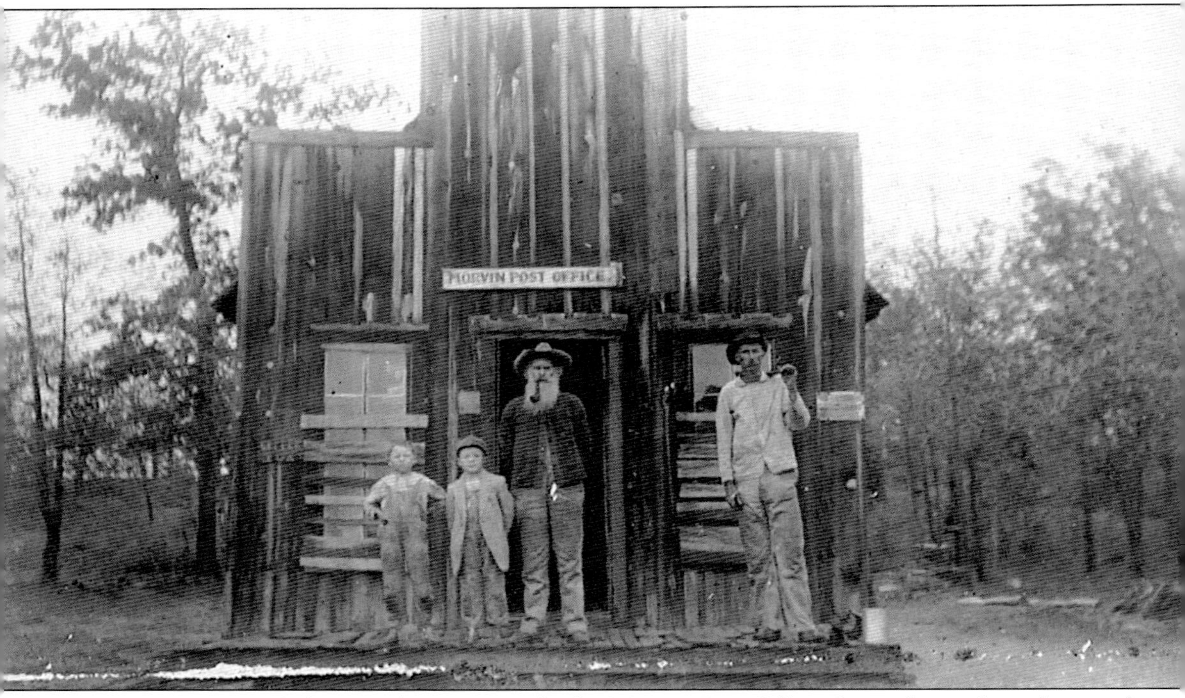

Ghost Town. A few people pose outside the Morvin Post Office. It was located northwest of Macomb and existed from 1898 to 1905. The town had a general store, a blacksmith shop, and a cotton gin. Towns like Morvin often sprang up to meet the needs of oilfield workers. When the oil dried up, the town often did too, thereby creating one of many ghost towns in the county. (Courtesy of Pottawatomie County Historical Society.)

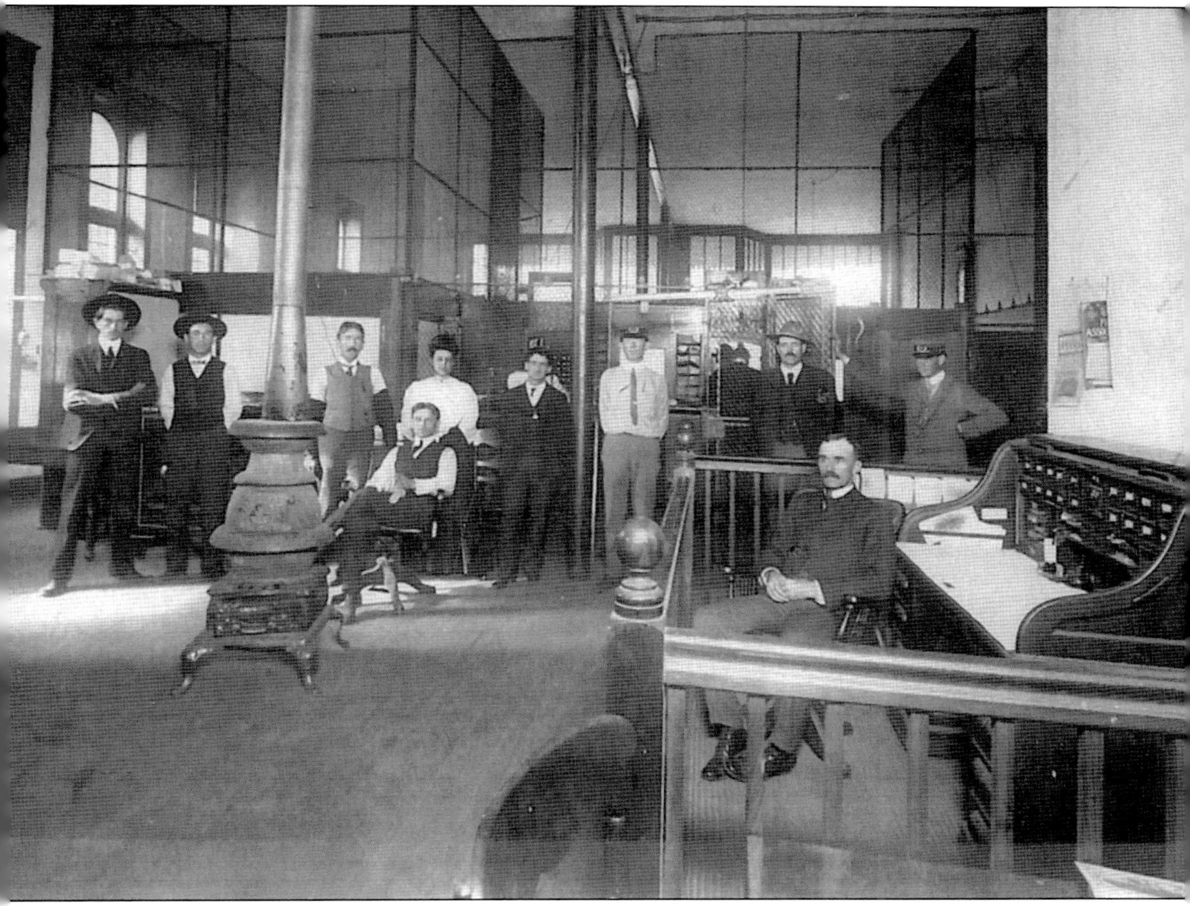

SHAWNEE POST OFFICE, 1900s. Above, several Shawnee Post Office employees pose for a picture on November 14, 1905. From left to right are Boyd Cade, Hubert Allnutt, Frank Hyde, Will Becker (seated), Pearl Darnell, Henry Moyle, Vic Shane, Bob Wallace, and Sam Malahy. A.E. Kennedy, the assistant postmaster, is behind the desk. The post office at this time was located at 113 North Broadway Avenue. (Courtesy of Pottawatomie County Historical Society.)

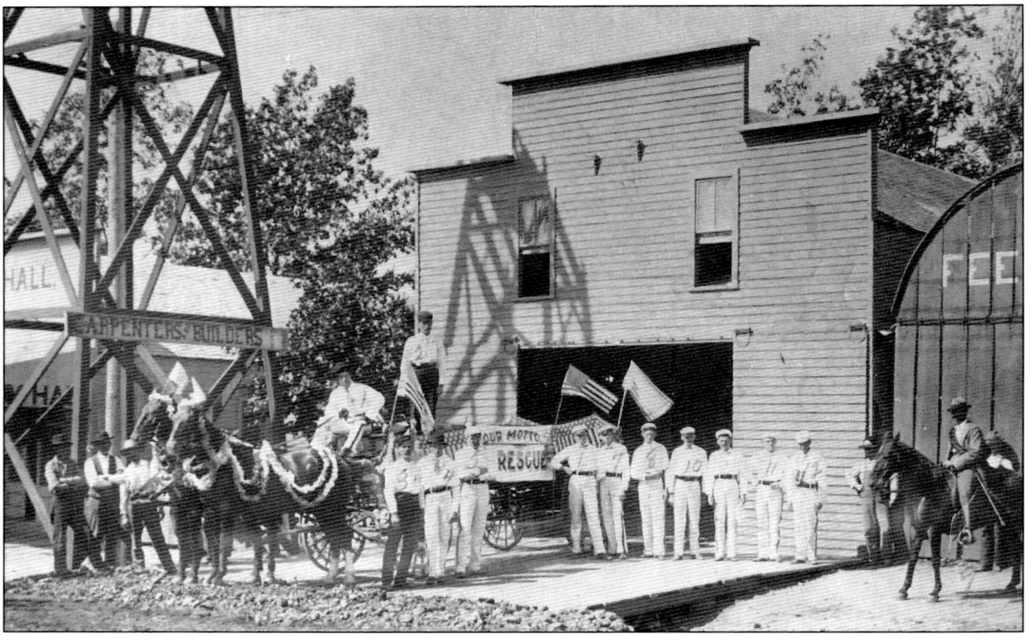

Fire Station, c. 1900. A wagon and horses are decorated outside an early Shawnee fire station. This 1900s station was located at 100 South Bell Street. To the left is the city hall of the time, before it moved to Ninth Street and Broadway Avenue a few years later. (Courtesy of Pottawatomie County Historical Society.)

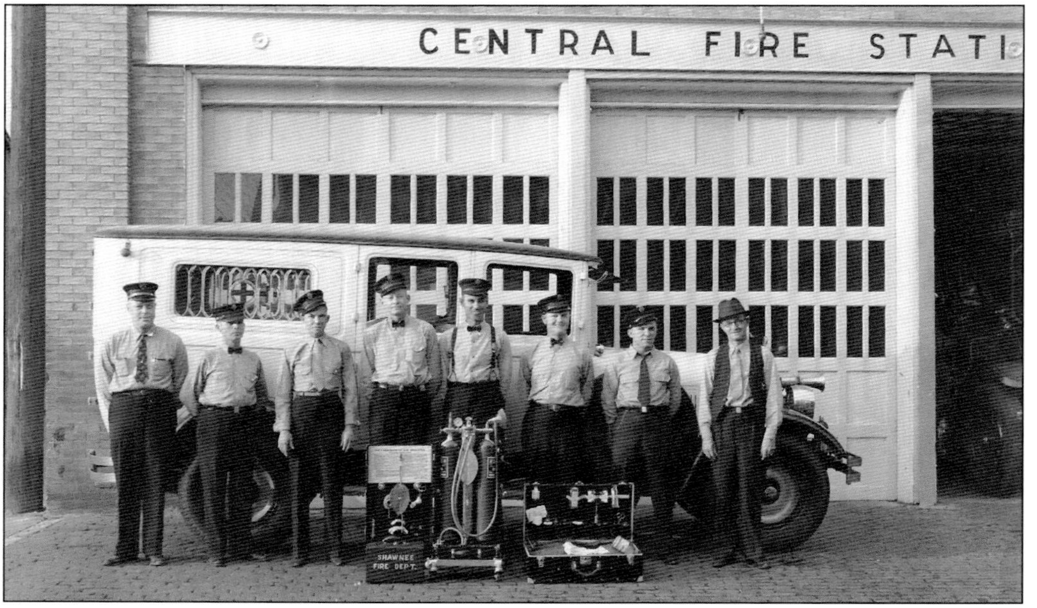

Shawnee Rescue No. 1. A group of men shows off a fire truck along with some firefighting apparatus of the late 1930s. They are standing outside the Shawnee Central Fire Station, which was located at Ninth Street and Broadway Avenue. It was destroyed by a tornado in 1970. The brass pole from the fire station hangs in Station No. 1. (Courtesy of Pottawatomie County Historical Society.)

Six

Schools and Activities

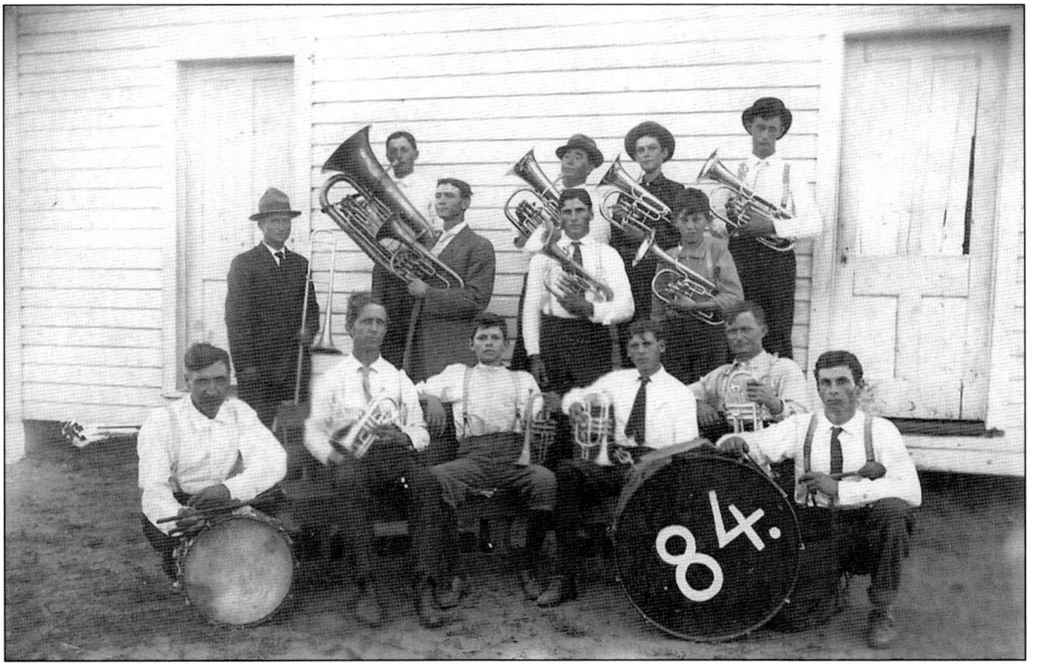

Gravel Hill Band, 1910. In the early days of Pottawatomie County, many small schools—some only miles from each other—dotted the county, mainly due to the fact that many students had to walk to school. Gravel Hill, northeast of Asher, was one of those schools. This photograph is of the Gravel Hill band members, many proudly displaying their instruments. Eventually, smaller rural schools like Gravel Hill were lost as transporting students became easier and schools consolidated. (Author's collection.)

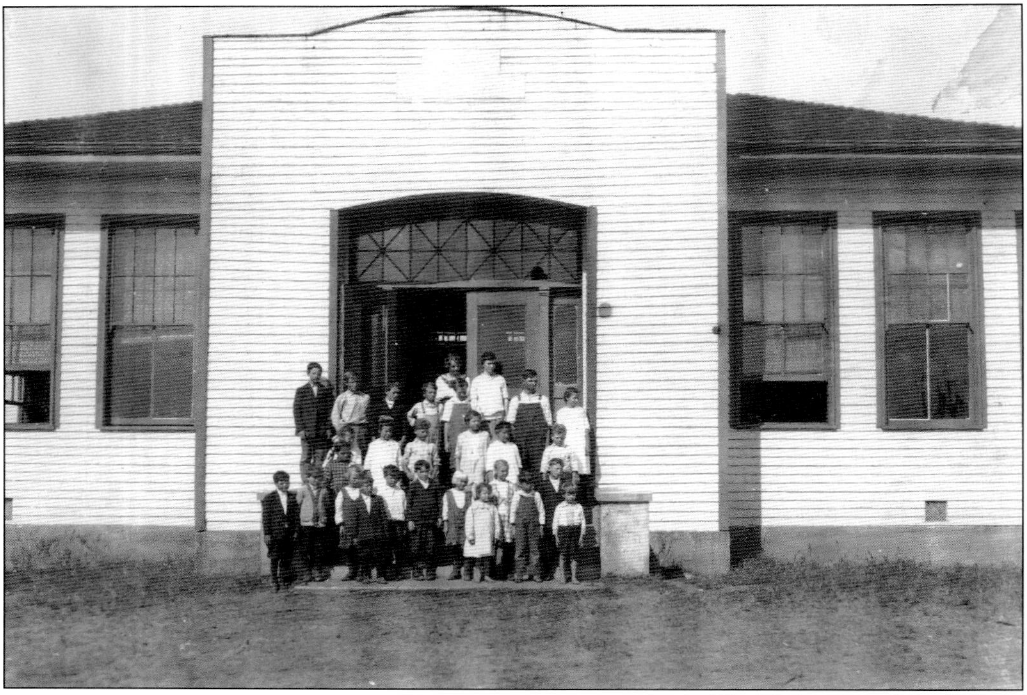

ACME SCHOOL. Acme School District No. 24 was located four miles northwest of Shawnee; Lois Millard was principal when this photograph was taken. According to the Library of Congress's records, 26 students are present, but 40 will be expected after all families return from the southern part of the state, where they have been picking cotton. (Courtesy of Library of Congress.)

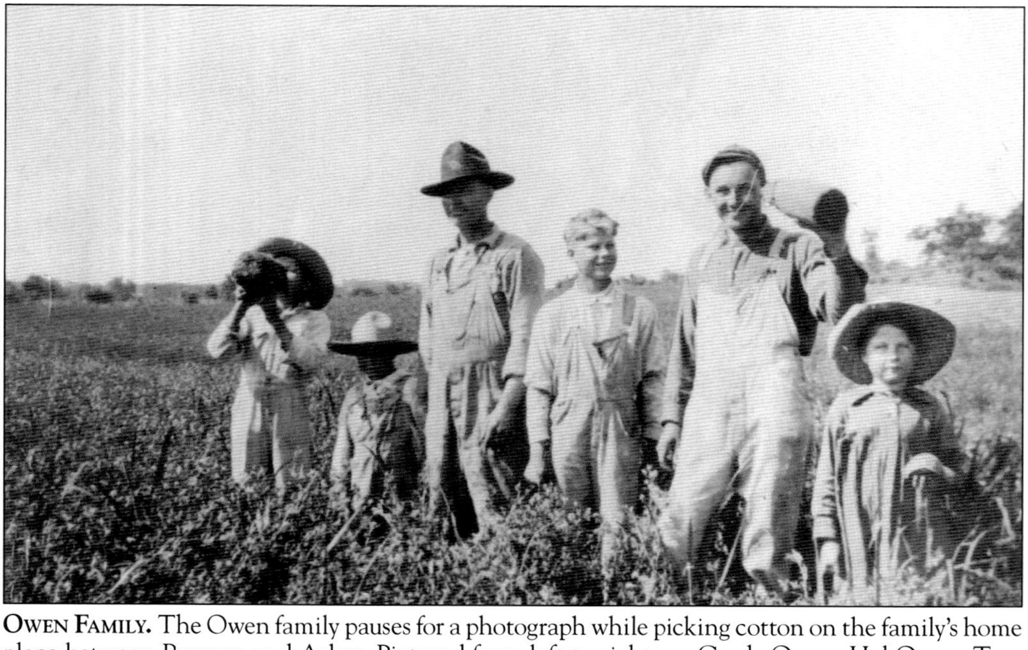

OWEN FAMILY. The Owen family pauses for a photograph while picking cotton on the family's home place between Pearson and Asher. Pictured from left to right are Grady Owen, Hal Owen, Tom Owen, Eulie Owen, John Merrill (a neighbor), and Margaret Owen. (Courtesy of Reta Bowen.)

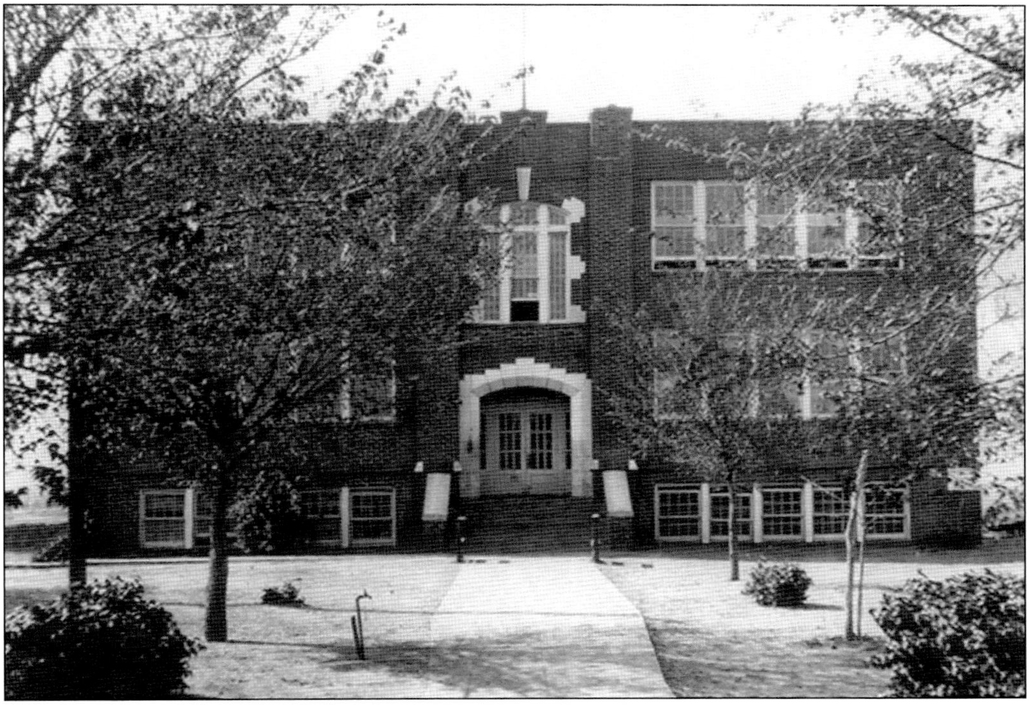

DALE SCHOOL. The Dale school building above was constructed in 1919. The building was a two-story brick structure with a basement and was in use until 1938. Below, students from Dale School District No. 17 are pictured in March 1898. (Both, courtesy of Pottawatomie County Historical Society.)

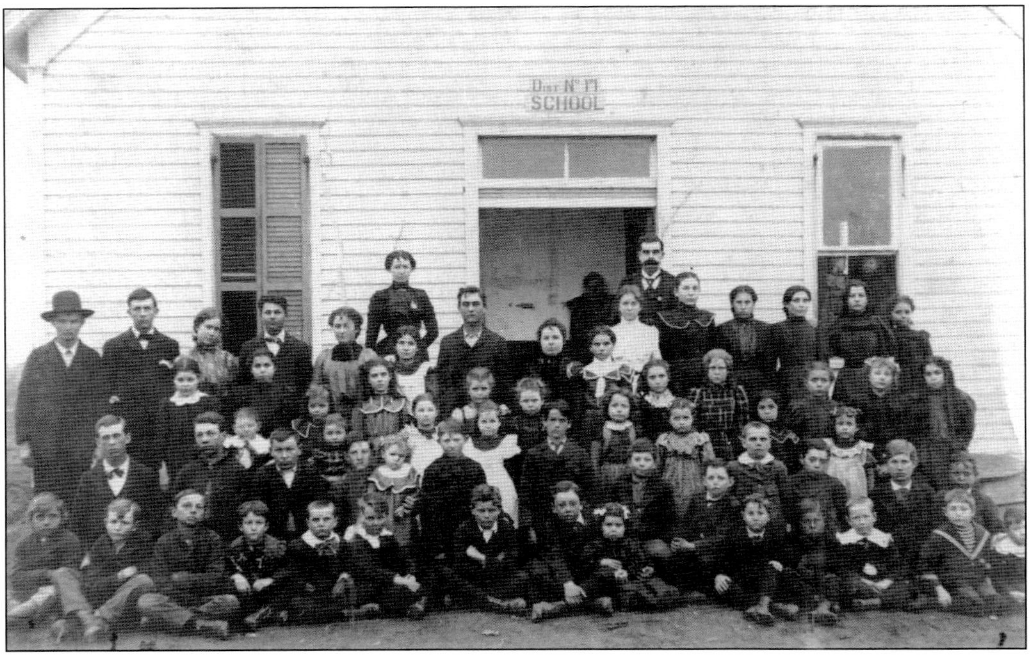

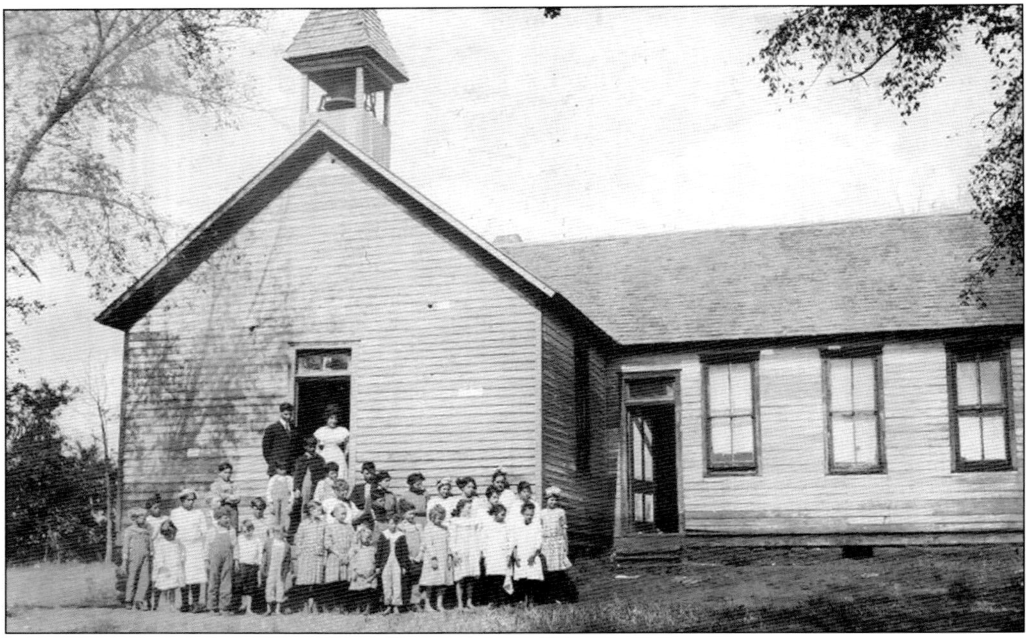

ROCK CREEK SCHOOL NO. 32. Rock Creek School District No. 32 was located five miles east of Shawnee. Thirty-four students are present in this 1916 photograph. J.W. Evans, the principal at this time, commented that he expected twice as many students when cotton picking was over. (Courtesy of Ron Olson.)

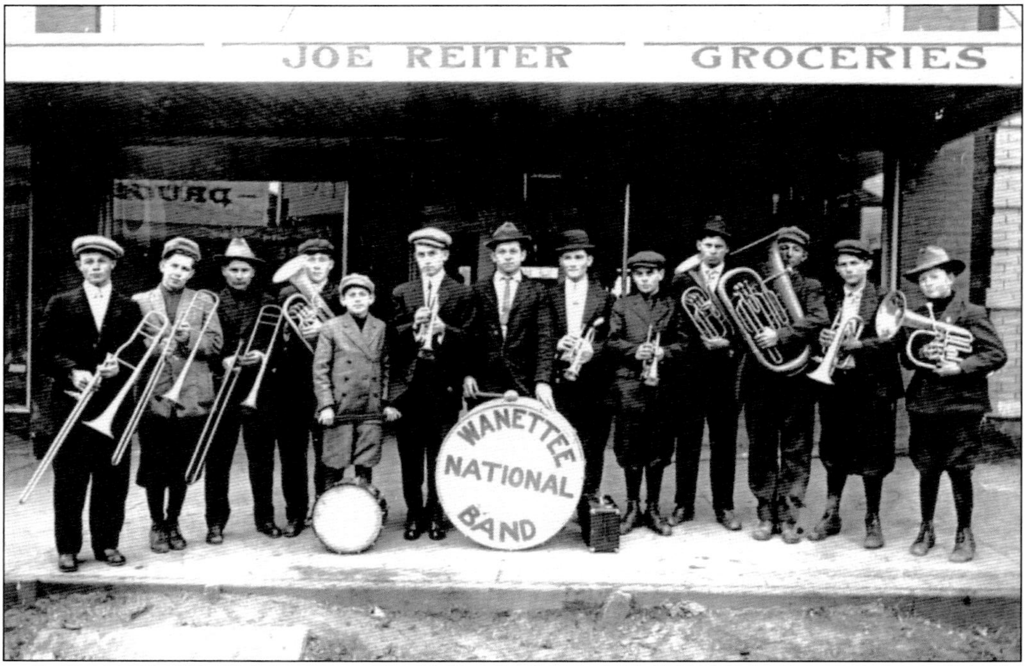

WANETTE NATIONAL BAND. Members of the Wanette National Band pose with their instruments outside Joe Reiter Groceries in Wanette. (Courtesy of Pottawatomie County Historical Society.)

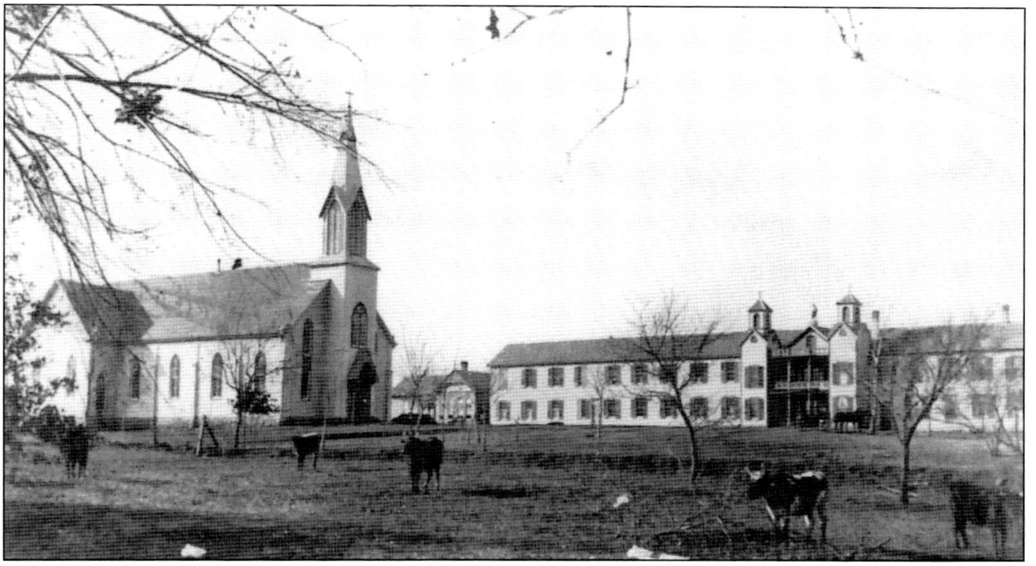

Sacred Heart. The photograph above shows Sacred Heart Mission east of Asher as it looked before a disastrous fire that destroyed several buildings in 1901. Additional structures are shown below. The first mass at Sacred Heart was celebrated on Sunday, May 13, 1877. The church was rebuilt by 1914 (and still stands beautifully), but educational and monastic endeavors transferred to St. Gregory's in Shawnee by 1930. (Both, courtesy of Pottawatomie County Historical Society.)

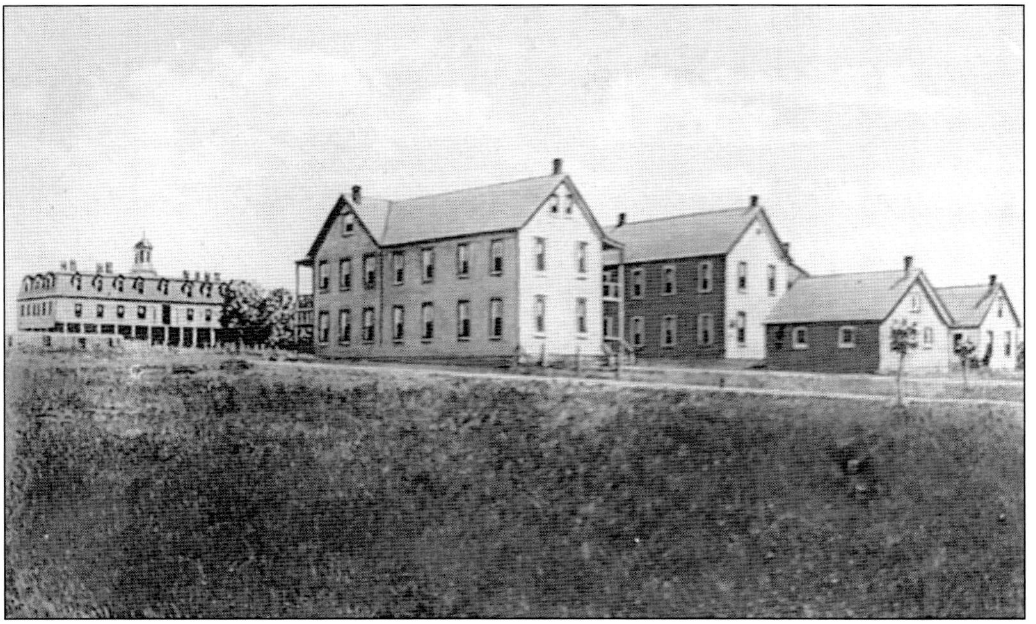

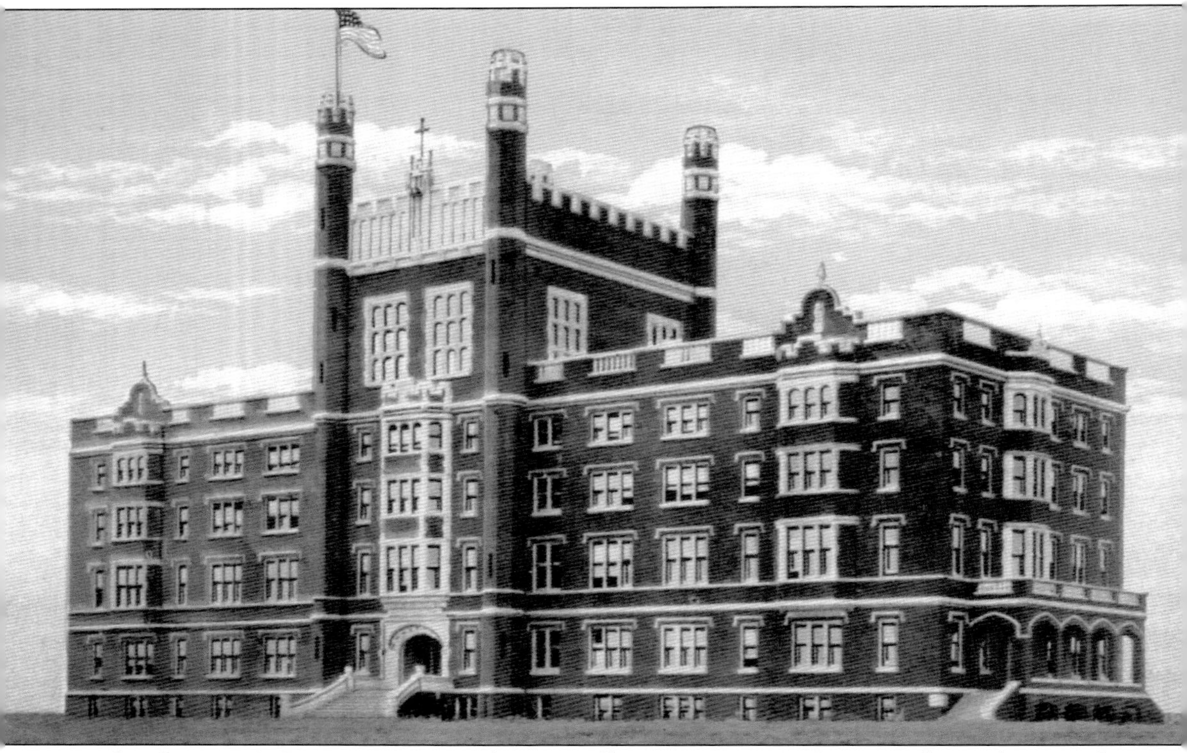

St. Gregory's University. Benedictine Hall at St. Gregory's University looms large in this photograph. St. Gregory's traces its roots to the Sacred Heart Mission. After that mission near Asher suffered a disastrous fire, the monks began planning and construction in Shawnee. St. Gregory's opened its doors in 1915 and is now one of the oldest institutions of higher learning in Oklahoma. This building was damaged by a 5.6 magnitude earthquake in 2011 that caused the loss or partial loss of all four of its landmark turrets. They were rebuilt by 2013. (Courtesy of Pottawatomie County Historical Society.)

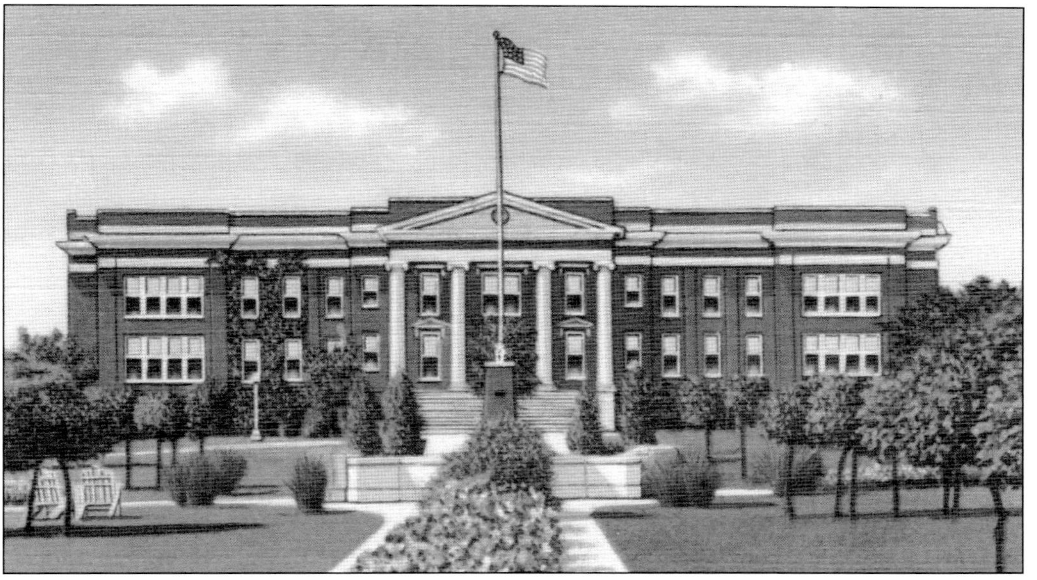

Oklahoma Baptist University. Oklahoma Baptist University (OBU) opened in Shawnee in September 1911. The first classes were held in the basement of the First Baptist Church and in the Shawnee Convention Hall. Due to financial exigency, OBU operations were suspended for three years after graduating its first class. Shawnee Hall, pictured, was the first building on the new campus and opened in September 1915. The college has operated continuously ever since. (Author's collection.)

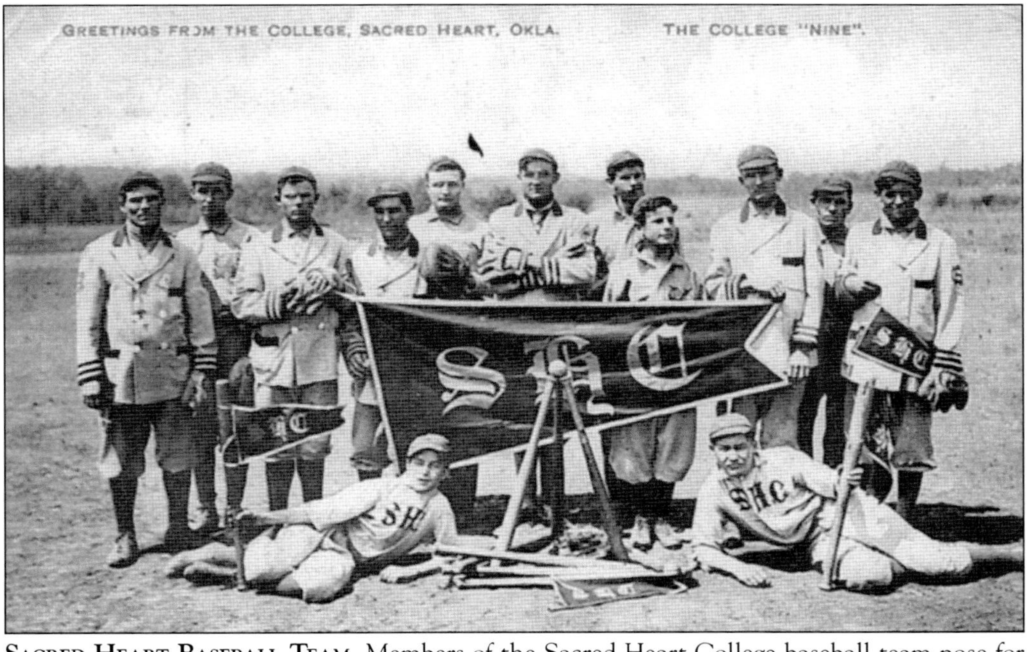

Sacred Heart Baseball Team. Members of the Sacred Heart College baseball team pose for a c. 1911 photograph. Sacred Heart was located east of Asher toward Konawa just inside the county line. The high school and college endeavors moved to St. Gregory's in Shawnee about 1915. (Courtesy of Don Taylor.)

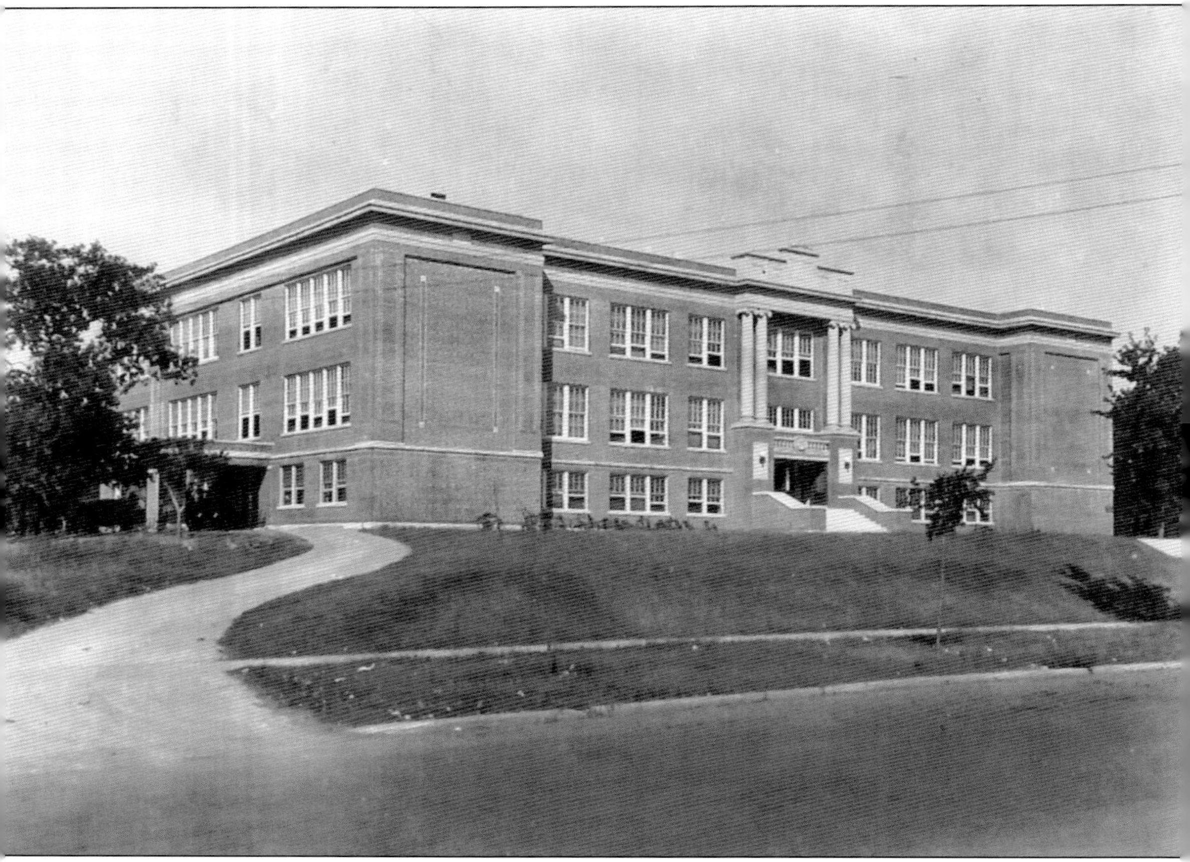

Shawnee Junior High School. The junior high school in Shawnee was built on Union Street in Woodland Park about 1920. It replaced Central School, which was also once located in the park. The junior high building was eventually adapted for use as an administration building and still serves in that capacity. (Author's collection.)

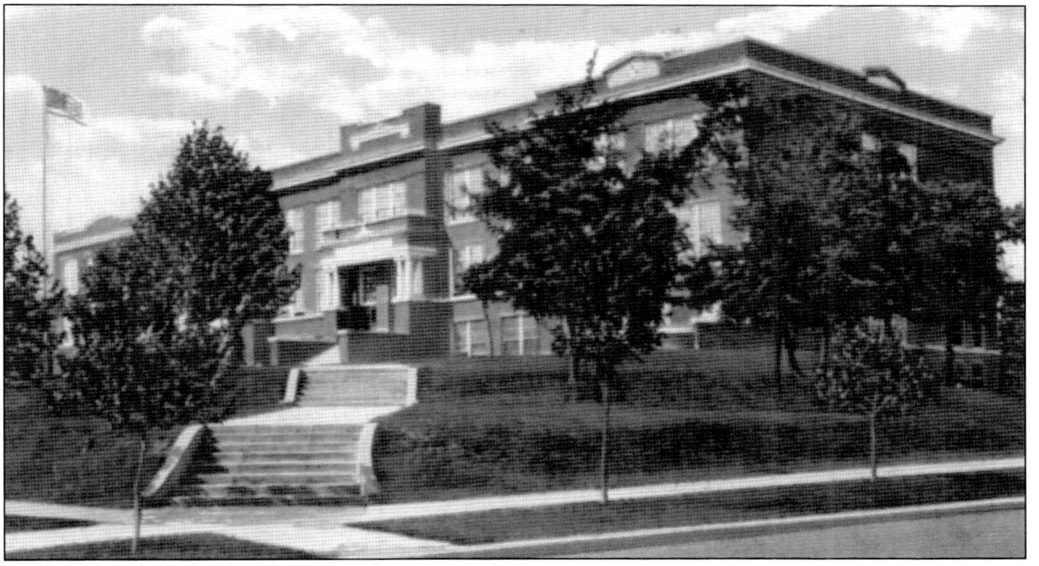

SHAWNEE HIGH SCHOOL. The Shawnee High School building can be seen above from a postcard postmarked in 1942. This building was located at Union and Highland Streets and was built around 1909. It was destroyed in a 1948 fire, and a replacement high school was built on the site. (Above, author's collection; below, courtesy of Pottawatomie County Historical Society.)

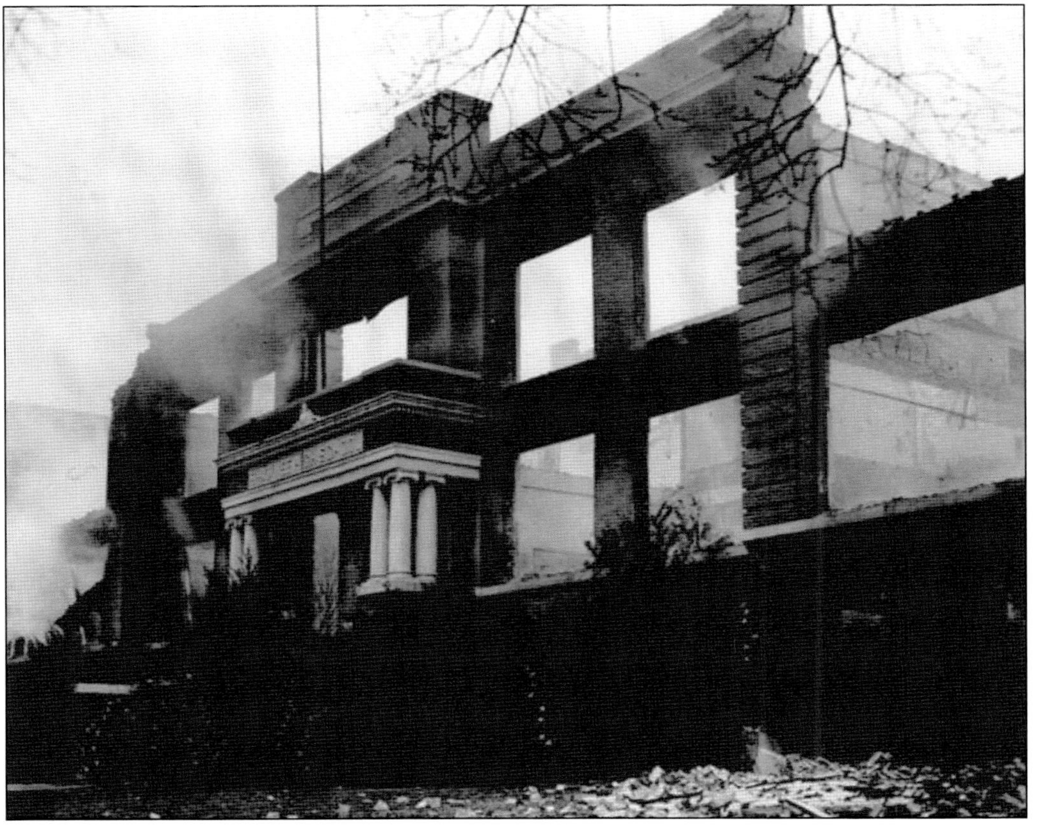

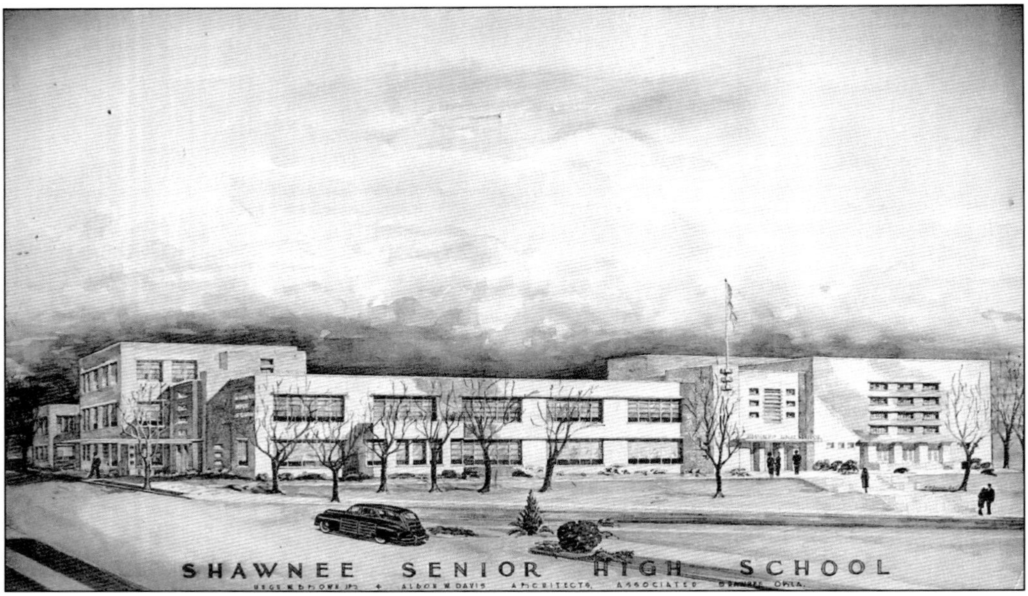

A New High School. This contemporary-looking high school building replaced the one that burned in 1948 at the same Union and Highland Street site. It was opened in the mid-1950s. The building is now used for Head Start educational programs. (Courtesy of Pottawatomie County Historical Society.)

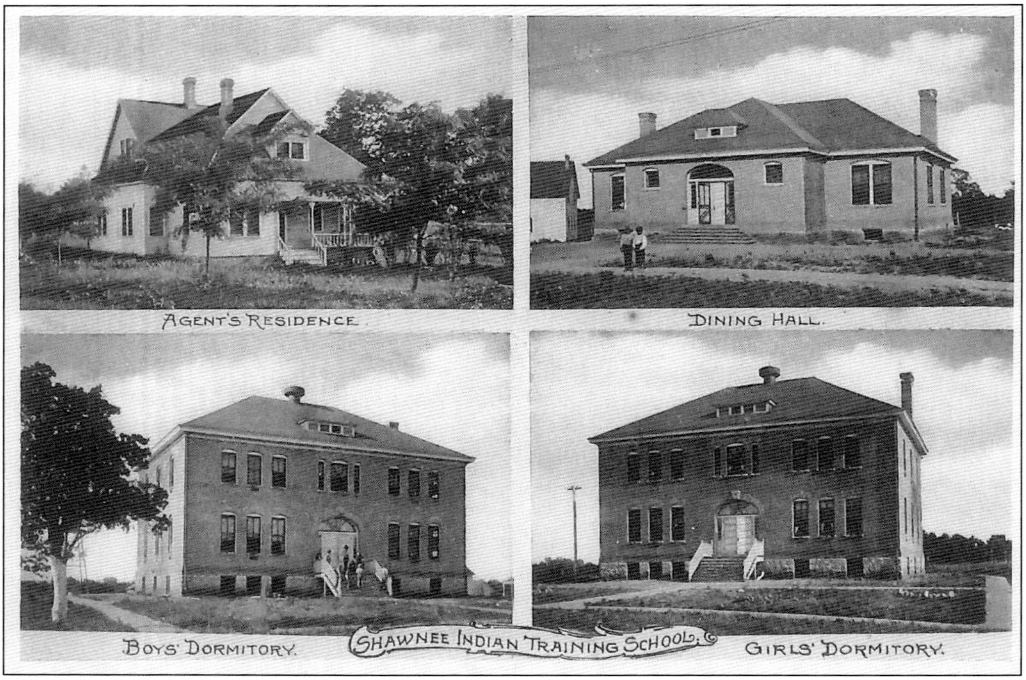

Shawnee Indian Training School. Four buildings of the Shawnee Indian Training School are presented on this postcard. Many American Indian boarding schools were established across Oklahoma in the early 1900s to educate Native American children according to European American standards. (Courtesy of Pottawatomie County Historical Society.)

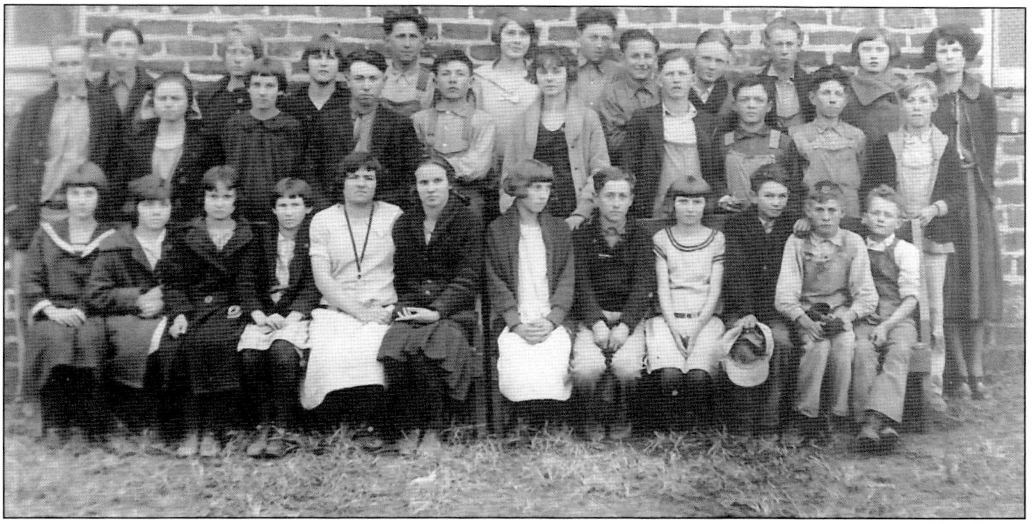

Centerview High School. Centerview High School was located south of Prague on Highway 99. Seventh- and eighth-grade students pose here for a group photograph during the 1924–1925 school year. Hazel Kyker is the teacher. (Courtesy of Pottawatomie County Historical Society.)

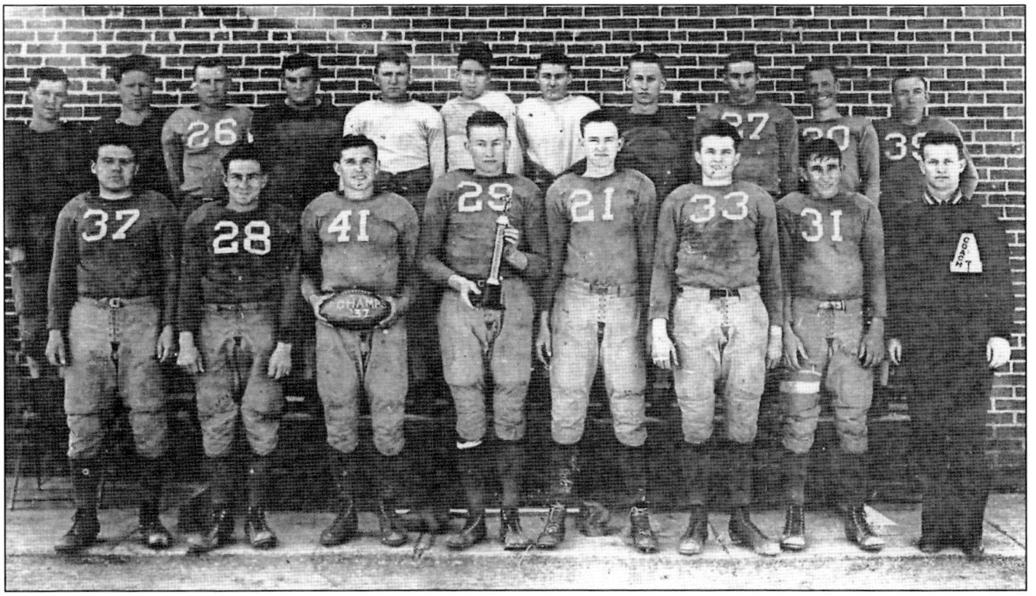

Asher Football Team. While Asher is known more for baseball today, in its early years it also had a football team. From left to right, team members are (first row) Floyd Cunningham, Leroy Youngblood, Ruey Burks, Les Giles, Wayne Boswell, Odell Bush, Eugene ?, and unidentified; (second row) unidentified, Albert Richardson, Monroe Bettis, Dempsey "Pudd" Kellum, Glen Morrison, Alvin ?, Lawton Hopkins, Stanley Giles, Raymond Williams, T.J. Sumpter, and ? Bowen. (Author's collection.)

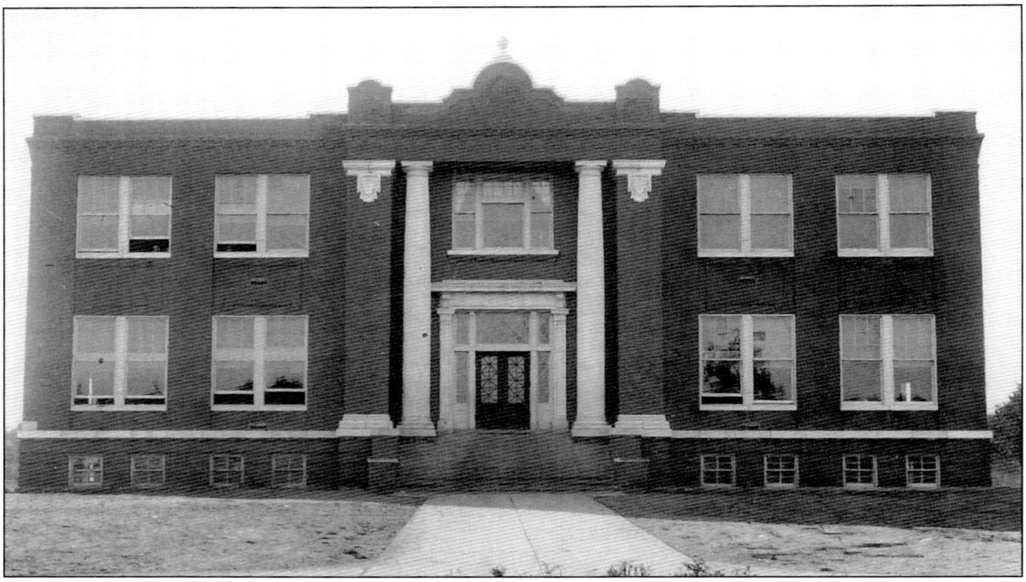

McLoud High School. Above, an early McCloud school building is shown. This building was constructed in 1909, and sometime prior to 1921 it was destroyed by fire. A similar building, pictured below, was constructed in 1921 to replace it. The beautiful shrubbery and green hedges trimmed out to spell "McLoud" were maintained for years. This new building served the community until 1993. After the decision was made not to remodel the building, it too was replaced with the current building that stands today. (Above, author's collection; below, courtesy of Pottawatomie County Historical Society.)

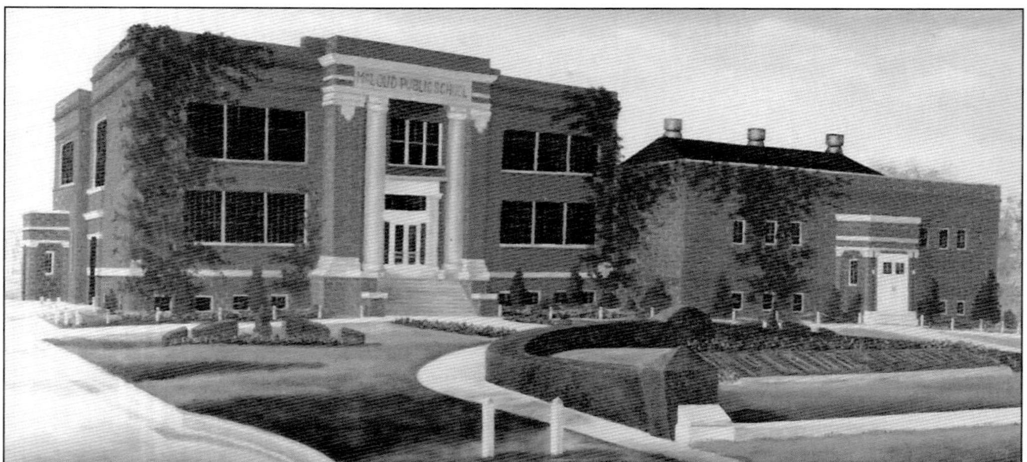

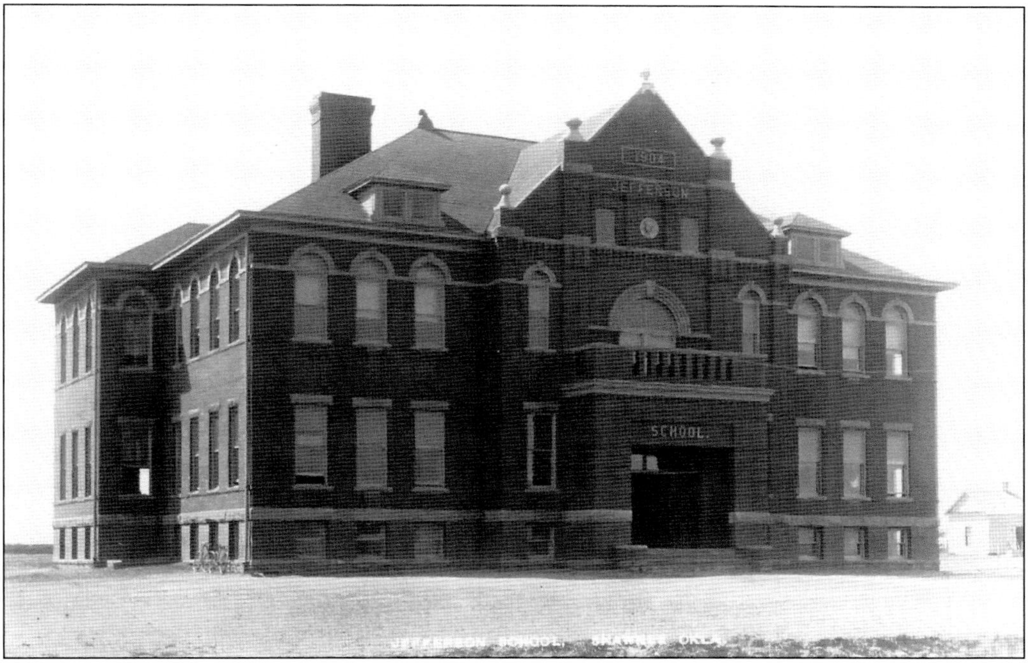

Jefferson School. Jefferson School, above, was built at the corner of Wallace and Kickapoo Streets in Shawnee and served as Shawnee Ward 6. In 1924, it was severely damaged by a tornado and removed. Another school was later built at this site, and that building continues to serve as an elementary school today. Below, Jefferson School lies in ruins after the March 28, 1924, tornado ripped off the upper floor of the building. According to the *Daily Oklahoman*, principal Glenn Smith dismissed classes just before the storm hit. (Above, author's collection; below, courtesy Bobbi Ross.)

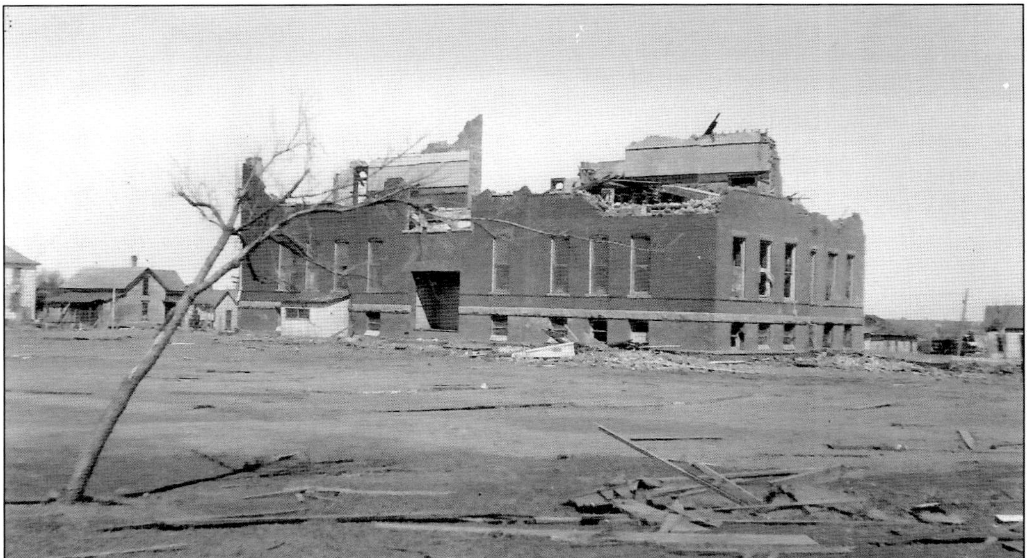

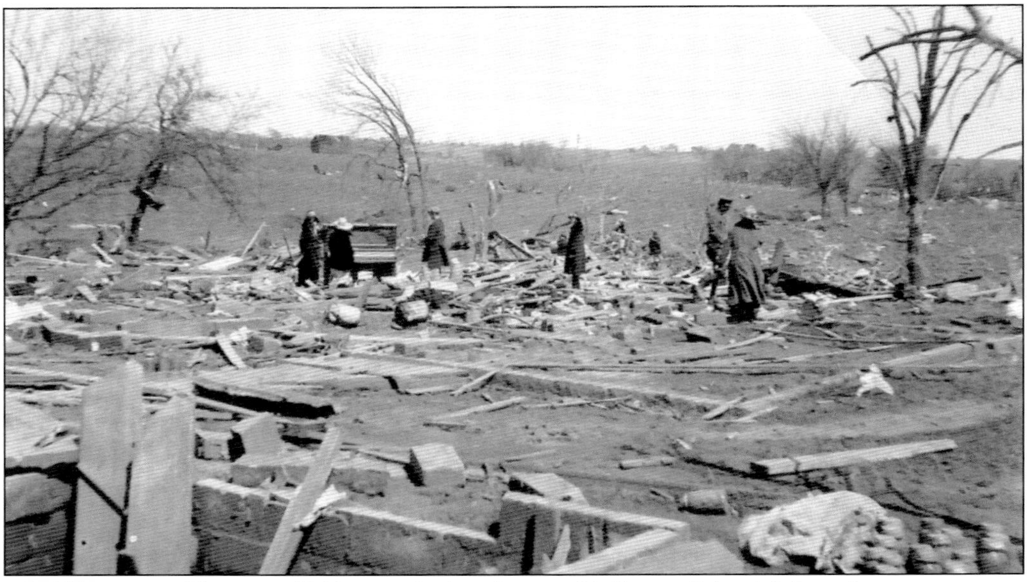

1924 Tornado. The same 1924 tornado that damaged Jefferson School did much worse to many other buildings. In this photograph, a few citizens inspect an organ that landed in this field virtually undamaged. The organ eventually found its way to the Santa Fe Depot museum. Several stories exist about which church it came from, but the truth may remain a mystery. (Courtesy of Bobbi Ross.)

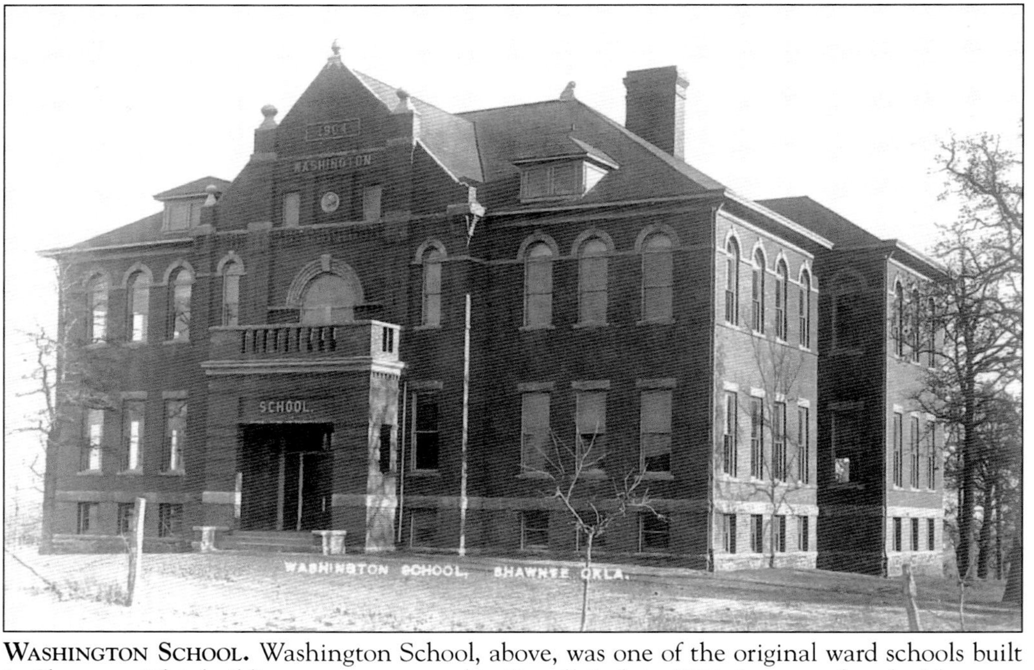

Washington School. Washington School, above, was one of the original ward schools built in Shawnee. This building was constructed in Farrall Park in 1904. It was replaced with a new building that was also built in the park in 1937. The replacement Washington School still stands, but after a stint as an alternative school, it is currently not in use. (Courtesy of Pottawatomie County Historical Society.)

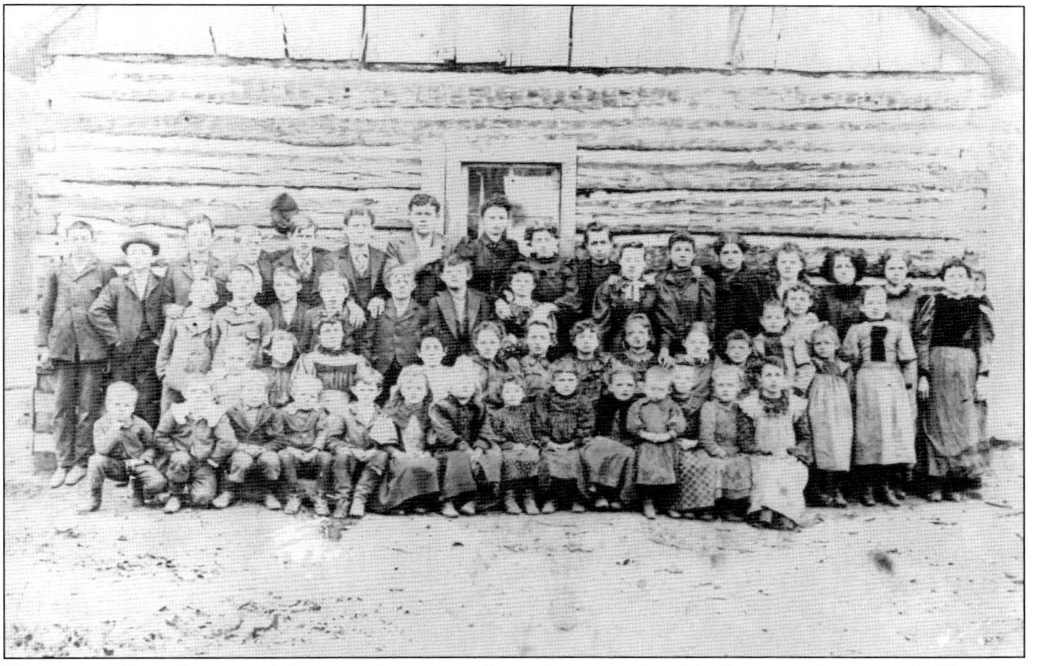

Pleasant Hill School. Many students pose for a photograph with their teacher outside Pleasant Hill School in 1896. Pleasant Hill was located between Wanette and Asher, south of the current highway. (Author's collection.)

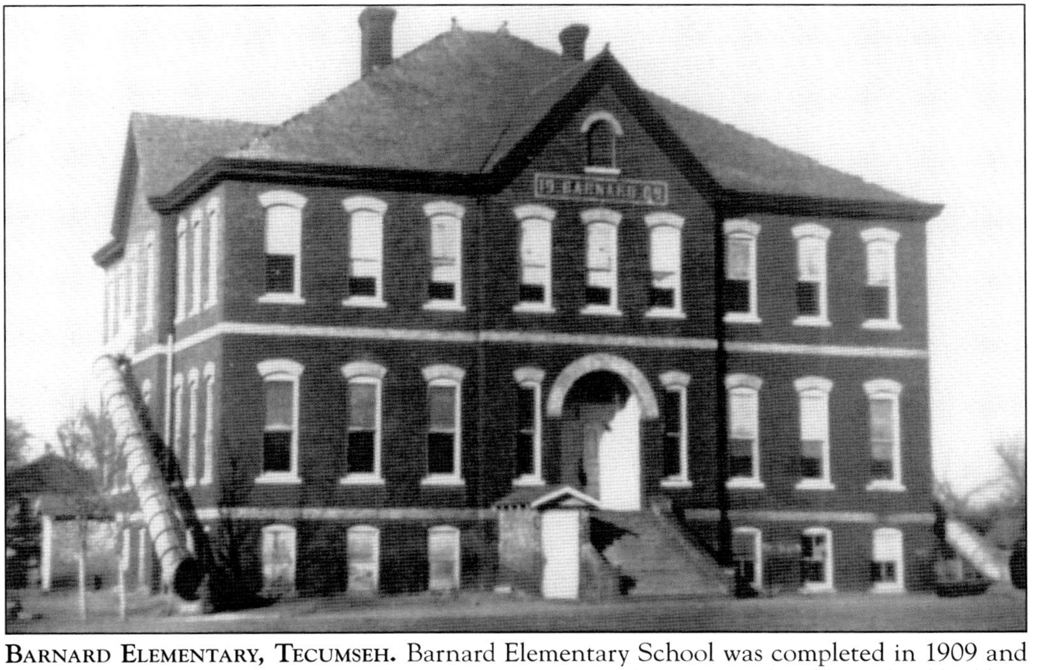

Barnard Elementary, Tecumseh. Barnard Elementary School was completed in 1909 and replaced the wood-frame ward school that previously sat on this site. It is the oldest school building that remains intact in Pottawatomie County. The building is still used as an elementary school for first and second grades. (Courtesy of Pottawatomie County Historical Society.)

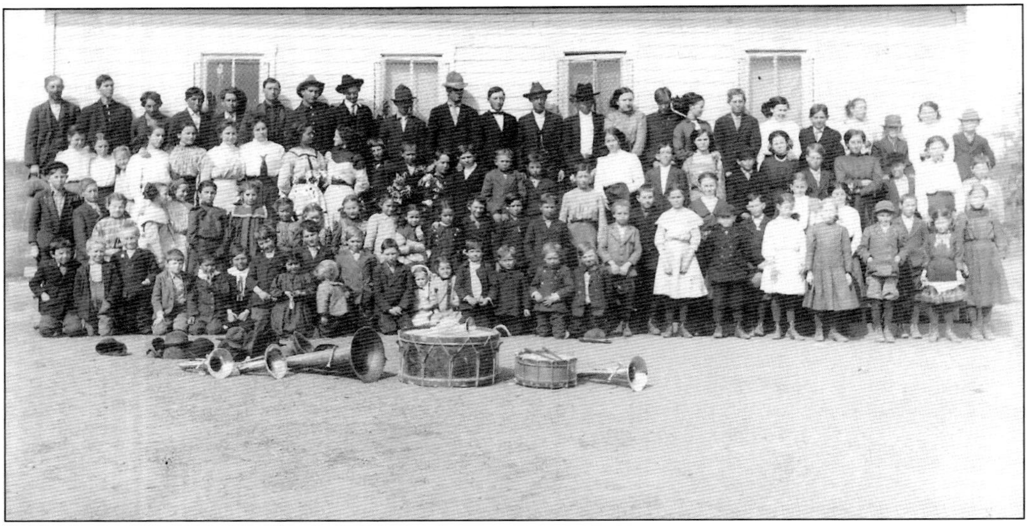

Gravel Hill. Gravel Hill was a small rural school district northeast of Asher. It was created in 1903 along with nearby Coulter School when the Lazell School closed. Gravel Hill schooled students through the eighth grade. Above, presumably the majority of the school poses for a photograph outside the schoolhouse in 1911. Below, a smaller group pauses for a photograph. Standing from left to right are Polly Douglas, Carl Hart, Barney Butts, Andy Yott, and two unidentified. Archie Butts is in the horn. Mozelle Butts, Mrs. Thrope, and Mrs. Lovelace are a few of the women photographed. (Both, author's collection.)

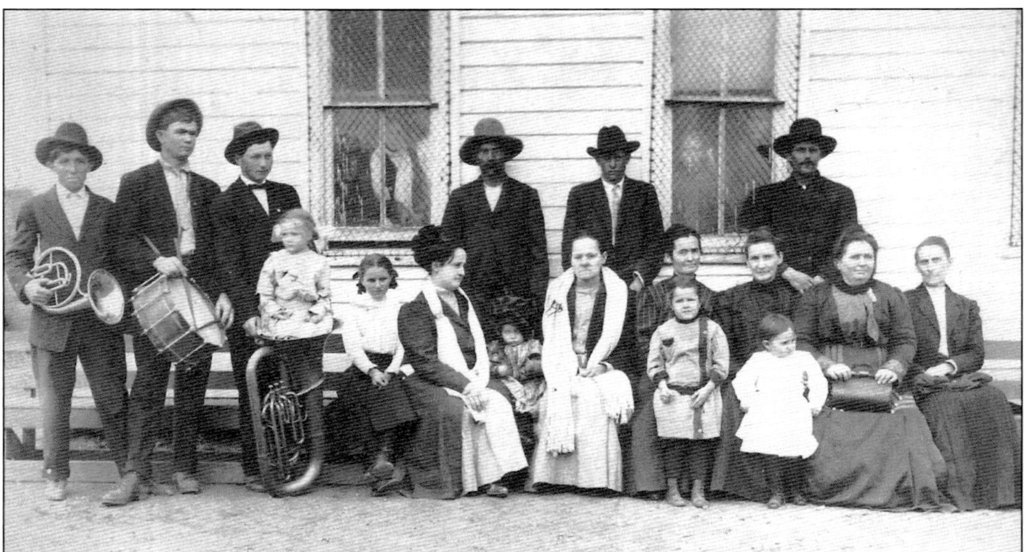

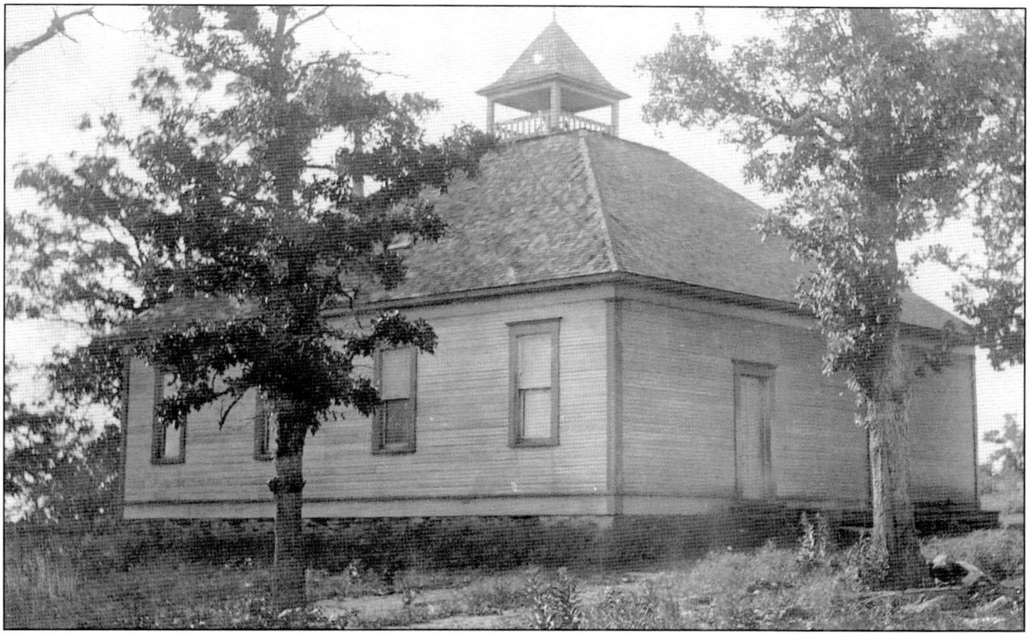

ROMULUS SCHOOL. Romulus School, above, was a small district located off Highway 18 (now Highway 177) north of Asher. Very little of Romulus can be found today, but the cemetery near the highway serves as a reminder of where it once was. Below, students gather for a group photograph outside the schoolhouse in 1923. (Both, courtesy of Pottawatomie County Historical Society.)

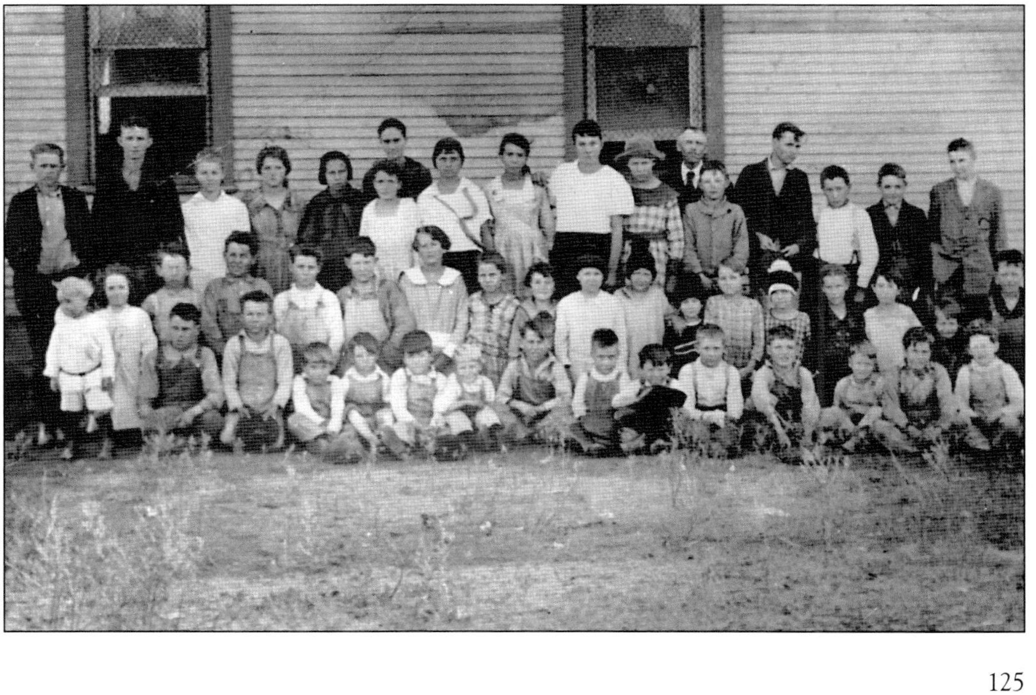

Bibliography

Fortson, John. *Pott County: And What Has Come of It.* Shawnee, OK: Eakin Press, 1936.

Pottawatomie County History Book Committee. *Pottawatomie County Oklahoma History*. Shawnee, OK: Pottawatomie County Historical Society, 1987.

About Pottawatomie County Historical Society

The Pottawatomie County Historical Society was an invaluable resource during the process of collecting photographs and information for this book. The society and museum are located in the old Santa Fe Depot at 614 East Main Street in Shawnee, have an abundance of photographs and artifacts of Pottawatomie County for viewing, and provide county citizens assistance with historical research.

The Pottawatomie County Historical Society was created on February 18, 1926, at the Carnegie Library in Shawnee, Oklahoma. People came from all sections of the county and enriched the meetings with their personal experiences of early-day happenings. A few turned in written statements and some valuable pictures, but little was done of a permanent nature. In 1936, under the guidance of Lola C. Durham, the society accepted as a gift the Old Friends Mission Church from the Philadelphia Society of Friends. The society then leased the land belonging to the church to an oil company and used the money to restore the building and do needed repairs.

The historical society began a fund drive to remodel the old Santa Fe Depot and convert it into a museum in 1979. After the depot was remodeled, the artifacts from the Old Friends Mission Church were moved to the depot, and the museum had its grand opening on May 30, 1982.

In 1991, in celebration of the 1891 Land Run, the park in front of the depot was named Centennial Park. A time capsule was placed in the park, and the Washington Irving Trail Monument can also be found here. In 1999, Beard Cabin (the first house built in Shawnee) was moved from Woodland Park to the depot grounds. In 2007, a monument was added to Centennial Park that recognized cities and organizations in the county that were at least 100 years old.

In 2008, the society began fundraising for an additional building to be located on land north of the depot. In May 2016, the society had the ground-breaking for the new building, to be named the Pottawatomie County Museum–Paul and Ann Milburn Center. It is expected to open in late 2017, and the museum artifacts and operations will move to the new building. The depot is to be restored as a railroad museum.

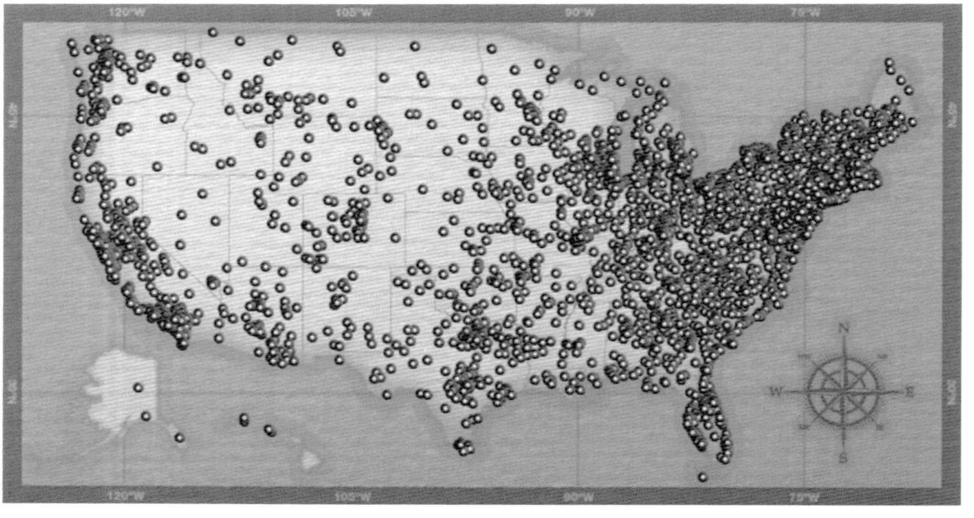

Consistent with our mission to preserve history on a local level, this book was printed in South Carolina on American-made paper and manufactured entirely in the United States. Products carrying the accredited Forest Stewardship Council (FSC) label are printed on 100 percent FSC-certified paper.

MADE IN THE USA